SACRAMENTO PUBLIC LIBRARY

D0201220

THE DARWIN ECONOMY

THE
DARWIN
ECONOMY

Liberty, Competition, and the Common Good

ROBERT H. FRANK

PRINCETON UNIVERSITY PRESS

Princeton and Oxford

Copyright © 2011 by Robert H. Frank
Requests for permission to reproduce material from this work should be sent to Permissions, Princeton University Press
Published by Princeton University Press, 41 William Street, Princeton, New Jersey 08540
In the United Kingdom: Princeton University Press, 6 Oxford Street, Woodstock, Oxfordshire OX20 1TW

press.princeton.edu

All Rights Reserved

Library of Congress Cataloging-in-Publication Data

Frank, Robert H.
    The Darwin economy : liberty, competition, and the common good /
    Robert H. Frank.
        p.   cm.
    Includes bibliographical references and index.
    ISBN 978-0-691-15319-3 (hardback : alk. paper)
    1. Free enterprise.   2. Competition.   3. Economics.   I. Title.
HB95.F723 2011
330.12′2—dc23   2011017346

British Library Cataloging-in-Publication Data is available

This book has been composed in Minion with Knockout display by Princeton Editorial Associates Inc., Scottsdale, Arizona

Printed on acid-free paper. ∞

Printed in the United States of America

10 9 8 7 6 5 4 3 2 1

For Tom and Karen Gilovich

CONTENTS

Preface ix

1 Paralysis 1
2 Darwin's Wedge 16
3 No Cash on the Table 30
4 Starve the Beast—But Which One? 46
5 Putting the Positional Consumption Beast on a Diet 64
6 Perpetrators and Victims 84
7 Efficiency Rules 100
8 "It's Your Money . . ." 119
9 Success and Luck 140
10 The Great Trade-Off? 157
11 Taxing Harmful Activities 172
12 The Libertarian's Objections Reconsidered 194

Notes 217
Index 229

PREFACE

BEHAVIORAL ECONOMICS HAS BEEN the economics profession's runaway growth area of recent decades. Scholars in this area work largely at the intersection of economics and psychology. Much of their attention has focused on systematic biases in people's judgments and decisions. As the late Amos Tversky, a Stanford University psychologist and a founding father of behavioral economics, liked to say, "My colleagues, they study artificial intelligence. Me? I study natural stupidity."

In the early 1980s, I taught one of the first undergraduate courses in behavioral economics. Because few students had heard of this nascent field, my first challenge was to come up with a course title that might lure some to enroll. In the end, I decided to call it "Departures from Rational Choice." Naturally, there was no standard syllabus then. After much thought, I decided to cover material under two broad headings: "Departures from Rational Choice with Regret" and "Departures from Rational Choice without Regret."

Under the first heading, I listed studies that document the many systematic cognitive errors to which people are prone. For example, although standard rational choice models say that people will ignore sunk costs (costs that are beyond recovery at the moment of decision), such costs often influence choices in conspicuous ways. Suppose you're about to depart for a sporting event or concert at an arena 50 miles away when an unexpected heavy snowstorm begins. If your ticket is nonrefundable, your decision whether or not to drive to the event should not be influenced by the amount you paid for it.

Yet a fan who paid $100 for his ticket is significantly more likely to make the dangerous drive than an equally avid fan who happened to receive his ticket for free. The first fan is probably guilty of a cognitive error. People typically seem to regret the decisions they make on the basis of such errors once they become aware of them.

Under the ". . . without Regret" heading, I listed studies that describe departures from the predictions of standard rational choice models that people do not seem to regret. A case in point is the way people typically react to one-sided offers in the so-called ultimatum game. In this game, the experimenter gives one subject some money—say, $100—and then tells him to propose a division of that sum between himself and a second subject. If the second accepts, each walks away with the amount proposed. For instance, if the first proposes "$60 for me and $40 for you" and the second accepts, the first gets $60 and the second gets $40. But here's the twist: if the second subject rejects the proposal, the $100 reverts to the experimenter, and each subject receives nothing.

Standard rational choice models predict that the first subject will make a one-sided proposal—such as $99 for himself and $1 for the second subject—since he knows that it would be in the second subject's interest to accept rather than get nothing. But such offers are rarely proposed, and when they are, they are almost invariably rejected. Subjects who reject one-sided offers seldom voice regret about having done so.

From the beginning, most of the work in behavioral economics has focused on departures from rational choice with regret—those caused by cognitive errors. My former Cornell colleague Dick Thaler collaborated with Cass Sunstein to write *Nudge*, a marvelous 2008 book summarizing the myriad ways in which such errors lead people astray and how policy makers might restructure environments to facilitate better choices. I enthusiastically endorse almost all the proposals they advocate in that book.

From the beginning, however, I've believed that much bigger losses result from departures from rational choice without regret. That's because people generally have both the desire and the ability to remedy cognitive errors unilaterally once they become aware of them. In contrast, we typically lack both the means and the motive to alter behaviors we don't regret, even when those behaviors generate large social costs.

Consider the assumption, standard in rational choice models, that the primary determinant of the satisfaction provided by any good is its absolute quality. That's clearly not true of the utility provided by an interview suit. If you're one of several similarly qualified applicants who all want the same investment banking job, it's strongly in your interest to look good when you show up for your interview. But looking good is an inherently relative concept. It means looking better than the other candidates. If they show up wearing $500 suits, you'll be more likely to make a favorable first impression, and more likely to get a callback, if you show up in a $2,000 suit than if you show up in one costing only $200.

When the ability to achieve important goals depends on relative consumption, as it clearly does in a host of domains, all bets regarding the efficacy of Adam Smith's invisible hand are off. Notwithstanding the uncritically enthusiastic pronouncements of many of Smith's modern disciples, unbridled market forces often fail to channel the behavior of self-interested individuals for the common good. On the contrary, as the pioneering naturalist Charles Darwin saw clearly, individual incentives often lead to wasteful arms races.

Darwin understood, for example, that peahens favored males with conspicuous tail displays, perhaps because such displays were a reliable signal of a robust immune system that could be passed along to offspring. (Parasite-ridden males are metabolically unable to support long, brightly colored tail feathers.) But Darwin also recognized that conspicuous tail displays made peacocks more vulnerable to predators and were hence wasteful from the perspective of the species. If all displays were smaller by half, the same males would pair with the same females as before, but each male would be less vulnerable. Yet no individual peacock would have reason to regret having a bright tail display, because without one his chances of landing a mate would be much diminished. Similarly, job applicants are no more likely to get the positions they seek if all spend $2,000 on interview suits than if all had spent only $300. But that's no reason to regret having bought the more expensive suit.

These are collective action problems, much like a military arms race. They have nothing to do with cognitive errors. Spending on interview suits is often excessive for the same reason that spending on armaments is excessive. In such situations, no individual or nation, acting alone, can profit by spending less.

In contrast, when individuals suffer losses because of their own cognitive mistakes, they have both the means and the motive to curtail their losses. They can seek additional information, for example, or employ experts to advise them. They can sign contracts that limit their ability to make such mistakes.

Not only are losses from collective action problems more difficult to remedy by individuals, they are also vastly larger than the losses caused by cognitive errors. But the good news, as I'll explain, is that simple, unintrusive changes in tax policy can eliminate many of the most important losses caused by collective action problems. In the process, I'll attempt to defend my prediction that economists a hundred years from now will be more likely to name Charles Darwin than Adam Smith as the intellectual founder of their discipline.

As I've read and listened to interviews with authors over the years, I've been struck by how frequently they've said something like "write about what you know" when asked to offer advice to young writers. The morning I sat down to begin work on the material that became chapter 9 of this book ("Success and Luck"), I thought to myself: Now *that's* a subject I know a bit about!

Indeed, among the many emotions I experienced as I began work on this book in May 2010, the strongest by far was a sense of wonder at being able to work on it at all. Chance events play an enormous role in every life, of course. But I've enjoyed vastly more than my share of improbable good fortune.

One experience in particular stands out. For many years, my good friend and colleague Tom Gilovich and I have had a ninety-minute slot every Saturday morning at an indoor tennis facility near Ithaca. As we sat during a changeover early in our second set one morning almost four years ago, I felt a sudden wave of nausea. Apparently, I then fell to the court unconscious, with no discernible pulse.

A few days later, as I lay in a hospital bed, the attending physician told me that I'd experienced an episode of sudden cardiac arrest—an event, he explained, that is almost always fatal, and almost always severely disabling to the few who survive it.

Tom later described to me in detail what had happened. When I collapsed, he immediately shouted for someone to call an ambulance. Although he'd had no previous training in CPR, he'd seen it done in movies and on TV. He flipped me onto my back and began pounding vigorously on my chest, with no apparent effect. But he kept at it, and after what seemed like a long time, he said, I coughed weakly.

Although the tennis facility is in an isolated location several miles from town, by chance an auto accident had occurred nearby just fifteen minutes earlier. Because of an administrative error, not one but two ambulances had been dispatched to the scene of that accident. As the second ambulance approached, its driver received instructions to divert to the tennis facility. It arrived shortly after my collapse, the attendants with paddles at the ready.

Although I'd been without oxygen for an undetermined number of minutes, the bottom line was that, against all odds, I was out of the hospital four days later, having suffered no lasting ill effects. Two weeks later, Tom and I were back on the tennis court. Resuming play wasn't a frightening step for me, since I'd passed a stress test with flying colors a few days earlier and had no firsthand recollection of my courtside collapse. But I know it was a trying experience for Tom.

In ways only slightly less dramatic, Karen Gilovich, Tom's wife, has also been a lifesaver. With deep fondness and gratitude, I dedicate this book to them.

This book's existence also owes much to my extraordinary good fortune to have landed my position at Cornell University. Shortly after I started teaching here in 1972, I learned that I'd been the seventh of the seven new professors hired by my department the previous year. In no other year has the department hired more than four. A colleague later told me that when he seconded the motion for me to be offered the seventh position, the department chairman, a volatile man who favored a different candidate, was so angry that he threw a piece of chalk at him. The only other offer I had at the time was from a much less prominent university in the Midwest, which is where I would have ended up in any normal year.

I was lucky not only to have landed the Cornell job but also to have been able to keep it. In my fourth year, my lone published paper was one I'd co-authored with a classmate in graduate school, and I had no other papers nearly ready for submission. That year, the economist (and later Federal Reserve Board Governor) Ned Gramlich left his position at the Brookings Institution to visit Cornell's economics department for two semesters. We quickly became close friends and, despite my conspicuous lack of tangible productivity, he seemed to think I had potential. When he asked whether I'd be willing to prepare a paper for a volume he was editing, I enthusiastically agreed. Eager to please, I worked really hard on the paper.

As it was nearing completion, Ned approached with a long face to apologize for the fact that his publisher had just canceled the volume. Disappointed, I sent the paper out for review, and six weeks later it was accepted by *Econometrica*—then, as now, one of the premiere economics journals. (For an economist, it is incomparably more advantageous professionally to publish a paper there than in a one-off edited volume.)

I was much more productive in my fifth year, but that would have made little difference except for the fact that each of the five papers I submitted that year was quickly accepted without revision by the *American Economic Review,* the *Journal of Political Economy,* or another leading economics journal. In the decades since, such quick turnaround never happened with any of my other papers. I was lucky, pure and simple.

For an academic, the opportunity to work with students and colleagues of the highest caliber is a rare privilege. The fact that I've been able to spend my career at a university like Cornell has made an enormous difference in the things I've been able to learn and do professionally. I'm sure I could have lived happily in many other places. But I never would have been able to write this book.

I also want to thank my wife, Ellen McCollister, for her incredible patience and support when I go into book mode. She's been through this many times now, but if she's grown weary of it in any way, she's done a remarkable job of concealing it. Many economists spend their days proving mathematical theorems. One of the things I like most about writing about the experiences of real people is the opportunity it's given me to discuss issues with Ellen and to benefit from her rich insights.

Others too numerous to mention have also been enormously helpful. But I would especially like to thank Bruce Buchanan, Gary Burke, Philip Cook, Tyler Cowen, Lee Fennell, Ted Fischer, Chris Frank, Herbert Gans, Srinagesh Gaverneni, Tom Gilovich, Marc Groeger, Maria Guadalupe, Henry Hansmann, Ori Heffetz, Moritz Heumer, Bob Hockett, Graham Kerslick, Mark Kleiman, Jim Luckett, David Lyons, Michael F. Martin, Rex Mixon, Sendhil Mullainathan, Tom Nagel, Matthew Nagler, Michael O'Hare, Sam Pizzigati, Kate Rubenstein, Tim Scanlon, Tom Schelling, Eric Schoenberg, Philip Seeman, Larry Seidman, Peter Singer, Jeff Sommer, Timon Spiluttini, Kai Tang, Steve Teles, Fidel Tewolde, Michael Waldman, David Sloan Wilson, Saskia Wittlake, and Andrew Wylie for their insightful comments. They of course bear no responsibility for any remaining errors.

Finally, I'm grateful to Peter Dougherty and Seth Ditchik at Princeton University Press for their early enthusiasm for this project and for their sage advice, which helped mold it into its current form. The title I'd originally chosen was *The Libertarian Welfare State*. If the book succeeds in finding its audience, I'll have Peter and Seth (plus a prod from Michael F. Martin) to thank for persuading me to abandon that title, which now survives as a section head in chapter 12.

The alternative I originally preferred was *Darwin's Wedge*, which eventually became the title of chapter 2. I liked the way it evokes the divergence between individual and group interests, which underlies my main thesis and whose importance Darwin understood so clearly. I also thought its unfamiliarity made it sound vaguely intriguing. Over dinner one evening, I asked several friends for their reactions. Before anyone else could respond, my wife said that the first thought that popped into her mind was "Darwin's wedgie." Peals of laughter ensued. The next morning, I wrote to Peter Dougherty suggesting that we go with his first proposal, *The Darwin Economy*.

ONE

Paralysis

PEOPLE OFTEN REMEMBER THE PAST with exaggerated fondness. Sometimes, however, important aspects of life really were better in the old days. During the three decades following World War II, for example, incomes were rising rapidly and at about the same rate—almost 3 percent a year—for people at all income levels. We had an economically vibrant middle class. Existing roads and bridges were well maintained, and impressive new infrastructure was being added each year. We cheered when President John F. Kennedy urged, "Ask not what your country can do for you, ask what you can do for your country." We were sure we could win the race to put a man on the moon. We were optimistic.

No longer. The economy has grown much more slowly during the intervening decades, and only those at the top of the income ladder have enjoyed significant earnings gains. CEOs of large U.S. corporations, for example, saw their pay increase tenfold over this period, while the inflation-adjusted hourly wages of their workers actually fell. The middle class is awash in debt.

Proposals to build desperately needed new infrastructure, such as high-speed rail systems or a smart electric grid, consistently fail in Congress, and existing infrastructure has been steadily falling into disrepair. Rich and poor alike now endure crumbling roads and unsafe bridges. Water supply and sewage systems fail regularly. Countless schools are in shambles. Many Americans live in the shadow of poorly maintained dams that could collapse at any moment. Funding has been cut for programs to lock down poorly guarded nuclear materials in the former Soviet Union.

More troubling, our political system seems almost completely paralyzed, even in the face of these genuinely urgent problems. This paralysis often stems from a seemingly willful ignorance of the basic facts and logic that govern human behavior.

A case in point is our failure to deal with the stubborn unemployment spawned by the financial crisis of 2008. As John Maynard Keynes explained during the Great Depression, economies mired in deep downturns seldom recover quickly on their own.[1] Consumers won't lead the way, he argued, because they're burdened with debt and fearful of losing their jobs, if they haven't already lost them. Nor will business investment spark recovery, because most firms already have more than enough capacity to produce what people want to buy. Government, Keynes concluded, is the only actor with both the ability and the motive to stimulate spending sufficiently to put people back to work.

Each new day of widespread unemployment is like a plane that takes off with many empty seats. In each case, an opportunity to produce something of value is lost forever. There was no good reason for failing to take every possible step to avoid such waste. Yet critics of economic stimulus were quick to denounce government spending itself as wasteful, even as a host of useful projects cried out for attention. According to the Nevada State Department of Transportation, for example, a worn 10-mile stretch of Interstate 80 would cost $6 million to restore if the work were done today; but if we postpone action for just two years, weather and traffic will eat more deeply into the roadbed, and those same repairs will cost $30 million.[2]

During the depths of the downturn, the workers and equipment necessary to do the work were sitting idle. And with considerable slack in markets worldwide, the required materials were available at unusually low prices. Interest rates for the money to finance these projects were near record lows. These were tasks that should have been tackled immediately, quite independently of the need for additional economic stimulus. Yet because of the profound ignorance that strangles our current political conversation, government could not act.

Stimulus opponents cited fear of deficits as a reason for inaction, but deficits are a long-run problem. No one argued that we could put off maintaining our infrastructure forever. Doing it right away meant doing it more cheaply, which meant smaller deficits in the long run, not bigger ones. Deficits must be dealt with, yes, but the time for doing so is when the economy has fully recovered.

The same leaders who cite concerns over deficits to explain their opposition to additional economic stimulus also voted to cut the enforcement budget of the Internal Revenue Service. Yet credible evidence says that each dollar cut from that budget causes tax revenue to fall by $10, for a net increase in the deficit of $9! That such cuts could be approved by the House of Repreentatives suggests that we're becoming, in the coinage of one pundit, an ignoramitocracy—a country in which ignorance-driven political paralysis prevents us from grappling with even our most pressing problems.

The same leaders voted to cut nutritional support for low-income women with small children by more than $1 billion and to reduce the Clean Water State Revolving Fund by $700 million. Those programs exist not only to help people in need, but also to prevent costly problems down the road. Cutting them will make future deficits larger, not smaller.

The same leaders also failed even to mention their deficit concerns when they opposed the scheduled expiration of the George W. Bush tax cuts for the wealthiest Americans in 2010. Because many of the wealthy already have more money than they can spend in their lifetimes, extending those tax cuts provided little economic stimulus. Letting them expire would have freed up revenue that could have been used for far more effective stimulus measures—such as grants to the states that could have prevented massive layoffs of teachers, police, and firefighters. Yet, as senate minority leader Mitch McConnell said without apparent irony in a CNN interview, "Raising taxes in the middle of a recession is not a good idea."[3]

A less immediate concern, but perhaps the most troubling one, is our political system's indifference, even hostility, to increasingly pessimistic scientific estimates of the pace of global warming. Climate change skeptics often base their case for inaction on the fact that the science underlying calls for change is so inexact. But our most distinguished scientists are themselves quick to acknowledge the uncertainty inherent in their projections. Temperature increases could of course be smaller than expected—but they could also be substantially larger, and quite possibly catastrophic. Given the range of possible temperature increases and their respective probabilities of occurring, uncertainty is actually the strongest possible case for action.

The most recent simulations by MIT's respected Integrated Global Systems Model, for example, estimate a 10 percent chance that the average global surface temperature will rise by more than 12°F by 2095.[4] An increase of that magnitude would spell the end of life on Earth as we know it. That threat could be eliminated by simple policy measures like a steep tax on carbon dioxide emissions. If it were phased in gradually, we could adapt to such a tax without painful sacrifices.

Any rational political process would address this problem with dispatch. But House leaders in charge of energy policy stubbornly deny that there's even a problem. Seasoned congressional observers say there's virtually no chance that meaningful climate legislation could win passage in the U.S. Senate anytime soon. In an ignoramitocracy, such legislation is apparently politically unthinkable.

How Did We Get Here?

It's prudent to be skeptical of unitary explanations. Yet it would be a mistake to downplay the importance of a powerful meme that has become entrenched in the public mind during the past three decades—namely that government is the source of all ills. Libertarians, who have always been vigilant against the misuse of government power, have been among the major propagators of this meme. And although those with formal ties to the Libertarian Party remain small in number, their influence on public discourse has been large and growing.

That influence has stemmed in large part from the enormous sums of money they've spent to spread the message that government is the problem. In a widely cited ten-thousand-word article published in the *New Yorker*, for instance, Jane Mayer traced how the multibillionaire libertarians Charles and David Koch, owners of Koch Industries, have donated more than $100 million in recent years to far-right-wing think tanks, organizers of the Tea Party, and other groups whose mission is to promulgate that message.[5]

Notwithstanding its claim to be fair and balanced, Rupert Murdoch's Fox News Channel has also worked tirelessly to promote the same message. Predating these efforts were substantial grants in support of right-wing think tanks by the billionaire Richard Mellon Scaife, owner of the Pittsburgh *Tribune-Review* and an heir to the Mellon fortune. Earlier still, the John M. Olin Foundation had distributed almost $400 million to conservative think tanks, media outlets, and law and economics programs at leading universities, all with the aim of spreading the beliefs that government is the problem and unfettered markets are the solution.

In total, these investments have been extraordinarily effective in fostering an inchoate but pervasive sense of anger that has made it all but impossible for government to act. Libertarians are correct, of course, that waste in government has a long and troubling history. And we can be grateful for their vigilance against the erosion of personal liberties and misuse of public funds. But does the fact that government is imperfect mean that complete policy paralysis is what most Americans really want? Markets, after all, aren't perfect either, and there are many important tasks that only government is well suited to perform. National defense is an obvious example, as are the construction and maintenance of public infrastructure. The definition and enforcement of property rights are also the province of government.

Government plays a prominent role in the economic and social life of every successful society. Countries whose citizens have the most favorable opinions of their governments tend also to be ones with the best public goods and services, the lowest levels of perceived corruption, and the highest per-capita incomes. In contrast, those with the weakest governments—think Haiti, Somalia, or Sudan—typically have poorly functioning markets, extremely low per-capita incomes, high levels of crime and violence, and citizens who regard their governments as ineffectual and corrupt. If forced to choose, most Americans would prefer to live in New Zealand than in Haiti.

Differences in the quality and scope of their respective governments are not the only reasons they'd make that choice. But they're important reasons.

The fact that many activities are best carried out collectively means that government must levy taxes to pay for them. Libertarians and other anti-government activists often decry mandatory taxation as theft, but no government could function if forced to rely exclusively on voluntary contributions. Without mandatory taxation, there could be no government. With no government, there would be no army, and without an army, your country would eventually be invaded by some other country that has an army. And when the dust settled, you'd be paying mandatory taxes to that country's government.

If there's no realistic alternative to living under a government with the power to levy mandatory taxes, our best option is to try to create one that will deliver the most value for our money. We must take seriously the question of how government institutions should be designed and monitored. We should have far-reaching conversations about what public services we want and how to pay for them. Yet we are doing none of those things at the moment.

This is clearly not how things should be in a resource-rich nation with the most educated and productive workforce on the planet. The good news is that it would actually be easy to move past our current gridlock. That's because it's the result not of irreconcilable differences in values but of a simple but profound misunderstanding about how competition works.

Why the Invisible Hand Often Breaks Down

Without question, Adam Smith's invisible hand was a genuinely groundbreaking insight. Producers rush to introduce improved product designs and cost-saving innovations for the sole purpose of capturing market share and profits from their rivals. In the short run, these steps work just as the producers had hoped. But rival firms are quick to mimic the innovations, and the resulting competition quickly causes prices to fall in line with the new, lower costs. In the end, Smith argued, consumers are the ultimate beneficiaries of all this churning.

But many of Smith's modern disciples believe he made the much bolder claim that markets *always* harness individual self-interest to produce the greatest good for society as a whole. Smith's own account, however, was far more circumspect. He wrote, for example, that the profit-seeking business owner "intends only his own gain, and he is in this, as in many other cases, led by an invisible hand to promote an end which was no part of his intention. *Nor is it always the worse for the society that it was not part of it* [emphasis added]."[6]

Smith never believed that the invisible hand guaranteed good outcomes in all circumstances. His skepticism was on full display, for example, when he wrote, "People of the same trade seldom meet together, even for merriment and diversion, but the conversation ends in a conspiracy against the public, or in some contrivance to raise prices."[7] To him, what was remarkable was that self-interested actions often led to socially benign outcomes.[8]

Like Smith, modern progressive critics of the market system tend to attribute its failings to conspiracies to restrain competition. But competition was much more easily restrained in Smith's day than it is now. The real challenge to the invisible hand is rooted in the very logic of the competitive process itself.

Charles Darwin was one of the first to perceive the underlying problem clearly. One of his central insights was that natural selection favors traits and behaviors primarily according to their effect on individual organisms, not larger groups.[9] Sometimes individual and group interests coincide, he recognized, and in such cases we often get invisible hand-like results. A mutation that codes for keener eyesight in one particular hawk, for example, serves the interests of that individual, but its inevitable spread also makes hawks as a species more successful.

In other cases, however, mutations that help the individual prove quite harmful to the larger group. This is in fact the expected result for mutations that confer advantage in head-to-head competition among members of the same species. Male body mass is a case in point. Most vertebrate species are polygynous, meaning that males take more than one mate if they can. The qualifier is important, because when some take multiple mates, others get none. The latter don't pass their genes along, making them the ultimate losers in Darwinian terms. So it's no surprise that males often battle furiously for access to mates. Size matters in those battles, and hence the evolutionary arms races that produce larger males.

Elephant seals are an extreme but instructive example.[10] Bulls of the species often weigh almost six thousand pounds, more than five times as much as females and almost as much as a Lincoln Navigator SUV. During the mating season, pairs of mature bulls battle one another ferociously for hours on end, until one finally trudges off in defeat, bloodied and exhausted. The victor claims near-exclusive sexual access to a harem that may number as many as a hundred cows. But while being larger than his rival makes an individual bull more likely to prevail in such battles, prodigious size is a clear handicap for bulls as a group, making them far more vulnerable to sharks and other predators.

Given an opportunity to vote on a proposal to reduce every animal's weight by half, bulls would have every reason to favor it. Since it's relative size, not absolute size, that matters in battle, the change would not affect the outcome of any given head-to-head contest, but it would reduce each animal's risk of being eaten by sharks. There's no practical way, of course, that elephant seals could implement such a proposal. Nor could any bull solve this problem unilaterally, since a bull that weighed much less than others would never win a mate.

Similar conflicts pervade human interactions when individual rewards depend on relative performance. Their essence is nicely captured in a celebrated example by the economist Thomas Schelling.[11] Schelling noted that hockey players who are free to choose for themselves invariably skate without helmets, yet when they're permitted to vote on the matter, they support rules that require them. If helmets are so great, he wondered, why don't players just wear them? Why do they need a rule?

His answer began with the observation that skating without a helmet confers a small competitive edge—perhaps by enabling players to see or hear a little better, or perhaps by enabling them to intimidate their opponents. The immediate lure of gaining a competitive edge trumps more abstract concerns about the possibility of injury, so players eagerly embrace the additional risk. The rub, of course, is that when every player skates without a helmet, no one gains a competitive advantage—hence the attraction of the rule.

As Schelling's diagnosis makes clear, the problem confronting hockey players has nothing to do with imperfect information, lack of self-control, or poor cognitive skills—shortcomings that are often cited as grounds for government intervention.[12] And it clearly does not stem from exploitation or any insufficiency of competition. Rather, it's a garden-variety collective action problem. Players favor helmet rules because that's the only way they're able to play under reasonably safe conditions. A simple nudge—say, a sign in the locker room reminding players that helmets reduce the risk of serious injury—just won't solve their problem. They need a mandate.

What about the libertarian's complaint that helmet rules deprive individuals of the right to choose? This objection is akin to objecting that a military arms control agreement robs the signatories of their right to choose for themselves how much to spend on bombs. Of course, but that's the whole point of such agreements! Parties who confront a collective action problem often realize that the only way to get what they want is to constrain their own ability to do as they please.

As John Stuart Mill argued in *On Liberty,* it's permissible to constrain an individual's freedom of action only when there's no less intrusive way to prevent undue harm to others.[13] The hockey helmet rule appears to meet this test. By skating without a helmet, a player imposes harm on rival players by making them less likely to win the game, an outcome that really matters to them. If the helmet rule itself somehow imposed even greater harm, it wouldn't be justified. But that's a simple practical question, not a matter of deep philosophical principle.

Rewards that depend on relative performance spawn collective action problems that can cause markets to fail. For instance, the same wedge that separates individual and group interests in Darwinian arms races also helps explain why the invisible hand might not automatically lead to the best possible levels of safety in the workplace. The traditional invisible-hand account begins with the observation that, all other factors the same, riskier jobs tend to pay more, for two reasons. Because of the money employers save by not installing additional safety equipment, they can pay more; and because workers like safety, they will choose safer jobs unless riskier jobs do, in fact, pay more. According to the standard invisible-hand narrative, the fact that a worker is willing to accept lower safety for higher wages implies that the extra income was sufficient compensation for the decrement in safety. But that account rests on the assumption that extra income is valued only for the additional absolute consumption it makes possible. When a worker gets a higher wage, however, there is also a second important benefit. He is able to consume more in absolute terms, yes—but he is also able to consume more relative to others.

Most parents, for example, want to send their children to the best possible schools. Some workers might thus decide to accept a riskier job at a higher wage because that would enable them to meet the monthly payments on a house in a better school district. But other workers are in the same boat, and school quality is an inherently relative concept. So if other workers also traded safety for higher wages, the ultimate outcome would be merely to bid up the prices of houses in better school districts. Everyone would end up with less safety, yet no one would achieve the goal that made that trade seem acceptable in the first place. As in a military arms race, when all parties build more arms, none is any more secure than before.

Workers confronting these incentives might well prefer an alternative state of the world in which all enjoyed greater safety, even at the expense of all having lower wages. But workers can control only their own job choices, not the choices of others. If any individual worker accepted a safer job while others didn't, that worker would be forced to send her children to inferior schools. To get the outcome they desire, workers must act in unison. Again, a mere nudge won't do. Merely knowing that individual actions are self-canceling doesn't eliminate the incentive to take those actions.

Shallow Thinking about Freedom

As a high school student, when I first read Mill's passage that preventing harm to others was the only legitimate reason for restricting individual liberty, I enthusiastically agreed with it. I still do. Although Mill was no libertarian, libertarians are often quick to cite his harm principle approvingly.[14] But the list of restrictions of liberty that can be persuasively defended in its name is far longer than libertarians and other antigovernment activists commonly suppose.

Because the strongest objections to the kinds of policies needed to put our economy back on track have come from libertarians and others on the political right, their arguments merit careful scrutiny. Unlike most critics on the left, I will grant the libertarians' most important basic assumptions about the world—that markets are competitive, that people are rational, and that the state must meet a heavy burden of proof before restraining any individual citizen's liberty of action. Although there are reasons to question each assumption, the internal contradictions of the libertarian framework emerge clearly even if we accept these assumptions uncritically.

The fatal flaw in that framework stems from an observation that is itself completely uncontroversial—namely that in many important domains of life, performance is graded on the curve. A professional tennis player's earnings, for example, depend not on how well she plays in absolute terms, but on how well she plays relative to others on the tour. The dependence of reward on rank eliminates any presumption of harmony between individual and collective interests, and with it, the foundation of the libertarian's case for a completely unfettered market system.

But antigovernment activists are not the only ones who have failed to understand the logic that governs market exchange. Many beliefs long cherished by progressive thinkers are also at odds with that logic. Although many of the shortcomings that progressives have identified in our economic and political system are real, they're often wrong about the causes of those shortcomings, and therefore often wrong about how best to counteract them.

Many critics on the left, for example, attribute market failure to insufficient competition. But the problem is in fact a fundamental property of competition itself. Markets are more competitive now than they've ever been, yet that fact has done little to narrow the scope of market failure and much to exaggerate it.

Indirect Harm

The specific issue on which my libertarian friends and I are quickest to part company concerns how we think about what constitutes harm to others. We all agree that it's legitimate for government to restrain people from stealing others' property or from committing violence against them. The difficult cases involve more indirect forms of harm.

For example, although a sprinter who consumes anabolic steroids may make no physical contact with his closest rival, he nonetheless imposes heavy costs on him. The rival can either abstain from taking steroids, thereby losing the race and forfeiting any return on his substantial investment of time and effort, or he can restore the competitive balance by consuming steroids himself, thereby courting serious long-term health risks. Either way, the original sprinter's action will have caused him far greater harm than if he had been physically assaulted or had his bicycle stolen.

Yet many self-described libertarians insist that it should be a sprinter's right to take performance-enhancing drugs if he chooses. But why should that right trump the right of others to escape the resulting harm? Why should harm be discounted merely because it is indirect?

If Mill's harm principle is to have any coherent meaning, indirect forms of harm must count. My conception of what constitutes harm to others may strike some as expansive. But it's one that even libertarians will find difficult to challenge in their own terms. We'll see that even if libertarians had complete freedom to join others in forming any sort of society they pleased, they'd find compelling reasons for joining one that gave indirect harm equal footing with direct harm. Confusion about this point sometimes arises because indirect harm is often harder to measure than direct harm. But direct harm is sometimes hard to measure, too, and in those cases there's usually no debate about whether it should count.

The bottom line is that if one adopts any reasonable conception of what constitutes harm to others, the regulatory apparatus of the modern industrial state—in concept if not in every detail—becomes completely consistent with—and is indeed even required by—Mill's harm principle.

Governing with a Lighter Touch

The fact that our political debate has been shackled by false beliefs has prevented us from grappling with serious problems. But if we can abandon those beliefs, many of our problems turn out to be far less daunting than they appear.

Burgeoning government deficits, for example, are hardly the insurmountable hurdle they often seem. Reduced spending alone clearly can't eliminate them. With baby-boomer retirements looming and the electorate unwilling to embrace large cuts in Social Security and Medicare, we must also raise additional revenue. The good news is that doing so will not require difficult sacrifices from anyone. But it will require a Congress that is willing to redesign tax policy from the ground up. Although Tea Partiers and others decry taxes of all kinds, many levies actually make the country richer, not poorer. The way forward lies in greater reliance on these kinds of taxes.

A tax on any activity not only generates revenue but also discourages the activity. The second effect, of course, underlies the claim that taxes inhibit economic growth. That's often true of taxes on useful activities, a primary source of current tax revenue. Job creation, for example, is discouraged by the payroll tax, and investment is discouraged by the income tax, which is also a tax on savings.

But the reverse is true when we tax activities that cause harm to others. By entering a congested highway, we increase delays that in turn cost others thousands of dollars—even though entering those highways may save us only negligible time when compared with alternatives. In buying a heavy vehicle, we put the lives of others at risk, even though a lighter one might have served us almost as well.

Taxes levied on harmful activities kill two birds with one stone. They generate desperately needed revenue while discouraging behaviors whose costs greatly outweigh their benefits.

Antigovernment activists reliably denounce such taxes as "social engineering"— attempts to "control our behavior, steer our choices, and change the way we live our lives."[15] Gasoline taxes aimed at discouraging dependence on foreign oil, for example, invariably elicit this accusation.

But it's a vacuous complaint, because virtually every law and regulation constitutes social engineering. Laws against homicide and theft? Because they aim to control our behavior, steer our choices, and change the way we live our lives, they're social engineering. So are noise ordinances, speed limits, even stop signs and traffic lights. Social engineering is inescapable, simply because narrow self-interest would otherwise lead people to cause unacceptable harm to others. Only a committed anarchist could favor a world without social engineering.

If outright prohibitions are an acceptable way to discourage harmful behavior, why can't taxes be used for the same purpose? Taxes are, in fact, a far cheaper and less coercive way to curtail such behavior than laws or prescriptive regulations. That's because taxes concentrate harm reduction in the hands of those who can alter their behavior most easily.

When we tax pollution, for instance, polluters with the cheapest ways to reduce emissions rush to adopt them, thereby avoiding the tax. Similarly, when we tax vehicles by weight, those who can get by most easily with a lighter vehicle will buy one. Others find it cheaper to pay the tax.

The list of behaviors that cause undue harm to others is long. When we drink heavily, we increase the likelihood that others will die in accidents. When we smoke, we cause others to suffer tobacco-related illnesses. When we emit carbon dioxide into the atmosphere, we increase the damage from greater climate volatility.

Every dollar raised by taxing harmful activities is one dollar less that we must raise by taxing useful ones. The resulting revenue would enable us to reduce not only the federal deficit, but also the highly regressive payroll tax. And cutting that tax would stimulate hiring and help low-income families meet the burden of new taxes on harmful activities.

Wasteful government spending, of course, should be cut whenever possible. Military spending and subsidies to oil companies have dodged recent budget cuts, as did the notoriously inefficient ethanol subsidy program. These and other outlays merit closer scrutiny, to be sure.

But again, poorly conceived spending reductions often do more harm than good. Postponing highway repairs actually increases future deficits, because costs escalate so rapidly when maintenance is deferred.

Taxing harmful activities is the best way to raise the revenue essential for reducing deficits. Only someone who thinks that people have a right to cause undue harm to others could object that such taxes violate anyone's rights. And because such taxes make the national economic pie bigger, it makes little sense to object that we can't afford them.

The new taxes should be phased in only after the economy is back at full employment. But even with federal taxes at their lowest level since the 1950s, we're unlikely to summon the political will to take that step until leaders stop insisting that all taxes are evil.

Shifting tax policy in this way would place additional resources at our disposal. Without having to sacrifice anything we value, we could generate more than enough revenue to eliminate government debt and refurbish long-neglected public infrastructure.

That's a bold claim. But as we'll see, it follows directly from logic and evidence that most of us already accept. The good news, in short, is that there's an enormous pot of free money available to any society that can bring itself to think more clearly about, and deal more intelligently with, activities that cause undue harm to others.

TWO

Darwin's Wedge

I WAS BORN IN 1945. When someone my age makes a forecast about something that will happen a hundred years from now, he needn't worry about being teased by friends if it doesn't pan out. Without trepidation, then, I offer the following prediction. One century hence, if a roster of professional economists is asked to identify the intellectual father of their discipline, a majority will name Charles Darwin.

If the same question were posed today, of course, more than 99 percent of my colleagues would name Adam Smith. My views about Darwin's significance reflect no shortage of admiration for Smith on my part. On the contrary, reading any random passage from the eighteenth-century Scottish moral philosopher's masterwork, *The Wealth of Nations,* still causes me to marvel at the depth and breadth of his insights.

Charles Darwin was himself no slouch, obviously, yet few people outside academic departments of biology and economics associate his name with ideas in economics. Those who have studied Darwin's theory of evolution carefully, however, realize that he was in fact heavily influenced by the works of the economists Thomas Malthus and David Ricardo. Malthus had been a student of Smith's, and Ricardo was heavily influenced by *The Wealth of Nations.* So even if my prediction comes true, Smith's fans can still justifiably think of him as the great-grandfather of economics.

I base my prediction on a subtle but extremely important distinction between Darwin's view of the competitive process and Smith's. Today Smith is best remembered for his invisible-hand theory, which, according to some of his modern disciples, holds that impersonal market forces channel the behavior of greedy individuals to produce the greatest good for all. As noted in chapter 1, this characterization is an oversimplification. But it captures an important dimension of Smith's understanding of the competitive process. In any event, it's fair to say that the invisible-hand theory's optimistic portrayal of unregulated market outcomes has become the bedrock of the antigovernment activists' worldview. They believe regulation is unnecessary because they believe unbridled market forces can take care of things quite nicely on their own.

Darwin's view of the competitive process was fundamentally different. His observations persuaded him that the interests of individual animals were often profoundly in conflict with the broader interests of their own species. In time, I predict, the invisible hand will come to be seen as a special case of Darwin's more general theory. Many of the libertarians' most cherished beliefs, which are perfectly plausible within Smith's framework, don't survive at all in Darwin's.

Giving the Invisible Hand Its Due

Even so, the invisible-hand theory remains a genuinely revolutionary insight, all the more so because in hindsight it seems so obvious. Why does a business owner go to the trouble of designing a new product that consumers are likely to find appealing? Why does he invest such effort to revamp his production process to reduce costs? The motive, as Smith and undoubtedly many before him clearly saw, was simply to make more money. What others did not see clearly was the responses those actions would provoke from rival business owners, and how the ensuing dynamic would produce outcomes very different from the ones intended.

If one producer comes up with a cheaper way of manufacturing a product, he can cut his price slightly and steal market share from his rivals. In the short run, his profits soar, just as he'd hoped. But the loss of market share by rival firms gives their owners a powerful incentive to mimic the original innovation. And once the innovation spreads industrywide, the resulting competition drives the product's price down to a level just sufficient to cover the new, lower production costs. The ultimate beneficiaries of all this churning are consumers, who enjoy steadily improved products at ever-lower prices.

The Wealth of Nations was published in 1776, not even 250 years ago. What an extraordinary narrative, Smith's invisible hand! Thousands of brilliant minds had earlier observed the same patterns that prompted Smith's insight, yet none had managed to appreciate their significance. Aristotle didn't see it. Copernicus didn't see it. Newton didn't see it.

Smith was well aware that unregulated markets didn't always produce the best outcomes. For the most part, the market failures that were his focus involved underhanded practices by business leaders in a position to wield power. Thus, he wrote, "To widen the market and to narrow the competition, is always in the interest of [those who live by profit]. . . . [Such interest] comes from an order of men, whose interest is never exactly the same with that of the public, who have generally an interest to deceive and even to oppress the public, and who accordingly have, upon many occasions, both deceived and oppressed it."[1]

When markets failed, in Smith's view, it was because of an absence of effective competition. A firm might deceive its customers about the quality of its offerings; or it might cut prices to drive rivals out of business, only to raise prices again once they were gone. Such abuses were common in Smith's day and, though less frequent now, remain part of the landscape.

Social critics on the left have long focused on anticompetitive behavior as the key to understanding why markets fail. The late John Kenneth Galbraith, for example, stressed the contrast between the "traditional sequence" envisioned by Adam Smith's modern disciples and a "revised sequence" that Galbraith saw as a more accurate portrayal of the modern marketplace.[2] In the traditional sequence, consumers enter the market with well-formed preferences, and firms struggle to meet their demands as well and cheaply as possible. But in Galbraith's revised sequence, powerful corporations first decide which products would be most convenient and profitable for them to produce, and then hire Madison Avenue hucksters to persuade consumers to want those products.

Many economists remain skeptical about this account, citing conspicuous examples of corporate failure, such as the Ford Edsel in Galbraith's day.[3] Ford introduced the Edsel with great fanfare in September 1957. It was named for Edsel B. Ford, son of company founder Henry Ford, and its outsized promotional budget included a widely viewed national television special, *The Edsel Show*. But customers never showed much enthusiasm for the car, and its production was discontinued in 1960.

More recently, Microsoft spent almost a billion dollars to develop and promote the Kin, a smartphone targeted at the youth market. The phone, which hit stores in April 2010, was unceremoniously pulled from shelves just forty-five days later because of abysmal sales.

Notwithstanding such failures, there is little doubt that advertising campaigns can shift consumer tastes. But from the perspective of those who are skeptical about markets, advertising wizardry is a two-edged sword. The driving force behind the invisible hand is greed, and if producers are currently selling inferior products at inflated prices, there's cash on the table. If a rival producer could let consumers know that a better, cheaper model was available, he could make lots of money. Modern marketing methods are surely up to that task. Competition is obviously still far from perfect, but today's markets are much closer to the perfectly informed, frictionless ideal than were those of Adam Smith's day.

Individual and Group Interests Often Diverge

Darwin trained his sights on competition not among merchants but among individual members of plant and animal species. But the two domains, he realized, share deep similarities. Darwin's analysis revealed a systemic flaw in the dynamics of competition. The failures he identified resulted not from too little competition, but from the very logic of the process itself. The central premise of his theory was that natural selection favored variants of traits and behaviors insofar as they enhanced the reproductive fitness of the individual animals that bore them. If a trait made the individual better able to survive and reproduce, it would be favored. Otherwise, it would eventually vanish. In many cases, Darwin recognized, the same variant that served the individual's interest would also serve the interests of its species. But he also saw that many traits promoted individual interest to the detriment of the species.

As an example in the former category, consider the speed of the gazelle. Mature members of this species can sustain speeds of 30 mph for extended periods and can reach 60 mph in short bursts. How did they become so fast? It might seem that being faster would be unambiguously better from an evolutionary point of view, but that can't be true or else all species would be fast. Tapeworms are slow. In their particular environmental niche, however, being fast never really mattered. Gazelles are fast because they evolved in an environment in which being faster than others was often decisive for survival. The gazelle's predators, which include the cheetah, are also very fast, and there are few places to take shelter on the terrain where both groups evolved. Slower genetic variants among the modern gazelle's ancestors were more likely to be caught and eaten.

Since the selective pressure that forged speed in gazelles was the threat of being caught by predators from other species, greater speed posed no conflict between the interests of individual gazelles and those of gazelles as a species.[4] Up to some point, being faster conferred advantages for both individual and species. With respect to this particular trait, then, Darwin's natural selection narrative closely tracks Smith's parallel invisible-hand narrative about the proliferation of cost-saving innovations and attractive new product designs.

Many other traits, however, increase the reproductive fitness of each individual while simultaneously imposing significant costs on large subgroups of the species. Such conflicts are especially likely for traits that confer advantage in an individual's head-to-head competition with members of its own species.

A case in point is the outsized antlers of bull elk. These antlers function as weaponry not against external predators but in the competition among bulls for access to females. In these battles, it's relative antler size that matters. Because a mutation that coded for larger antlers made a bull more likely to defeat its rivals, it was quick to spread, since winning bulls gained access to many cows, each of whose calves would then carry the mutation. Additional mutations accumulated over the generations, in effect creating an arms race. The process seems to have stabilized, with the largest antlers of North American bull elk measuring more than 4 feet across and weighing more than 40 pounds.

Although each mutation along this path enhanced individual reproductive fitness, the cumulative effect of those mutations was to make life more miserable for bull elk as a group. Large antlers compromise mobility in densely wooded areas, for example, making bulls more likely to be killed and eaten by wolves. A bull with smaller antlers would be better able to escape predators, but because he'd be handicapped in his battles with other bulls, he'd be unlikely to pass those smaller antlers into the next generation.

In short, bull elk face a collective action problem. One bull's larger antlers make him more likely to win a fight, but they also make his rivals more likely to lose that same fight. The individual payoff to having larger antlers is thus substantially larger than the collective payoff. As a group, bull elk would be better off if each animal's antlers were much smaller.

The conflict between individual and species arises because reproductive fitness is essentially a relative concept. Under natural selection, the traits that succeed are those that confer relative advantage. To spread, it's not sufficient that a genetic variant be helpful. It must be *more* helpful than the other variants with which it's competing. A trait that evolves because it helps the individual prevail in battles against members of the same species typically constitutes a handicap for the species as a whole. Antlers are such a trait. At every stage of the arms race that molded them, the relative advantages to individuals canceled one another out, and when the race finally stabilized, the species was saddled with a substantial absolute handicap.

Darwin's insight does a lot of the heavy lifting in my project to take the libertarian's basic principles as my starting point and then explore what those principles imply about the kind of government that freedom-loving people might choose for themselves. Their choice clearly depends heavily on the kinds of outcomes they can expect from unbridled competition in the marketplace. Libertarians' expectations have been guided by Smith's invisible-hand narrative and its presumption of perfect competition. In the natural environments that were Darwin's concern, the kinds of impediments to competition that worry traditional market skeptics were almost completely absent. Yet Darwin's understanding of the competitive process itself supports a profound measure of skepticism about market outcomes. It's instructive to examine more closely how that understanding causes the invisible-hand account to falter.

The libertarian's faith in unregulated markets rests on several premises. Two of the most important are that consumers are well informed and that markets are competitive. Unless we insist on reading these premises literally, there is nothing in Darwin's framework that challenges either of them. Of course, with so many millions of products and services on offer, no consumer could possibly be well informed about every option that might be worth considering. But consumers are reasonably well informed, or could choose to become so, about the options most likely to be important. Similarly, no market could possibly satisfy all the stringent conditions required for perfect competition—completely free entry and exit and a large number of firms producing identical, standardized products, each serving only a small share of the market. Yet most markets are workably competitive, in the sense that if a clearly better option were possible, some entrepreneur would eventually step forward and make consumers aware of it.

In short, Darwin's challenge has nothing to do with the kinds of competitive imperfections traditionally invoked by market skeptics. If libertarians were going to empower the state to regulate firms in any way, it would not be because of any evidence that markets were insufficiently competitive.

But Adam Smith's invisible-hand narrative also requires some additional assumptions, ones that available evidence should lead any reasonable person to question. One is that people are rationally attentive to all relevant costs and benefits of the various options they consider. Another is that, to the extent that material resources matter for well-being, it's absolute income that counts, not relative income. Compelling evidence suggests that both assumptions fail in ways that undermine the invisible-hand narrative. The implications of the second assumption's failure, we will see, are especially problematic.

As concerns the first assumption, a large body of research has demonstrated that people are not attentive to costs and benefits in the manner required by traditional theories of rational consumer behavior.[5] For example, people are generally attentive even to small costs and benefits that are certain to affect them immediately, but they tend to give short shrift to even large costs and benefits that either are uncertain or occur with significant delay. People also exhibit a systematic tendency to treat gains very differently from losses. That asymmetry is not irrational per se, but its magnitude often leads to outcomes that are unattractive from the decision maker's own point of view.

Failure of the rationality assumption might lead people to empower government to restructure the decision environment in various ways that would foster better choices. But the question of how government might respond to those failures is not my focus here. That question has already received comprehensive treatment from Thaler and Sunstein in *Nudge*. Instead, my focus will be on the question of what kind of government a fully empowered libertarian would choose if she were persuaded by the evidence that people's concerns about relative position figure prominently in their economic decisions. Such concerns, as we'll see, don't constitute a departure from rationality at all.

The Importance of Relative Position

As Darwin saw clearly, much of life is graded on the curve. For a genetic mutation to be favored, it's not sufficient that it enable the individual to generate large numbers of offspring. It must enable him to produce more offspring than rivals who do not carry the mutation. Reproductive fitness is thus a quintessentially relative concept. To survive and prosper, an individual need not be the strongest, fastest, or smartest animal in the universe. He may be weak, slow, and stupid. What matters is that he be able to compete successfully against members of his own species vying for the same resources.

To do so, his nervous system must absorb information about the local environment and calculate the extent to which different behavioral options will contribute to his ability to achieve various goals. But his nervous system must also perform another important function, which is to rank those goals. Which goals are most important? Which ones should be abandoned during times of duress?

We can't pretend to understand how markets function unless we begin with a reasonably accurate portrait of the structure of human motivation. Human motivation resides in the brain, which has been evolving for millions of years. Its proximate purpose in every generation was to guide its bearer to take the actions that would best promote the transmission of its genetic blueprint into the next generation. The Darwinian framework is the only scientific framework available for trying to understand why humans and other animals are motivated to behave as they do.

To think of the brain as an evolved organ is not to deny the importance of culture in human behavior. Humans and their cultures obviously evolved in tandem, each exerting substantial influence on the other.[6] Many have found it instructive to view the evolved brain as the hardware of the human motivational system and culture as the corresponding software.[7] As this more nuanced view emphasizes, human motivation is extremely complex and multidimensional.

When economists try to model it in an attempt to understand how markets work, we're forced to adopt stick-figure simplifications. But some of those simplifications have been extreme. Most economists, for example, assume that people are purely selfish, even though there is compelling evidence for motives that transcend narrow self-interest.[8] Most also assume that the satisfaction people take from consumption depends only on the absolute amount of it, even in the face of compelling evidence that relative consumption also matters.[9]

Since reproductive success has always depended first and foremost on relative resource holdings, it would be astonishing if the evolved brain didn't care deeply about relative position. Most vertebrate societies, including the vast majority of early human societies, were polygynous, meaning that males claimed more than one mate when they could. It was the high-ranking males in those societies who claimed multiple mates. And given the inexorable logic of musical chairs, it was the low-ranking males who were left with none.

Famines were also a frequent survival threat in the environments in which humans evolved. But even in the worst famines, there was always some food available. And the question of who got fed was almost always settled by relative income. Then as now, it was the poorest in every group who were most likely to starve.

Against the backdrop of this payoff structure, imagine two genetic variants —one that codes for a brain that cares strongly about relative position, and the other for a brain that doesn't care at all about it. In general, caring more strongly about something inclines you to expend more mental and physical energy to acquire it. So individuals who care more about relative position would be more likely to muster the behaviors necessary to acquire and defend positions of high rank. That, in turn, would make them more likely to survive famines and marry successfully, thus increasing their genotype's frequency in the next generation.

The current environment is of course very different from the ones in which our ancestors evolved. But relative position still matters, often for purely instrumental reasons. When you go for a job interview, for example, you want to dress presentably, but the standards for looking good are almost purely relative. An interviewer many have no conscious awareness of how different candidates were dressed. But if you show up in a $500 suit, you'll be more likely to get a callback if other candidates were wearing $200 suits than if they were dressed in $2,000 suits. And as discussed earlier, parents who want to send their children to good schools must outbid other parents for houses in good school districts. Their ability to do so depends almost entirely on relative income. Here, too, we see the logic of musical chairs: no matter how much money people earn, only half of all children can attend schools in the top half.

Context and Evaluation

Experience confirms that psychological reactions to many consumption experiences depend heavily on the context in which those experiences occur. Some people, for example, derive pleasure from the experience of driving a fast car. But how fast does a car have to be to deliver that pleasure? It's impossible even to think about that question without knowing something about the relevant context. In the 1920s, a car would have seemed fast if it could eventually reach 60 mph. But as the years have passed, the standards that define fast have changed considerably.

The first sports car I ever drove was a 1955 Ford Thunderbird. Its 292-cubic-inch V8 engine generated almost 200 horsepower and propelled the car from 0 to 60 mph in 11.5 seconds. I'll never forget how blisteringly fast it seemed at the time. In recent years, I've been driving a 2001 Mazda Miata. Although its engine has less than half the displacement of the '55 Thunderbird's, it can reach 60 mph in less than 8 seconds. It's a great little car, but even though it's significantly faster than the old Thunderbird, it doesn't seem nearly as fast. That's because in the current sports car constellation it isn't fast. The 2011 Miata will reach 60 mph in 6.5 seconds. Nearer the top of the performance ladder, the 2011 Porsche 911 Turbo reaches that speed in less than 3 seconds. *That's* fast. But it won't seem fast forever.

The hypothesis that concerns about relative position are part of the evolved circuitry of the human brain is supported not just by everyday experience, but also by evidence of specific neurophysiological processes that respond to local rank. For example, local rank appears to both affect, and be affected by, concentrations of the neurotransmitter serotonin, which regulates moods and behavior. Within limits, elevated serotonin concentrations are associated with enhanced feelings of well-being. (The drug Prozac, widely prescribed for depression and other mood disorders, increases the effective concentrations of serotonin in the brain.)

In males, concentrations of the sex hormone testosterone appear to have a similar relationship with local rank. Reductions in local rank tend to be followed by reductions in plasma testosterone levels, whereas these levels tend to rise following increases in rank. A player who wins a tennis match decisively, for example, experiences a postmatch elevation in plasma testosterone, and his vanquished opponent experiences a postmatch reduction. As with serotonin, elevated concentrations of testosterone appear to facilitate behaviors that help achieve or maintain high local rank.[10]

Further evidence of the importance of relative position comes from studies of the determinants of happiness, or subjective well-being. Early investigators found that whereas measured average happiness levels within a country tend to be highly stable over time, even in the face of significant economic growth, individual happiness levels within any country at a given moment of time depend strongly on income.[11] And recent work documents a robust negative association between individual happiness measures and average neighborhood income.[12]

In sum, no economic model can hope to capture how markets actually function unless it begins with the assumption that context shapes evaluation in significant ways. Yet the models that underlie Adam Smith's invisible-hand narrative assume, preposterously, that context doesn't matter at all. And it's not just libertarians and right-wing zealots who embrace that assumption. All economic forecasting and policy analysis done in government for more than a century have relied on the very same models.

Our task in the next three chapters will be to explore how explicit recognition of the importance of context alters our understanding of how markets function. As we'll see, adding this simple feature is the key to understanding why the invisible hand breaks down, even when consumers are fully informed and interact with employers and sellers under conditions of perfect competition. We'll also see that failure to understand why markets fail has led many on the left to invent spurious explanations for why we need to regulate them. Their claim is that regulation is necessary to protect us from exploitation by sellers and employers with market power. But the real reason we regulate is to protect ourselves from the consequences of excessive competition with one another.

Why Are Traditional Economic Models Context-Free?

As we'll see, wasteful competition follows from the simple fact that evaluation depends strongly on context in many domains. That context shapes evaluation is completely uncontroversial. Would any sane person really want to stand before an informed audience to defend the assertion that context doesn't matter? What could possibly persuade someone, for example, that perceptions about whether a car is fast are completely independent of the performance of other cars in the same local environment? It would be an utterly hopeless task. But that very fact raises the question of how we came to embrace context-free economic theories in the first place. So before we explore how context shapes economic behavior, it will be useful to consider that question.

In recent years, I have posed it to a number of economists. One suggested that the importance of context will be fully embraced once it can be shown conclusively that it helps us track the data better than traditional models. Experience, however, suggests otherwise. In earlier work, for example, I've pointed out that economists have been reluctant to abandon theories of saving based on absolute income, even in the face of compelling evidence that theories based on relative income do a much better job of tracking the data.[13]

Another economist speculated that many of our colleagues fear that taking context seriously might signal a certain lack of rigor. After all, many economists take considerable pride in their ability to formalize their theories mathematically. Some in that camp might fear that taking positional concerns seriously could cause them to be mistaken for sociologists. Yet as past work has amply demonstrated, there is no barrier to formalizing models that incorporate positional concerns.[14] Those models can be as complex as economists want to make them.

Still another economist suggested that the unwillingness to take context seriously might be rooted in the fact that doing so would undermine the celebrated invisible-hand narrative. This explanation may well account for the attitudes of at least some economists. But it's not sufficient. The profession, after all, has incorporated numerous other forms of market failure into its arsenal of policy recommendations. Even the most ardent market enthusiasts, for example, are quick to concede a productive role for government intervention to curb pollution when transaction costs are high.

A final possibility I consider is the one that strikes me as most plausible. In the more than thirty years I have been writing about positional concerns, the most frequent response of libertarians and others on the right has been to accuse me of trying to incite class warfare. They dismiss positional concerns for the same reason they dismiss the preferences of sadists. But bringing positional concerns into the conversation is nothing remotely like giving policy weight to the preferences of sadists. We can all agree that society has a legitimate interest in discouraging negative emotions like envy and jealousy. Because there will always be someone out there with more and better stuff, being preoccupied with that fact would be a sure recipe for unhappiness. Teaching our children not to envy the good fortunes of others is a worthwhile project. But such teachings, even if completely successful, will not eliminate the consequences of wasteful spending prompted by concerns about relative position. Such waste stems far less from envy than from the fact that many important rewards in life depend on relative consumption. In any event, tax remedies for collective action problems are no more an endorsement of envy than speeding tickets are an endorsement of driving too fast.

THREE

No Cash on the Table

ADAM SMITH'S CONCERNS ABOUT THE efficacy of the invisible hand focused on the ability of powerful actors to limit competition. Liberal skeptics of the marketplace were quick to embrace those concerns and continue to see limited competition as the most important cause of market failure. But as Charles Darwin saw clearly, even perfect competition will not always guide behavior in ways that promote the common good. Individual and group interests often diverge sharply, he realized, and in such cases individual interest generally carries the day.

An important feature of Darwin's narrative is that market failure can occur even when all individuals have taken full advantage of all available opportunities for potential gain. Recall Thomas Schelling's hockey players who skate without helmets when permitted to do so, yet vote overwhelmingly in favor of rules that require them to wear helmets. As in that example, the kinds of market failure Darwin envisioned can happen even when individuals are fully informed and rational. Even though it would be better for all bull elk if each animal's antlers were smaller, it would not be in any individual bull's interest to have smaller antlers.

In contrast, imperfect competition can lead to market failure only if some individuals persistently fail to take advantage of available options that would benefit them. In the familiar economist's metaphor, some individuals must be leaving cash on the table. And that, I'll argue, is a fatal flaw in conventional accounts of market failure.

Why Haven't Labor-Managed Firms Proliferated?

My first exposure to this particular flaw came during discussions with a group of economists in my department during my early years at Cornell. Members of this group had developed a research program focused on worker-managed firms. They were deeply committed to ideals of social justice and extremely skeptical about conventional hierarchical capitalist firms. Such firms, they believed, were the source of pollution, alienation, and a long inventory of other serious social ills. They were confident that the surest way to eliminate those ills was to replace the traditional model of industrial enterprise with a new model—one that placed employees at the helm.

In light of evidence that people place high value on personal autonomy, this view did not seem totally implausible.[1] Studies suggest that happier workers are also more productive,[2] and it's easy to see how working for a firm whose mission you don't believe in and being ordered around all day by an autocratic boss might undermine your morale. Proponents of labor-managed economic systems felt sure that things would change dramatically for the better once workers were placed in charge. As three senior researchers in this nascent field put it at the time,

> Workers in more participatory workplaces are not only more productive but also more satisfied with their jobs. We could apparently increase hourly output by at least 15 percent without pushing workers harder or exposing them to greater workplace hazards. This waste elimination would come from greater work commitment, not speedup. It would capitalize on all the current worker effort currently WASTED in capitalist enterprises through working to rules, through slowdown and shirking, through direct worker resistance.[3]

It's a remarkable claim. If any firm could achieve the productivity increases described in this passage while simultaneously making its workers happier, it would enjoy a prodigious competitive advantage. Since wages account for about 70 percent of a typical firm's total cost, increasing productivity by 15 percent would reduce total cost by more than 10 percent. The firm could cut its prices by almost that amount and still remain profitable, which would enable it to peel off most of its rivals' customers. And because its workers would be happier, it would have its pick of the best talent, which would further increase its competitive advantage. In short, this narrative implied that there were prodigious sums of cash on the table. Any firm that enjoyed these advantages should sweep the market like a prairie fire, reaping enormous profits in the process.

Labor-managed firms in fact have a long history in the United States and other industrial economies. Small family businesses are perhaps the most widespread example. But many other cooperative ventures also populate this category. When I was a graduate student in Berkeley in the late 1960s, many of us shopped at Leopold's, an employee-managed record store. Many cities have cooperatively owned and managed food retailers.

Yet these organizations occupy an extremely circumscribed niche in the economy. There is absolutely no evidence that they're poised to sweep the marketplace. That observation raises a basic question: If labor-managed firms are so great, why don't we see more of them?

I once put this question to several of my colleagues in the Cornell labor-managed systems group—a collection of very smart people who appeared to take it seriously. After much discussion, their considered response was that labor-managed firms had failed to proliferate because financial markets refused to make capital available to them on fair terms. Banks, they explained, had a long history of dealing with conventional capitalist firms. They knew the players in that community well and felt they understood the risks well enough to be able to evaluate loan applications intelligently. In support of this explanation, one of my colleagues produced a copy of a bank's loan application form that a local labor-managed firm had been required to fill out. It was twice as long as the same bank's normal application form and asked many more probing questions.

My response was that this handicap couldn't possibly explain why labor-managed firms had failed to proliferate. If these firms enjoy more than a 10 percent cost advantage over conventional firms, they can certainly afford to spend the extra time it takes to fill out longer loan application forms. Indeed, they should be able to grow and prosper even if the banking system were to cut them off completely. Most businesses start out small. One with a significant cost advantage might have to grow more slowly for a while if it were denied outside sources of credit, but a 10 percent cost advantage is itself a substantial source of internal capital for expansion.

More important, the very idea that a capitalist banking system might persistently deny funds to creditworthy borrowers strains credulity. All business loans entail at least some risk. But any firm with a 10 percent cost advantage over its rivals would be at the extreme low end of the risk scale. If bankers were frightened because they weren't accustomed to dealing with labor-managed firms, their traditional response would be not to deny credit altogether, but rather to charge a higher interest rate. And any firm with a 10 percent cost advantage could easily absorb a higher interest rate.

Others have written that banks might be reluctant to lend to labor-managed firms because they believe that enabling that ownership structure to spread over time would severely threaten the long-run interests of the capitalist system.[4] But to suppose that a banker would pass up the opportunity to make a profitable loan for that reason is to completely misunderstand the very essence of capitalism. Capitalism begins with the assumption that people are greedy. In the most widely quoted passage from *The Wealth of Nations*, Smith wrote, "It is not from the benevolence of the butcher, the brewer, or the baker that we expect our dinner, but from their regard to their own interest."[5] Bankers aren't altruists on a mission to promote the interests of their class at their personal expense. They're just capitalists trying to make a buck. So even if we grant the implausible assumption that loans to labor-managed firms would eventually undermine the capitalist system, a rational banker would still have no motive to refrain from making them.

The problem is analogous to the tragedy of the commons that leads to overfishing, which I will discuss in more detail in chapter 10. This is another form of market failure that results from the wedge between individual and group incentives described by Charles Darwin. Fishermen don't deplete their fisheries because they're stupid. It happens because no single person's decision to enter the fishing industry has any measurable effect on the ultimate outcome. Similarly in banking, if enough bankers lend money to labor-managed firms, the resulting prosperity of those firms might cause the capitalist system to crumble, but nothing would have played out differently if any particular banker had held back. Under the circumstances, there's simply no rational motive for a greedy banker to pass up a profitable lending opportunity, even if she is deeply committed to the goal of preserving the capitalist enterprise in its current form. Her own restraint would cost her some profits, but it wouldn't make capitalism's survival any more likely.

And why would a banker feel committed to a goal like that in the first place? Banks could survive quite nicely in a world in which most of their clients were labor-managed firms. And if costs were really 10 percent lower in a world like that, banks themselves would eventually become labor managed. So a bank that gained early experience with that type of enterprise would actually enjoy a powerful competitive advantage.

As noted, however, there is no compelling evidence that labor-managed firms enjoy a competitive advantage at all. On a visit to Berkeley years after I had finished my graduate work there, I noticed that Leopold's, the employee-managed record store, was no longer in the storefront location it had occupied during my student days. When I asked a friend what had become of it, he said it had gone out of business a few years earlier. But its main competitor, an outlet of the Discount Records chain located nearby, was still a going concern.

Again, labor-managed firms have been around for a long time, but they have never occupied more than a small portion of the economic terrain. There is no indication whatsoever that they're poised to take over the marketplace. The only way to make sense of these facts is to conclude that the labor-managed firm may have some advantages over conventional firms on some of the critical dimensions of performance that predict and explain market success, but that it must also perform less well on other dimensions.

The employees at Leopold's, for example, may have enjoyed the sense of empowerment that came from having a voice in day-to-day management decisions, which in turn may have made them more productive. But over time, perhaps they grew weary of having to attend so many meetings. Or perhaps the difficulty is that workers who are put in charge produce the kinds of products they think would be good for people, rather than those that people actually want.

Markets Don't Ignore Profit Opportunities for Long

My exchanges with the evangelists for labor-managed firms were an object lesson in the power of ideology to disable the capacity for critical thinking. My colleagues knew there were grave shortcomings in the market system, and they were equally sure that capitalist exploitation was the cause of those problems. But it was precisely that faith that made them unwilling or unable to examine the broader implications of their theory.

Over the years I have urged my students to disengage their ideological leanings as completely as possible when thinking about questions of market failure. If they have a hypothesis about why a market has failed in some particular way, the first and most important test of that hypothesis is whether it implies that people have been leaving cash on the table. The narrative put forward by the evangelists for labor-managed firms fails that test unambiguously. If those firms deliver the kinds of advantages claimed by their proponents, entrepreneurs could make billions of dollars by buying conventional firms and reorganizing them as labor-managed units. They'd need only buy up the stock of an existing conventional firm, shift decision authority to workers, then sell shares in the restructured firm to the new worker-owners. Because the new firm would be much more efficient than the one it replaced, those shares would sell for much more than they cost to acquire. And yet, as noted, the predicted stampede to reorganize firms in this way never materialized.

In short, theories that imply that vast sums of cash are being left on the table for extended periods are bad theories. Any market situation that has remained stable for an extended period is overwhelmingly likely to be one in which there are *not* large sums of cash on the table. Yet many of the explanations offered by those who have denounced market outcomes from the left fail the no-cash-on-the-table test. These critics, for example, often claim that we must regulate workplace safety because workers would otherwise be exploited by powerful economic elites. At first glance, the claim may sound plausible. The owners of the enterprise, after all, often have more money than they can possibly spend, while their workers risk life and limb each day for barely a living wage. That certainly *looks* like exploitation. But as I'll explain, it's also an account that implies vast amounts of cash on the table.

Suppose there were a woodworker at risk of injury because the employer's table saw had no guard over the blade. Should the employer have installed one? Any intelligent answer to that question must rest on a comparison of the costs and benefits of the device. If the worker owned the business and had to make the decision on his own, the calculation would be straightforward. The cost of the device is easy to measure, and for the sake of discussion let's assume it to be $50 a week. The benefit of the device is the largest dollar amount he'd be willing to sacrifice to gain the blade guard's protection, which of course depends on how dangerous it is to operate the saw without one. If he'd pay up to $100, say, then installing the blade guard would clearly make sense. But if it's worth, say, only $30 to him, then he'd choose not to install it.

The logic of the decision is no different when the woodworker is employed by a firm. It's still necessary to compare the blade guard's cost with its benefit. The fact that the employer would be writing the check for the device does nothing to change its cost. And its benefit is still the value, in the worker's eyes, of the protection it would provide. Let's suppose the blade guard meets the cost-benefit test, since that's the more interesting case. If it's worth $100 a week to the woodworker and costs only $50 a week to install and maintain, then the employer has every incentive to provide it. Failure to do so would be to forgo the $50 of economic surplus it could have created.

Skeptics of the invisible hand insist the capitalist employer's greed motivates him to withhold the device. But that charge misses the essence of Adam Smith's argument. If an employer failed to install a safety device that met the cost-benefit test, there would be cash on the table available to any rival employer willing to install one. The device costs only $50 a week, remember, and the woodworker values it at $100 a week. It's fair to assume that his current employer isn't losing money by employing him at his current salary. So if a rival offered him a saw with a blade guard at a salary only $75 less than his current salary, the offer would be accepted. After the move, the woodworker would enjoy $25 in additional economic surplus each week (the $100 value he assigns to the blade guard less the $75 cut in salary). And his new employer would also be better off by $25 a week (assuming his costs were otherwise similar to the current employer's). Any time an employer refuses to install a piece of safety equipment that passes the cost-benefit test, then, there will always be cash on the table.

Many critics of the market system respond that it's morally reprehensible to use cost-benefit analysis for deciding whether a safety device should be installed. But that objection fails to withstand even minimal scrutiny. Safety devices cost money that could be used to purchase other things people value. It's impossible to create a world in which the risk of unfavorable outcomes is zero. When deciding which safety steps to take, we must compare costs and benefits.

If you disagree, I pose two simple questions: Did you get your car's brakes checked today? If so, do you plan to get them checked again tomorrow? No sensible person answers yes to both questions. If the brakes on your car have just been found to be in good working order, the odds of them failing the next day are vanishingly small. Getting them checked takes time and costs money, so reasonable people do it only at intervals. States that have automobile inspection programs usually specify yearly checks. Most people don't get their brakes checked more often than that because doing so would be expensive and wouldn't yield significant benefits. If the cost-benefit framework is the right way to think about how often to get your brakes checked, why isn't it also the right framework for thinking about whether there should be a blade guard on a table saw?

Other skeptics of the market respond that the invisible-hand argument might be persuasive if labor markets were truly competitive, but go on to insist that labor markets are not, in fact, competitive. Without doubt, there is less mobility in labor markets than in many other markets. Once someone signs on with an employer, for example, many of the skills she develops over time are of more value to that employer than to rival employers, which makes it steadily less likely that she'd garner an attractive outside offer. At some point she becomes, in effect, a captive employee.[6]

But even if she were forced to stick with the same employer forever, it still wouldn't make sense for her employer to withhold a safety device that met the cost-benefit test. Both she and her employer would do better if the employer bought the device and then cut her salary by enough to cover its cost. Market skeptics might respond that captive workers are paid so little that they couldn't afford as much as they'd be willing to pay if they earned a truly competitive wage. In that case, however, a country that was inclined to regulate would have a far better option. It could simply require that firms pay higher wages. Employees could then decide for themselves whether additional safety measures were worth their cost.

In any event, the claim that labor markets are not competitive must not be pushed too far. Mobility isn't perfect, but people change jobs far more frequently than in the past. And even when firms know that most of their employees are unlikely to move, some do move and others eventually retire or die. So employers must maintain their ability to attract a steady flow of new applicants, which means they must nurture their reputations. There are few secrets in the information age. A firm that exploits its workers will eventually experience serious hiring difficulties.

In sum, to insist that a worker's saw is "too dangerous" is to insist that the cost of making it safer would be less than the corresponding benefit. If labor markets were competitive and workers valued a safer saw enough to cover its additional cost, the employer would have a strong incentive to provide it, lest a rival employer poach his worker. If neither happens, the presumption is that the worker does not, in fact, value the safer saw enough to cover its additional cost. He might be glad to have it for free, but he is not willing to pay for it.

More detailed accounts of the invisible-hand story go on to explain how the market serves up a broad menu of choices regarding workplace safety. Some firms offer high wages and low safety, others offer low wages and high safety, and still others offer intermediate values of the two. Faced with this menu, workers sort themselves across firms as their individual preferences dictate. Tastes differ along many dimensions, of course, but for present purposes the two that matter are attitudes toward risk and desires for the things that money can buy.

For the most cautious people who happen also to care least about money, the best option is a job at the extreme low end of the risk scale. That job gives them the safety they crave, and because money doesn't loom especially large in their eyes, the lower wage is acceptable. At the other extreme are those with the least cautious attitudes toward risk and the most pressing desires for additional income. For them, the riskiest job is the best option. It maximizes their pay, and they're relatively tolerant of its extra risk. People with less extreme preferences on these two dimensions do best by choosing jobs with intermediate values of wages and safety.

According to the traditional invisible-hand account, then, workers get as much safety on the job as they're willing to pay for. Since making jobs safer requires real resources that could be used for other things we value, that's as it should be. If a worker doesn't get the extra safety he claims he wanted, that must mean he didn't value it enough to be willing to pay its cost.

Why Skepticism about the Invisible Hand Persists

Market skeptics often respond, tellingly, by citing behavior by employers that seems transparently at odds with the invisible hand's rosy portrayal of market outcomes. Walmart, the nation's largest retailer, has often been their target. On numerous occasions, for example, the company has locked overnight maintenance workers into stores with no supervisor present to let them out in case of emergency. Walmart defended this step as necessary to control theft, but it has led to at least some instances in which employees were unable to receive timely care for medical emergencies. The company has also been accused and convicted of a host of other violations of labor laws, including altering employee time records to avoid overtime payments. If that's not exploitation, it's a convincing simulacrum.[7]

Of course, Walmart has also brought many benefits to the communities it serves, most notably a broad array of products at low prices made possible by its tireless cost-cutting. Yet throughout its history, the company has also moved aggressively to oppose various laws and regulations that libertarians and other antigovernment activists view as unwarranted intrusions on the invisible hand of the marketplace.[8] Many of the behaviors that these laws and regulations aim to prevent certainly *seem* to be ones worth preventing. And yet, by all available evidence, the marketplace is more competitive now than it's been at any point in history.

If the market is truly competitive, what makes those regulations necessary? What prevents the invisible hand from working its magic?

An Alternative Explanation of Market Failure

The explanation I propose is simple.[9] It rests on Darwin's central insight that the interests of individuals are often in conflict with those of broader groups. In the standard invisible-hand account, as noted in chapter 1, the fact that a worker is willing to accept lower safety in exchange for higher wages implies that the extra income was sufficient compensation for reduced safety. But the invisible-hand narrative assumes that extra income is valued only for the additional absolute consumption it supports. A higher wage, however, also confers a second benefit for certain (and right away) that safety only provides in the rare cases when the guard is what keeps the careless hand from the blade—the ability to consume more relative to others.

That fact is nowhere more important than in the case of parents' desires to send their children to the best possible schools. As noted in chapter 1, a worker might well accept a riskier job at a higher wage because doing so would cover the monthly payments on a house in a better school district. But the same observation applies to other workers. And because school quality is an inherently relative concept, when others also trade safety for higher wages, no one will move forward in relative terms. They'd succeed only in bidding up the prices of houses in better school districts.

Hence the attraction of safety regulations, even in perfectly competitive labor markets in which all workers are perfectly informed about the risks they face. Workers confronting these incentives might well prefer an alternative state of the world in which all enjoyed greater safety, even at the expense of all having lower wages. But workers can control only their own job choices, not the choices of others. If any individual worker accepted a safer job while others didn't, that worker would be forced to send her children to inferior schools. To get the outcome they desire, workers must act in unison.

But merely knowing that individual actions are mutually offsetting doesn't eliminate the incentive to take those actions. Societies around the globe have settled on a similar set of policies to encourage greater workplace safety than unregulated private labor markets would provide. In the United States, for example, the Occupational Safety and Health Administration prescribes detailed safety procedures that must be followed in different industries. Firms are also required to carry workman's compensation insurance, whose rates rise sharply with the number of injury claims filed. These instruments are far from perfect, but there's little doubt that workplace safety levels are higher because of them.

Skeptics of big government often denounce such policies as unjustified violations of individual liberty. For example, as Thaler and Sunstein describe safety regulations, "they impose flat bans, and they undoubtedly do hurt some people. Such laws do not permit individual workers to trade their right to (what the government considers to be) a safe work environment in return for a higher salary, even if sophisticated and knowledgeable people might like to do that."[10] The implication is that, for well-informed workers at least, Adam Smith's invisible hand would provide the best combinations of wages and safety even without regulation. Yet that belief is indefensible when people care strongly about relative position.

As Darwin clearly recognized, many of the most important domains of life are graded on the curve. It's relative income, not absolute income, that predicts who will be able to buy a house in a good school district, or one with a breathtaking view. And when relative income is important, the invisible hand breaks down. There's no longer any reason to believe that individual incentives guide resources to their most valuable uses.

Again, note the striking similarity between my proposed explanation for safety regulation and Thomas Schelling's proposed explanation for hockey helmet rules.[11] As discussed in chapter 1, Schelling began with the observation that hockey players who are left to their own devices invariably skate without helmets, yet voice a strong preference for rules that require helmets. The discrepancy, he explained, is the result of a conflict between individual and group incentives. When an individual player removes his helmet, he gains a slight competitive edge, something he considers far more than enough to trump the slight increase in his odds of being seriously hurt. And because other players confront those same incentives, the inevitable result is that all players skate without helmets. Neither team's players gain the competitive edge they were seeking, yet all end up facing increased risk of serious injury, hence their support for the helmet requirement.

Merely understanding the incentive structure that produced their problem does not solve it. They need a forceful way to change individual incentives. And that's exactly what they get when the league adopts a helmet requirement. The only recourse open to players who insist on skating without a helmet is to form a league of their own. It's the same with safety regulation in the workplace. Those who don't want to be coerced by safety regulation can move to a country that doesn't regulate safety. But as we'll see in chapter 12, the only such countries are probably ones they wouldn't want to live in.

Note also that the explanation I propose for safety regulation does not imply that people were leaving cash on the table before safety was regulated. As in Schelling's helmet example, the market outcome in the absence of regulation was one in which each individual had chosen the best option available. If a rival firm came along and offered a safer job at a lower wage, no one would have taken it, because that would have meant having to move to an inferior school district.

My explanation also does not require that people be poorly informed about their options. It does not require imperfect mobility. It does not require that anyone be irrational. Nor, finally, does it require powerful actors with the ability to impose their will on reluctant subordinates. All it requires is the basic Darwinian observation that individual incentives often differ from collective incentives. That condition is met when the ability to achieve important outcomes in many domains depends significantly on relative income.

The resulting wedge between individual and collective incentives also helps us understand other ways in which the invisible-hand account might break down. According to libertarians and other proponents of the invisible hand, market forces guide people not only to the best possible combinations of safety and wage income, but also to optimal combinations of other job characteristics and wage income. Consider, for example, the question of task specialization. As Adam Smith emphasized, the explosive productivity growth observed since the start of the Industrial Revolution is a consequence of greater division and specialization of labor. Smith also recognized, however, that as tasks became more specialized, they often took an increasing toll on the human psyche. Karl Marx insisted that capitalism pushed the process much too far, arguing that division and specialization "mutilate the laborer into a fragment of a man, degrade him to the level of an appendage to a machine, destroy every remnant of charm in his work and turn it into hated toil."[12]

Libertarians and other proponents of the invisible hand challenge Marx's claim by pointing out that it implies cash on the table. The argument is precisely analogous to their argument in the case of safety. If the claim that there is too little variety in the workplace is to be coherent, it must mean that the value workers place on having additional variety in their daily work routines is larger than the corresponding loss of output that would be caused by reduced specialization. But if workers care about relative income, that claim simply doesn't follow. Workers as a group might be happier if all had a little more variety and a little less income, for that shift wouldn't jeopardize anyone's ability to achieve goals that depend on relative income. But no individual worker could move to a job with more variety without jeopardizing his ability to achieve such goals.

In like fashion, the wedge that separates individual and collective incentives can also be invoked to explain why people might end up in jobs that offer too little of other desirable working conditions. The labor market offers opportunities for people to earn additional income by accepting jobs that offer less autonomy, or that require them to perform tasks they find morally objectionable.[13] The lure of additional relative income is an important reason people accept such tasks. Yet when absolute incomes rise in tandem, relative purchasing power is little affected.

The fact that individual and collective incentives diverge when relative income matters also calls into question the traditional economic doctrine of revealed preference. This doctrine holds that we learn more about people's preferences by observing their behavior than by listening to what they say.[14] According to the doctrine, if someone could have bought additional variety by sacrificing $100 a week in wages yet chose not to, the additional variety must have been worth less than $100 to him. In terms of his individual valuation, that statement is true. But individual valuations and collective valuations need not coincide. When relative income matters, people who refuse to pay $100 for an increment in variety might find that increment worth far more than $100 if everyone made the same move in tandem.

No one can dispute that, beyond some point, the ability to achieve many important goals in life depends on relative purchasing power. A direct consequence of that fact is that when someone acquires additional income, she not only enhances her ability to achieve those goals, she simultaneously makes others less able to attain them. Or, to put the same point in the economist's parlance, the same activities that put additional income into one person's pocket impose negative externalities on others.

Many movement libertarians will be content either to ignore this problem or to insist that they have a right to cause indirect harm to others as they please. But as I will argue in chapter 6, the problem of indirect harm confronts the honest libertarian with a difficult choice. If he wants to claim a right to cause indirect harm to others, he must offer a cogent justification for that right, and that proves a difficult hurdle indeed.

I hope it's fair to assume that an honest libertarian would not object to a hockey helmet rule on the grounds that it deprives individual hockey players of the right to decide for themselves whether to wear helmets. Of course the rule denies them that right! But that's the very reason hockey players support it! They know that if they're permitted to skate without helmets, they'll feel they must. And they don't *want* to skate without helmets.

It's clearly a more serious matter to be restrained by the government than to be restrained by a hockey league. That fact alone might dictate more stringent standards for approving governmental restrictions. But the difference is one of degree, not kind. The reassuring news, as we'll see in coming chapters, is that it's often possible to mitigate harm to others without having to enact prohibitions at all.

FOUR

Starve the Beast—But Which One?

B Y MEANS OF THREE SEPARATE congressional earmarks in 2005, a total of $320 million was proposed for the construction of a bridge linking the town of Ketchikan, Alaska, with its airport on Gravina Island. Dubbed "The Bridge to Nowhere," the project quickly became a celebrated symbol of waste in government.[1]

This particular bridge was a terrible idea from the beginning. Ketchikan's population at the time was less than 9,000 and Gravina's was only 50. Ferry service provided transportation between the town and the island at a fee of $6, at fifteen- to thirty-minute intervals, depending on the time of day. Having bridge access would have been more convenient, obviously, but nowhere enough so to justify the enormous cost of the project.

Yet if the bridge was such an obvious loser, why was it slated for construction in the first place? The answer to that question reads word-for-word from the dog-eared script of antigovernment crusaders. The politicians who proposed the project hoped to curry favor with the local voters who would directly benefit from it, while foisting the bill on millions of distant and unsuspecting taxpayers, who would never even notice, much less complain about, the eventual small increment in their tax bills. Legislators from other states supported the proposal in the rational expectation of receiving reciprocal support for their own pork projects when the time came.

The encouraging coda to this story is that a firestorm of unfavorable national publicity eventually forced the project's cancellation. In each congressional budget, however, a host of other proposals survive because they're too small to make it onto the public's radar screen.

Some boondoggles eventually make the news after the fact. In the 1980s, for example, the Project on Military Procurement (now called the Project on Government Oversight) publicized examples in which private defense contractors were said to have billed the government $435 for a claw hammer, $640 for a toilet seat, and $7,600 for a coffee maker.[2] The revelations were deeply troubling. If inattentive or corrupt government officials could be induced to pay such prices for familiar items, how much greater might the potential for abuse be in contracts involving complex and difficult-to-understand equipment?

Starve the Beast

Antigovernment crusaders are clearly onto something. There *is* waste in government. But the interesting question is what to do about it. Many libertarians believe that the best strategy is to "starve the beast." Or, as Grover Norquist, president of the antitax advocacy group Americans for Tax Reform, colorfully put it, "I don't want to abolish government. I simply want to reduce it to the size where I can drag it into the bathroom and drown it in the bathtub."[3]

Starve-the-beast proponents make a simple point. Since money sent to Washington (or Sacramento or Albany) will inevitably be wasted, the solution is to send as little money as possible to those places. California has been fertile ground for proponents of the starve-the-beast approach because of the state's unique constitutional provision that permits legislative proposals to be decided directly by voters.

It's been said that if you want to see where America is headed, you should study California. The state was the first jurisdiction seriously to tackle the problem of air pollution from auto emissions. It led the way in promoting energy-efficient appliances. It was a forerunner in the expansion of rights for women and minorities. It was among the first to confront the issue of secondhand smoke. And it also spawned the antitax crusade that has dominated public discourse for the past three decades.

On June 6, 1978, Proposition 13 won the approval of almost 65 percent of Californians who voted in an election with near-record turnout. Officially called the People's Initiative to Limit Property Taxation, this measure was popularly known as the Jarvis-Gann Amendment, after the two men who spearheaded the referendum. Howard Jarvis was an Orange County businessman and long-standing tax protestor; Paul Gann was a Sacramento conservative activist. The main provision of their amendment was to limit California property taxes to 1 percent of a property's assessed valuation, which in turn would be prohibited from rising more than 2 percent in any year.

Debate continues about the specific details of Proposition 13's impact on the state. But no one seriously questions that it significantly dampened what had been a long-run upward trend in tax revenues. Unlike the federal government, state governments are generally not permitted to run persistent budget deficits. There is thus little question that Proposition 13 also prevented much government spending that otherwise would have occurred.

Since at least some of that spending would have been wasteful, the supporters of Proposition 13 can claim, without fear of contradiction, to have eliminated some government waste. But it's a much harder task to persuade neutral observers that Proposition 13 made California a better place to live. All government programs exist because legislators have constituents who favor them. Some of these programs deliver good value for the money. Others are boondoggles. When revenue shortfalls force government to make budget cuts, the best predictor of which programs get the ax is the power of the particular constituents who support them. As Alaska's Bridge to Nowhere clearly demonstrates, however, the mere fact that a group supports a project does not mean that it serves the broader public interest. The inescapable conclusion, then, is that Proposition 13 has also caused many worthwhile programs to be cut.

What's been the net effect? In his 1998 book *Paradise Lost,* Peter Schrag grappled with that question.[4] Schrag, who had been the editorial page editor of the *Sacramento Bee* for nineteen years, offered a meticulously researched and studiously nonpartisan account of the state's economic and social history during the two decades following passage of Proposition 13 and numerous other ballot initiatives aimed at curbing the scope of government.

The portrait that emerges is of a state dramatically different from the one that had been "both model and magnet" for the nation during the generation immediately following World War II. The California government's fiscal position has continued to deteriorate sharply in the years since *Paradise Lost* was published, and the state's overall prosperity relative to other states has fallen spectacularly. In 2009 alone, for example, revenue shortfalls forced the state to make some $20 billion in additional budget cuts. But even the first twenty years of Proposition 13 had left the state a very different place. Thus, Schrag wrote,

> California's schools, which, thirty years ago, had been among the most generously funded in the nation, are now in the bottom quarter among the states in virtually every major indicator—in their physical condition, in public funding, in test scores—closer in most of them to Mississippi than to New York or Connecticut or New Jersey. . . . Its once celebrated freeway system is now rated as among the most dilapidated road networks in the country. Many of its public libraries operate on reduced hours, and some have closed altogether. The state's social benefits, once among the nation's most generous, have been cut, and cut again, and then cut again. And what had once been a tuition-free college and university system, while still among the world's great public educational institutions, struggles for funds and charges as much as every other state university system, and in some cases more.[5]

Proponents of Proposition 13 counter that other factors have been important in the state's long-run relative decline. Undoubtedly so. Yet the fact remains that chronic revenue shortfalls have been at the core of the state's problems.

Antigovernment activists insist that the best way to deal with revenue shortfalls is to eliminate wasteful government spending. Who, other than the direct beneficiaries of a wasteful program, could possibly object? The difficult question is how to eliminate wasteful spending without inflicting even more costly collateral damage. Experience suggests that the starve-the-beast strategy is not the answer.

The Parasite-Host Analogy

Starve-the-beast proponents might be likened to a doctor who treats a patient suffering from intestinal parasites by ordering him to stop eating. The patient's food intake, he explains, is the very lifeblood of the parasites. Cut that off, and they will eventually die. Well, yes. But the patient himself may die first, or be seriously damaged in the process. That's why the approved strategies for attacking parasites all take a much more targeted approach. They attempt to inflict damage on the parasites directly, while minimizing collateral damage to their host.

It's instructive to push the parasite-host analogy a step further, by noting that no complex organism is ever completely free of parasites. Yes, the organism benefits from reducing its parasite load, and that's why natural selection has always favored organisms with effective immune systems. But natural selection has always favored the most effective parasites, too. The battle against parasites entails costs as well as benefits. The rule of thumb for how to wage such battles is the same as that for battles in other domains: Use the most cost-effective weapons first, and use them to attack the most dangerous parasites. But eventually a point comes at which the cost of the next weapon exceeds the costs imposed by the most dangerous remaining parasite. Beyond that point, additional parasite reduction actually leaves the organism worse off.[6]

The same logic applies to the problem of waste in government. The best way to reduce it is surely to reach first for the most cost-effective weapons at our disposal and deploy them against the most important causes of waste directly. To do that, of course, we must ask why waste exists in the first place.

Often the answer is that politicians support wasteful programs because of demands from important campaign donors.[7] A good place for opponents of waste to focus might thus be on legislation that could reduce legislators' dependence on large campaign contributions. (Small donations pose a less serious threat because the individuals who make them are in no position to extract major concessions from legislators.) The cost of enforcing stricter campaign finance laws would be relatively low, and such laws would be likely to curb some of the most important sources of government waste. But the U.S. Supreme Court has shown little inclination to support stricter campaign finance laws in recent years. On the contrary, its controversial ruling in the *Citizens United v. Federal Election Commission* case appears to signal the court's intention to roll back even long-standing limits on corporate campaign contributions.[8]

Unless the court reconsiders, opponents of government waste will have to continue working their way down the list of alternative strategies. One lesson of the Bridge to Nowhere episode, for example, was that boondoggles are less likely to survive politically when more voters learn about them. The information revolution has greatly reduced the cost of putting information in front of voters, so we might make some progress there. But the same revolution has also caused explosive growth in the total amount of information that bombards us each day. Thus it may be just as hard as ever to draw voters' attention to any particular wasteful program.

In short, attacking government waste is a project that will be with us forever. Going forward, new technologies and better institutional design may facilitate significant progress, but they will never eliminate waste entirely.

Spending Cuts That Backfire

For now, our most pressing issue is that although many extremely important tasks remain to be done, government has no money. In July 2010, for example, the *Wall Street Journal* reported that budget shortfalls around the nation had forced many states to downgrade many asphalt roads to gravel:

Paved roads, historical emblems of American achievement, are being torn up across rural America and replaced with gravel or other rough surfaces as counties struggle with tight budgets and dwindling state and federal revenue. State money for local roads was cut in many places amid budget shortfalls. In Michigan, at least 38 of the 83 counties have converted some asphalt roads to gravel in recent years. Last year, South Dakota turned at least 100 miles of asphalt road surfaces to gravel. Counties in Alabama and Pennsylvania have begun downgrading asphalt roads to cheaper chip-and-seal roads, also known as "poor man's pavement." Some counties in Ohio are simply letting roads erode to gravel.[9]

The problem is that such moves not only do not end up saving any money, they actually end up costing us. Potholes and other road-surface irregularities cause an average of more than $100 in damage each year to every car and truck on the road, not to mention many needless deaths and serious injuries.[10] When road maintenance is postponed by even two to three years, the cost of repairs more than doubles. Spending $1 now on road maintenance thus keeps us from having to spend $2 three years from now. Even if we ignore the savings from prevented pothole damage, deaths, and injuries, that's an investment with a rate of return of more than 18 percent a year.

The federal government can borrow at much lower rates than that. The interest rate on ten-year Treasury bills, for example, has not exceeded 5 percent since 2001. Selling T-bills and investing the proceeds at more than 18 percent would immediately make the nation's balance sheet stronger. Any private business would leap at the opportunity to make an investment like that. And there is no shortage of such opportunities. Some 50 percent of the nation's major roads and highways are in backlog, meaning that they're "cracked, crumbled and overdue for repaving."[11]

But the stranglehold of antitax, antigovernment rhetoric on American political discourse has made it difficult to discuss investments of this sort, even in an economic climate that cries out for additional public investment. I refer, of course, to the deep economic downturn spawned by the financial crisis of 2008.

Before late 2007, total spending was sufficient to create jobs for almost everyone. But then the housing boom began to unravel. Consumption, which had been unsustainably inflated by home equity loans based on illusory housing prices, fell sharply. Businesses began to lay people off, which produced further declines in consumption. Falling consumption, in turn, caused a parallel decline in investment, because most businesses already had the capacity to produce more than people wanted to buy. And with the economics of most other countries also in the doldrums, demand for American exports also fell. By late 2008, output and employment were plummeting even faster than they had at the beginning of the Great Depression.

When the world economy plunged into deep depression in the 1930s, many economists believed that the best policy response was to balance government budgets. And since falling incomes had caused tax revenues to fall sharply, that meant some combination of reduced government spending and higher tax rates. President Herbert Hoover's approach to the Great Depression was informed by that prevailing economic orthodoxy. So it seems hardly fair to fault him for having implemented policies that actually made the depression worse, not better.

President Franklin Roosevelt appeared to understand intuitively that the prevailing orthodoxy was mistaken. Ignoring it, he vigorously expanded government spending for public construction projects that put the unemployed to work directly. But it was only when John Maynard Keynes published *The General Theory of Employment, Interest, and Money* in 1936 that economists had a coherent theoretical framework within which to understand why Roosevelt's intuition was correct.[12] Keynes, widely viewed as the greatest economist of the twentieth century, earned his reputation by explaining why a deeply depressed economy generally wouldn't recover quickly on its own.

Consumers won't lead the way, he argued, because even those who still have jobs are fearful they might lose them. Nor will businesses invest, since they already have more capacity than they need. Only government, Keynes concluded, has both the motive and opportunity to boost spending significantly during deep downturns.

Although most economists now favor the Keynesian approach to combating deep economic downturns, an influential group of dissenters has inspired libertarians and other antigovernment activists to oppose all economic stimulus measures. On many occasions, I have pressed members of this group to explain why boosting government spending won't speed the recovery of a depressed economy. In most cases, they have been either unwilling or unable to offer a clear response. So I was grateful when I saw the economist Lee Ohanian's attempt to explain why government spending won't help. The crux of his argument is that "the higher taxes on incomes or expenditures that ultimately accompany higher spending depress economic activity."[13]

The stimulus opponents' argument thus boils down to this striking claim: When the government spends borrowed funds now, consumers will realize that the resulting debt spells higher taxes in the future, which will lead them to curtail their current spending. Those cutbacks will offset the increased government spending dollar for dollar, leaving no net stimulus.

Such claims have led many psychologists to describe economists as having "high IQ but no clue." There may be people who would actually spend less now to hedge against uncertain future tax liabilities. It's unlikely, though, that you know any of them. As behavioral economists have been pointing out for decades, that's just not the way most people behave. Hardly any consumers even know how big the national debt is, much less how it might affect their future tax bills.

Standard economic models predict that people will save enough during their working lives to avoid having to reduce their standard of living in retirement. Evidence suggests, however, that most people save far too little to meet that goal.[14] Even the prospect of having to eat pet food in retirement is not enough to spur them to save more. Yet antigovernment activists want us to believe that the possibility of facing unspecified tax liabilities at some unknown future date would cause people to increase savings by enough to offset every penny of additional government spending.

It's an absurd claim, but in a climate dominated by antitax, antigovernment rhetoric, the mere fact that some people say economic stimulus won't work is enough to halt conversation. We're told that economic stimulus financed by borrowed money will raise the national debt, which will impoverish our grandchildren. And since most people don't want to impoverish their grandchildren, the discussion ends there.

But prudent public investment does not impoverish our grandchildren at all. On the contrary, when the government borrows money at 4 percent and invests it in a project that yields 18 percent during an economic downturn, the effect is not only to put people to work who otherwise would have been sitting idle but also to enrich our grandchildren.

In an economy at full employment, it would of course be even better to pay for such investments with tax revenue rather than with borrowed money. But antitax rhetoric has apparently ruled out that option, even for residents who would directly benefit from the specific government investments being paid for. Thus, as *Wall Street Journal* reporter Lauren Etter notes, many of the North Dakota residents who complain most bitterly about the deteriorating quality of their roads seem disinclined to consider the obvious remedy: "In June, Stutsman County residents rejected a measure that would have generated more money for roads by increasing property and sales taxes. 'I'd rather my kids drive on a gravel road than stick them with a big tax bill,' said Bob Baumann, as he sipped a bottle of Coors Light at the Sportsman's Bar Café and Gas in Spiritwood."[15]

It's not uncommon for stones thrown up by a car on a gravel road to crack a trailing car's windshield, which can cost $1,000 to replace. Such events happen much less frequently on asphalt roads. That's just one among a host of good reasons for having paved our roads in the first place. Refusing to maintain them is a false economy, plain and simple. But that's what happens when public discussion of taxes is off limits.

Obstacles to Creating Good Government

To repeat, my point is not that governments are never wasteful. Waste happens. Many antigovernment activists arrive at their position in the sincere belief that government does more harm than good. And indeed there can be little doubt that many governments around the world have caused enormous harm. Even today, there are many countries in which ordinary citizens are afraid to call the police when someone steals their property. In these countries, corruption is the norm rather than the exception.

Transparency International, a Berlin-based nonprofit group, conducts periodic surveys to assess the quality of the world's governments. The organization publishes a Corruption Perceptions Index (CPI), based on its definition of corruption as "the abuse of public office for private gain." Its surveys ask respondents to report "the degree to which corruption is perceived to exist among a country's public officials and politicians."[16] Some countries, such as Myanmar and Somalia, are perennially near the bottom of Transparency International's CPI. It's no accident that they and other persistently low scorers on that index—which include Afghanistan, Haiti, Tonga, and Uzbekistan—are among the poorest nations on the planet.

Yet no matter how bad the typical government might seem to be, it's striking to note that there are no countries without a government. The territory of any such country would have long since been invaded and claimed by some other country with a government and an army. If government is unavoidable, our challenge is to come up with the best one possible.

Notwithstanding the rhetoric of antigovernment crusaders, there seem to be some governments that are relatively free from corruption and do at least a reasonable job of responding to their citizens' demands for public goods and services. In a three-way tie for the least corrupt government on Transparency International's 2007 list were Denmark, Finland, and New Zealand. Singapore, Sweden, Iceland, The Netherlands, Switzerland, Canada, and Norway rounded out that year's top ten in that order.[17] Here, too, it's surely no accident that most of these countries are among the richest on the planet.

The causality undoubtedly runs in both directions. Having a more honest and effective government helps support activities that raise per-capita income. And being richer generally makes citizens more able and willing to support more effective forms of governance. But the correlation between per-capita income and the CPI is far from perfect. For example, the United States, which had higher per-capita income than any of the top ten on the

2007 CPI, ranked only twentieth-best on that list, primarily because of perceptions that our campaign finance system had corrupted Congress.

In countries with honest and effective governments, the view that promoting good government is a worthwhile investment would not strike most observers as absurd. Yet that does not seem to be the position of antigovernment evangelists in the United States, many of whom view government service with thinly veiled contempt. As Ronald Reagan often remarked, "Government's view of the economy could be summed up in a few short phrases: If it moves, tax it. If it keeps moving, regulate it. And if it stops moving, subsidize it." The foundation of honest and effective government is a professional civil service that takes pride in its work. Fostering a climate in which government is viewed with contempt inevitably makes it more difficult to recruit talented and dedicated civil servants.

But when antigovernment evangelists themselves assume the reins of state power, it's not clear that those are the kinds of civil servants they're looking to appoint. It's easy to see how someone whose core philosophy is that government has no useful mission might see no harm in appointing cronies with little interest in the task at hand. But as experience in the wake of Hurricane Katrina vividly demonstrated, appointing incompetent friends who don't care about the mission of the government agencies they head often plays out poorly.

No sensible person believes that eliminating government is an option. If we must have a government, then, it's surely worth thinking seriously about how to promote good government. What public goods and services do we want? How can we best raise the money to pay for them? And how can we attract the kinds of civil servants we're willing to install in positions of trust?

Our immediate problem, however, is a more pressing practical one—namely that existing financial commitments far exceed current tax revenues. With the baby boom generation swelling the ranks of retirees during the next two decades, this fiscal gap will grow dramatically. We should of course continue searching for creative ways to bridge as much of that gap as possible by reducing waste in government. But when pressure to trim budgets starts turning asphalt roads into gravel ones, that's a credible signal that cuts have gone too far.

Antigovernment crusaders are right that eliminating waste is a better way to free up resources than eliminating things we value. They take it as given that the lion's share of all waste in a market economy resides in government. As they're fond of saying, people spend their own money far more carefully than the bureaucrats in Washington do.

Maybe so. On a closer look, however, not all of the famous examples of government waste turn out to be as shocking as they first appear. For example, the $7,600 coffee pot mentioned at the beginning of this chapter was produced at Lockheed at the time Ronald Dubose, a college classmate of mine, was working for that company. Lockheed also produced the famous $640 toilet seats. Dubose describes himself as a libertarian, and he is inclined to view government spending as extremely wasteful in general. But in an email exchange about these particular projects, he had this to say:

I was at Lockheed when the infamous coffee pot story surfaced. In fact, I was in charge of testing the coffee pot. Here is the rest of the story:

Airplanes have two types of power: 28 volts, direct current; and 115 volts, alternating current, 400 Hz. The coffee pot had to be designed to run on the 400 Hz power, which made it completely different from your kitchen version. 400 Hz is used because it makes motors and things smaller and lighter than 60 Hz versions. The lifetime cost of every pound of airplane weight is enormous, given that fuel must be provided to carry it everywhere for 40 years or so. So this is a sensible economic decision. The next thing to remember is that the C5 total production run is only about 120 units, so development costs have little in the denominator. Finally everything on an airplane must be tested to be sure it will work under military conditions and won't start a fire or something. These tests usually include MIL STD 810 Environmental Testing. This includes shock, vibration, high/low temp, and so on.

So the unit has to take being dropped (hard landing) and shaken violently for hours. Just running these tests is very expensive and getting it to pass also adds cost. So it has always been misleading to complain about the coffee maker. I'm surprised it was so cheap considering the initial cost and the low run numbers. I suppose they could bring a thermos, which most military planes require but the C5 was a troop carrier and I'm sure the guys appreciated the "investment."

The famous "toilet seat" was not my responsibility because it was on the C130; however, it was not the seat one sees at Ace Hardware. What they refer to is the molded Fiberglas "surround" that you see in commercial planes. It is about 3′ cubed and it covers the bowl assembly. The actual "seat" attaches to it. Anyway, the cost was completely reasonable considering that low runs require custom molds and hand layup methods.

Even if the most famous examples of government waste turn out to have been misleading, however, there must be many other examples in which government purchasing agents did, in fact, fail to negotiate reasonable prices on their orders. Everything we know about human nature suggests that someone would be more likely to search out low prices when spending his own money than when spending someone else's. And the private sector is also intensely competitive, which helps keep prices reasonably close to actual production costs.

Waste in the Private Sector

Even though most people shop pretty carefully for the things they want, there's actually considerably more waste in the private sector than in the public sector, and not just because the private sector is so much larger. Most waste in the private sector occurs not because people pay too much for any given good or service, but because the outlays required to achieve many important goals often depend on how much other people in similar circumstances are spending. This is yet another instance of Darwin's insight that individual and group incentives often diverge sharply.

Consider the task of staging a coming-of-age party for your son or daughter. It's a special occasion, and you want it to seem like one. But what that means, exactly, is heavily dependent on context. In 2005, a New York CEO spent $10 million to stage a coming-of-age celebration in which more than 150 of his daughter's friends gathered in the Rainbow Room atop Rockefeller Center. At the end of the evening, after having been serenaded by 50 Cent, Don Henley, Aerosmith, Stevie Nicks, and other headliners, each guest went home with a bag of party favors that included a $300 video iPod, the must-have object of that moment.[18]

Though he was roundly criticized for his extravagance at the time, it's possible to imagine that this father's motives were completely benign. He may have wanted merely to stage a party that would communicate to the world the depth of his love for his daughter, an event that she'd remember as having been truly special. But special is a relative concept. And because others in his financial circle were also spending large sums to stage special parties for their own children, the standard that defined special in his case was very high. It was much higher, certainly, than the corresponding standard thirty years earlier, for the simple reason that wealthy families now have so much more money than they did then.

Middle-income consumers and wealthy CEOs travel in largely non-overlapping social circles, but the standards that define special occasions have been rising for middle-income families, too. Consider, for example, MaryEllen Fillo's account of recent trends among such families in Connecticut:

> "I read an article about parties for teenagers titled 'Don't You Wish Your Party Was Hot Like Mine,' and that said it all," said Susan Reardon, a Litchfield County mother who is planning a $12,000 birthday party for her nearly 16-year-old daughter, Grace. Those plans include specially designed invitations, a tented backyard with linen-covered round tables, a dance floor, a band, an ice cream sundae bar and DVDs of the celebration for all the guests.[19]

Families up and down the income ladder are spending more each year to celebrate special occasions for loved ones. The average cost of an American wedding in 2009 was $28,082.[20] The corresponding figure in 1980 (also in 2009 dollars) was $11,213.[21] The collective effect of all this extra spending has been largely just to raise the bar that defines special occasions. The events end up costing substantially more than they used to, but no one walks away feeling any more special than before.

Rising Income Inequality and Expenditure Cascades

The libertarian's faith in Adam Smith's invisible hand rests on the assumption that consumer spending is essentially independent of context. Yet context is often decisive, and when it is, the incentives that drive individual spending often produce results that are profoundly wasteful. The explosive growth of CEO pay in recent decades, for example, has led many executives to build larger and larger mansions. But those mansions have long since passed the point at which greater absolute size yields additional utility. Most executives need or want larger mansions simply because the standards that define large have changed.

The driving force behind that change has been a fundamental shift in the pattern of income growth. During the generation immediately following World War II, incomes grew at about the same rate—just under 3 percent—for families all along the income scale. But sometime around 1970, that pattern shifted. Since then, income growth has been significantly slower on average, except for families near the top of the income distribution, whose incomes have been growing at almost record high rates. CEOs of the largest corporations in the United States, for example, earned roughly 40 times as much as the average American worker in 1980, but now earn more than 400 times as much. The same pattern shows up no matter how we slice the data. The higher up people are on the income ladder, the faster their incomes have grown.[22]

This shift has spawned a phenomenon I call expenditure cascades.[23] Top earners build bigger mansions simply because they have more money. The middle class shows little evidence of being offended by that. On the contrary, many seem drawn to photo essays and TV programs about the lifestyles of the rich and famous. But the larger mansions of the rich shift the frame of reference that defines acceptable housing for the near-rich, who travel in many of the same social circles. Perhaps it has become the custom in those circles to host dinner parties for thirty-six rather than twenty-four, or to host wedding receptions at home rather than in a hotel or club. So the near-rich build bigger, too, and that shifts the relevant framework for others just below them, and so on, all the way down the income scale. By 2007, the median new single-family house built in the United States had an area of more than 2,300 square feet, some 50 percent more than its counterpart from 1970.[24]

Today's median earners don't build bigger houses and spend more to celebrate special occasions because they have more money. The incomes of families in the middle have actually grown very little during the past three decades. They're building bigger and spending more because other people like them are also building bigger and spending more, and that, in turn, is happening because of the changing pattern of income growth. Similar expenditure cascades have been taking place not just in housing and parties for special occasions, but in a host of other domains as well.

Not all of the extra spending has been for naught, of course. A bigger, clearer diamond, for example, refracts the light in ways that even a solitary inhabitant of a desert island would be likely to find more pleasing. But much of the extra spending has been profoundly wasteful. Once mansions pass a certain size, the demand for additional space is driven almost exclusively by social forces having nothing to do with the intrinsic utility of the extra space itself. Yet owning a bigger mansion entails considerable extra hassle. At the very least, one must recruit and oversee a bigger staff to operate and maintain it, which increases the risk that a disgruntled employee will publish an unflattering tell-all memoir. And so on. If all of the biggest mansions were a little smaller, the people who own them would actually be happier than before.

If we add to that observation the fact that total consumer spending is more than twice as large as total government spending, my assertion that there is more waste in the private sector than in the public sector should not strike any reasonable observer as implausible.

The Way Forward

The important question, in any event, is not whether private waste is larger than public waste, but rather where we should focus our search for additional resources to address pressing budget shortfalls. Efforts to eliminate government waste have been under way for a long time, and experience cautions against expecting sudden major breakthroughs on that front. Starving that particular beast often appears to have done more harm than good. The shifting standards that define what people feel they must spend to achieve their goals constitute a very different kind of beast. To emphasize the role that context plays in many important consumption decisions, I'll call it the positional consumption beast. It's a dramatically more voracious beast than government ever was.

The search for ways to eliminate private waste is still in its infancy. The good news, as I'll explain in the next chapter, is that private waste is actually much easier to eliminate than public waste. The positional consumption beast, it turns out, can be starved by relatively simple, unintrusive changes in incentives.

FIVE

Putting the Positional Consumption Beast on a Diet

DARWIN'S INSIGHT THAT INDIVIDUAL INCENTIVES often conflict sharply with those of larger groups is nowhere more clearly illustrated than in the context of military arms races. Yet, despite its familiarity, the parable of the military arms race remains imperfectly understood.

The Logic of Military Arms Races

In a stripped-down version of an arms race, one nation gains advantage over a rival by building additional armaments, which prompts the rival to build additional armaments of its own to restore the balance. The first nation then acquires still more weaponry, provoking yet another response from its rival, and so on. When the dust settles, neither side enjoys greater security, despite having spent a substantial share of its national resources on armaments.

If we assume that the antagonists were evenly matched to begin with, there's essentially universal agreement that this process is wasteful. It would have been far better for both nations if each had spent less on arms and more on schools, housing, hospitals, roads, and other nonmilitary goods.

The standard solution is a military arms control agreement, under which both sides pledge to reduce their spending on armaments. Lack of trust is perhaps the biggest barrier to reaching such agreements, and successful ones have almost always granted liberal inspection rights to both sides. As Ronald Reagan liked to say, "Trust, but verify."

So far, so good. But this account leaves an important question unanswered. What conditions must be met, exactly, for a military arms race to occur? If someone says there is too much of something, the unspoken implication is that there must be too little of something else. In the military arms race, there are too many bombs and not enough domestic consumption goods. But why was the imbalance in that direction and not the other way around? That is, why didn't nations try to outdo one another by building more and better hospitals and roads, in the process shortchanging their spending on armaments?

The answer to this question is both simple and instructive. It's that, although context matters for a nation's abilities to achieve its goals in both domains, it matters much more for armaments. In the two-nation example, the question of whether our stock of armaments is adequate depends almost entirely on how it compares with their stock. If theirs is bigger, our political independence is in jeopardy. If ours is bigger, we're safe.

Context matters for consumption goods, too, *but much less than for military goods.* Consumers may be displeased, for example, on learning that citizens of a rival nation have better TV sets and fancier cars. But such displeasure is far less costly than losing your political independence.

Except for this asymmetry, we'll never see a military arms race. Suppose, in contrast, that context mattered more for consumption goods than for armaments. One nation might try to get ahead of its rival by building more bombs, but the immediate consequence would be to have less money available to spend on toasters. And if falling behind a rival nation in toasters were more costly than falling behind on armaments, there would be no tendency to build too many bombs in the first place. On the contrary, there would be a "positional arms race" focused on toasters. Each nation would spend more and more on toasters in an effort to outdo its rival, in the process siphoning off resources from its armaments sector. That this doesn't happen is purely a consequence of the fact that context matters more for weaponry than for consumption goods generally.

Several other points are worth noting about military arms races. One is that they don't stem from irrational behavior. From the perspective of any individual nation, it's perfectly sensible to place high priority on being as well armed as rivals. Maintaining your political independence depends on your ability to defend yourself, which would be jeopardized by having an inferior stock of armaments.

Nor do military arms races stem from any absence of competition. On the contrary, they have historically pitted nations against the rivals with whom they compete most directly for important resources. More intense competition among nations makes military arms races more likely, not less.

Nor, finally, is there anything mysterious about military arms control agreements. A libertarian would make a fool of himself by objecting to such agreements on the grounds that they rob signatories of the right to decide for themselves how many bombs to build. That's precisely their intent! The signatories embrace these agreements because they understand that if they retain the right to decide individually, they'll end up spending far too much on bombs.

Each of the features of military arms races described thus far is completely uncontroversial. But that doesn't mean that arms control agreements themselves are always uncontroversial. For example, it may be perfectly rational for a nation's leaders to refuse to participate in such an agreement if they have no practical way to prevent the opposing side from cheating.

It may also be rational to refuse to sign an arms control agreement if leaders believe an arms race would play out to their own side's advantage. Ronald Reagan, for example, was said to have embraced the development of strategic missile defense systems in the 1980s in part because he believed that pressuring the USSR to follow suit would hasten the economic collapse of America's principal rival.

In sum, there's all but universal agreement that military arms races between closely matched rivals are wasteful, and that all parties can gain from collective agreements to limit spending on armaments. When nations are reluctant to enter into such agreements, it's generally because of practical concerns linked to verifiability or resource asymmetries. They don't refuse to sign military arms control agreements because of abstract philosophical concerns about the value of maintaining their freedom of individual action.

Arms Races in Other Domains

As in the domain of military competition, so also in the domain of economic competition. In sports, for example, both individual and team rewards depend heavily on relative performance. If one sprinter takes anabolic steroids, he improves his chances to land a spot on the medal stand. If a team bids successfully for an outstanding player, it's more likely to win a championship. There are also obvious downsides to these moves. Steroid users confront serious long-term health risks, for example, and bidding for star players is costly. But from each individual's or team's perspective, the gains loom large relative to the losses. The rub, of course, is that if all sprinters take steroids or if all teams bid for star players, all pay a price, yet none gains a competitive edge.

As in the domain of military competition, the solution in sports has been to forge positional arms control agreements. Some governing bodies conduct random drug tests and impose stiff sanctions on violators. Other leagues impose salary caps and roster limits in an effort to limit payrolls. Soapbox derby organizers impose spending limits. Auto racing associations impose engine displacement limits. And so on. Each of these restrictions is an attempt to solve a problem exactly analogous to a military arms race. Libertarians apart, there don't seem to be many people who view such steps as deeply troubling violations of individual rights.

When teams or individual competitors fail to implement positional arms control agreements, it's often for practical reasons similar to those that prevent military arms control agreements. The late New York Yankees owner George M. Steinbrenner, for example, successfully fought off attempts by other baseball owners to impose greater revenue sharing and stricter salary caps in Major League Baseball. Steinbrenner had access to New York's enormous local cable television revenue stream, which he knew would enable him to outbid other teams for star free agents. He also knew that although blocking salary caps and revenue sharing would substantially increase each team's payroll, including his own, maintaining his ability to field consistently winning teams would more than compensate for that disadvantage.

Steinbrenner's opposition to salary caps and revenue sharing imposed substantial costs on other team owners, and ultimately on fans. In the economist's parlance, those policies created "positional externalities."

All this, again, is familiar and uncontroversial. Much less familiar, however, is the fact that similar positional externalities produce analogous waste in everyday consumption spending patterns. In chapter 4, I discussed pressures that have led people to spend wastefully on housing and celebrations of special occasions. But implicit in that claim is a parallel claim that they must be spending too little on at least some other things. What are those other things, and why do people spend too little on them? The logic that governs military arms races suggests a systematic way of exploring these questions.

Context Matters More in Some Domains Than Others

A series of simple thought experiments provides a convenient way to evoke intuitions about the importance of context in different settings. In each case, you're asked to imagine the choice between two situations that are identical in all respects except for the one difference explicitly described. You're also supposed to assume that the two situations will remain as described forever.

The first thought experiment explores the importance of context for evaluations of housing:

Which world would you choose?

World A: You live in a neighborhood with 6,000-square-foot houses, others in neighborhoods with 8,000-square-foot houses;

or,

World B: You live in a neighborhood with 4,000-square-foot houses, others in neighborhoods with 3,000-square-foot houses.

Even by current standards in the United States, all the options in this thought experiment involve houses that are large in absolute terms. Again, don't assume that you could go to world A and move up to a neighborhood with larger houses by working a little harder. Choosing A means being in a relatively small house forever.

The standard economic models that underlie Adam Smith's invisible-hand theory say that this choice should be a no-brainer. In those models, context doesn't matter at all. Your evaluation of your house is assumed to depend only on its absolute characteristics, and since you'd have a bigger one in world A, that's necessarily the better choice. Yet when actual people are asked to make this choice, it's not a slam-dunk. Typically they take a while to think things over, and most end up picking world B.

Now consider a second thought experiment with exactly the same structure:

Which world would you choose?

World A: Your probability of dying on the job is 2 in 10,000 each year; others' is 1 in 10,000;

or,

World B: Your probability of dying on the job is 4 in 10,000 each year; others' is 8 in 10,000.

Like the first thought experiment, this one gives you a chance to choose between absolute and relative advantage. If you pick world A, your absolute probability of dying on the job each year will be only half as great as in world B. But your job in A would be the more dangerous job there, whereas your job in B would be the safer one in that world.

I have posed this thought experiment in numerous classes, with students ranging from freshmen to retirees. In almost every case, 100 percent of subjects chose world A. Unlike the first thought experiment, subjects in this one voice a consistent preference for absolute advantage over relative advantage.

What does this pattern tell us? When describing the reasons for their choices, the majority of subjects who chose B in the first experiment typically say they thought they'd be more likely to feel satisfied with their house in that world, even though it was smaller in absolute terms. Absolute house size also matters, of course, but once it crosses a certain threshold, context seems to loom larger in most people's evaluations.

Similar follow-up discussions with subjects about their choice in the second thought experiment make clear that they wouldn't like the fact that their chosen job would entail twice the risk of other jobs in world A. But typically they're quick to add that they'd much prefer to live with that fact than to choose B, where their job would be twice as risky as in A.

Following terminology coined by the late economist Fred Hirsch, the modal choices in these thought experiments identify housing as a "positional good" and workplace safety as a "nonpositional good."[1] Positional goods are ones whose evaluations are particularly sensitive to context. Since evidence suggests that context matters for virtually every evaluation, a positional good is thus one whose evaluation is *relatively* heavily shaped by context. In contrast, a nonpositional good is one whose evaluation depends relatively weakly on context.

As we saw in the example of the military arms race, a wasteful distortion results when context matters more in some domains than others. Nations tend to build too many bombs because the adequacy of their arsenals depends heavily on how they compare in size with those of rivals. Context matters for consumption goods, too, but much less so than for armaments.

The same logic implies a wasteful distortion toward spending on positional goods. Let's flesh out the details of how that distortion would unfold for the specific categories considered in the two thought experiments—namely housing and workplace safety. Both are desirable, and both are costly to produce. As discussed in chapter 3, the standard invisible-hand story holds that competitive markets allow workers to purchase the mix of safety and housing that best suits them. If they're highly averse to risk, they can choose a safer job, but that means a lower wage (since blade guards on saws are costly), which in turn means having less to spend on housing. Or, if risk doesn't much bother them, they can opt for a higher wage in a riskier job, which will enable them to spend more on housing.

Libertarians and other invisible-hand enthusiasts argue that when government regulates safety in the workplace, it makes workers worse off by forcing them to buy more safety than they'd have chosen to buy on their own. Consider, for example, the decision confronting someone trying to decide whether to accept a riskier job at higher pay so he can buy a more expensive house. The standard invisible-hand story says he'll accept the job if the value of the extra absolute house size outweighs the cost of having lower absolute safety. So he'll accept risk only up to the point at which the last small increment in absolute house size was worth just enough to cover the cost of the last small decrement in absolute safety. Forcing him to buy more safety than that, say the invisible-hand proponents, would be to force him to buy safety that's worth less to him than he must pay for it.

But that claim no longer holds if evaluations of housing are more context-sensitive than evaluations of safety. To see why, note that when context matters, two additional factors enter the cost-benefit calculus. Taking the riskier job will not only put the worker in an absolutely bigger house, it will also put him in a relatively bigger one; the same decision also means having less safety, both in absolute terms and relative to other workers.

Adding context to the story matters because the two new terms in the decision are strikingly asymmetric. Having a relatively expensive house matters a lot, if only because it enables you to send your children to better schools. In contrast, having a relatively unsafe job is of only secondary concern. Adding the two relative terms to the traditional account thus tilts the decision sharply in favor of accepting the riskier job. That's problematic because the relative advantage people seek is mutually offsetting. No matter how many workers accept riskier jobs hoping to move forward in relative terms, there can never be more than 50 percent of them in the top half.

That simple observation deals a heavy blow to traditional invisible-hand claims. Even when all decision makers are fully informed and perfectly rational, and even when all labor and product markets are perfectly competitive, there can be no presumption that the invisible hand of the marketplace leads to outcomes that are best for society as a whole. If housing is positional and safety is nonpositional, as evidence consistently suggests, unregulated markets will serve up houses that are too big and jobs that are too dangerous.

If workers respond by electing legislators who enact regulations that limit workplace safety risks, it makes no sense for libertarians and others to complain that such regulations strip workers of the right to decide for themselves how much risk to take. If illusory relative gains are what drove individual decisions to accept additional risk in the first place, those decisions are perhaps better made collectively. Complaining that regulations restrict the freedom of individual workers is thus little different from complaining that helmet rules restrict the freedom of individual hockey players. Yes, they do—but that's the whole point in each case.

Of course, the mere fact that a market outcome is less than perfect does not mean that government intervention would necessarily lead to a better outcome. Governments are imperfect, too. The important point is that the ultimate decision about whether regulation makes sense should hinge on purely practical questions about the efficacy of proposed regulatory remedies. Slogans about the absolute primacy of individual freedom don't help answer such questions.

The lesson of the arms race metaphor is that we have too much positional consumption and not enough nonpositional consumption. But which goods are positional and which are nonpositional? The Darwinian framework provides guidance for thinking about this question. The ultimate measure of success within that framework is the individual's ability to pass copies of its genes into the next generation. A category is thus more likely to be positional in proportion to the extent to which additional investment in that category makes individual reproductive success more likely.

The antlers of the bull elk, for example, are advantageous only insofar as they help their bearers win battles for access to females, and that advantage in turn depends almost entirely on their relative size. Larger antlers are purchased at the expense of reduced mobility in densely wooded areas, which makes a bull more likely to be killed by wolves or other predators. But greater mobility would be cold comfort, in purely Darwinian terms, if it were purchased at the expense of *relatively* small antlers, for the genes of such a bull would be unlikely to make it into the next generation. For the bull elk, then, antlers are a positional good and mobility a nonpositional good. And that's why bull elk as a group overinvest in antlers and underinvest in mobility.

The Darwinian perspective provides similar guidance for assessing other investment opportunities. Suppose, for example, that the question is whether spending time generating additional income is more positional than spending that same time at leisure. As noted earlier, famines were a frequent occurrence when the human nervous system was evolving, and although there was always some food available, only those with the highest relative incomes were certain to get fed. Someone who was more strongly motivated to achieve high rank in the leisure distribution would thus have been more likely to starve than someone who was more strongly motivated to achieve high rank in the income distribution. So the Darwinian framework predicts that income should be more positional than leisure.

This prediction is consistent with the pattern of responses to a thought experiment similar to the two discussed earlier:

Which world would you choose?

World A: You have four weeks of vacation each year; others have six weeks;

or,

World B: You have two weeks of vacation each year; others have one week.

Given these choices, most respondents pick world A, thus voicing a preference for absolute advantage over relative advantage. Follow-up discussions suggest that most respondents wouldn't be pleased about having shorter vacations than others, but rather than give up half their vacation time, they'd prefer to live with that fact.

Similar logic predicts that other nonmaterial consumption amenities, such as freedom from noise and pollution, should also be less positional than the income sacrifices that are required to obtain them.[2] By the same token, workplace amenities—such as grievance procedures, additional variety of tasks, and comfort features—should be less positional than the wage cuts necessary to obtain them.

In contrast, the Darwinian perspective suggests that investments related to the raising of offspring should tend to be highly positional. Expenditure categories that are more easily observed—such as those for cars, clothing, and jewelry—should also tend to be more positional than those that cannot be observed, such as those for insurance.

Savings, too, cannot be observed easily, and for that reason would be predicted to be nonpositional. Working against that prediction, however, is the fact that saving less today means having less to spend on positional consumption in the future. But the general human tendency to discount future costs and benefits too heavily cuts the other way. Saving less today means less positional consumption tomorrow, yes, but a current deficit can be experienced directly, whereas a future deficit can only be imagined. More important, many expenditures early in life, such as buying a house in a good school district while children are young, are inherently more positional than those occurring later. Younger parents might plausibly say to themselves, "Let's send the children to the best schools we can now and worry about retirement when the time comes." On balance, then, the prediction is that savings is nonpositional.[3]

Public goods would also be predicted to be nonpositional by virtue of one of the basic properties that defines them. Unlike private goods, for which quantities and qualities can vary for different people, public goods are provided in the same quantity and quality to everyone. So they cannot be a source of relative advantage.

These predictions are largely consistent with empirical evidence reported across a broad range of studies.[4] They're also consistent with existing patterns of regulation, taxation, and public expenditure worldwide.

Regulations as Data

Regulations are data. Antigovernment activists insist that all regulation is bad, and there are certainly many vivid examples of bad regulation. But it's instructive to consider the alternative hypothesis that many regulations exist for good reasons. Taking that view, we can learn something about how things work by observing the kinds of regulations that democratically elected representatives choose to implement.

Most jurisdictions in the United States, for example, require a child to start kindergarten in a given school year if he or she will have turned 5 years of age before a specified date during the fall term of that year. What's the purpose of this regulation? If parents were free to choose their own child's enrollment date, each might see advantage in holding their child back a year. He'd then be older, smarter, bigger, stronger, and more emotionally mature than his classmates. And since school performance is graded on the curve, he'd be more likely to do well, more likely to succeed in athletic competition, more likely to win admission to a selective university, and so on. But once some parents began "redshirting" their kindergartners, others would feel pressure to do likewise. In the end, most children might start school a few years older, but no more of them than before would win admission to selective universities. Under the circumstances, it's easy to see why people might want their elected representatives to impose mandatory kindergarten start dates.

Most societies around the world also regulate workplace safety. Most have programs either to stimulate additional savings or to compensate for the fact that many people retire with inadequate savings. Many countries have programs that attempt to equalize expenditures on schooling across different geographic areas. Most make some attempt to limit the workweek, and many set minimum requirements for worker vacation allowances.

Such regulations are squarely consistent with the hypothesis that private expenditure patterns are distorted by the fact that evaluation is more sensitive to context in some domains than in others. And as I have argued elsewhere, most competing explanations for these regulations are self-contradictory.[5] Many suffer from the no-cash-on-the-table objection discussed in chapter 3. If markets are as competitive as evidence suggests, and if evaluation were equally sensitive to context across domains, there should be little need for most of these regulations. The invisible hand would have taken care of everything.

The Progressive Consumption Tax

Prescriptive regulation is fortunately not the only way to alter wasteful consumption patterns. If the problem is that people spend too much on positional consumption and not enough on nonpositional consumption, the least intrusive way to right that imbalance is by altering the relevant prices. In a world of complete information and perfect government, we could simply set a different tax rate for every good in accordance with the extent to which context shapes its evaluation. The most positional goods would be taxed most heavily, the next-most positional goods would be taxed at slightly lower rates, and so on.

But although researchers have begun to estimate the differences in the extent to which context influences demands for specific categories of goods,[6] existing knowledge is far too fragmentary to support such an ambitious approach. Even if we knew much more about these magnitudes, it would be politically costly to establish a separate tax rate for every good. Lobbyists would inundate legislators with studies purporting to show why their particular client's product or service was nonpositional and therefore entitled to tax-exempt status.

In earlier work I have argued that a simpler, more promising, approach would be to abandon the current progressive income tax in favor of a much more steeply progressive general consumption tax.[7] This approach rests on the observation that positional concerns are stronger for luxuries than necessities. There are obvious pitfalls in trying to identify specific goods as luxuries. But given that luxury is an inherently context-dependent phenomenon, it's uncontroversial to say that the last dollars spent by those who spend most are most likely to be spent on luxuries. A steeply progressive consumption tax is thus a luxury tax that completely sidesteps the need to identify specific goods as luxuries.

Implementing a progressive consumption tax would be straightforward.[8] Taxpayers would report their incomes to the tax authorities just as they do now. They'd also report how much they had saved during the year, much as they do now for IRAs and other tax-exempt retirement accounts. People would then pay tax on their "taxable consumption," which is just the difference between their income and their annual savings, less a standard deduction.[9] Rates at the margin would rise with taxable consumption. If the tax were revenue-neutral, marginal rates at the top would be significantly higher than current marginal tax rates on income, to make up for the revenue lost by exempting savings. But if we want to repair crumbling infrastructure, round up loose nukes in the former Soviet Union, and bring the government budget into balance as the baby boomers retire, we'll need additional tax revenue. That would require still higher top marginal rates.

Proposals to generate additional income tax revenue by raising top marginal rates invariably summon concern about possible negative effects on the incentive to save and invest. Under a progressive consumption tax, by contrast, people's incentives would be to save and invest more, even if top marginal tax rates on consumption were extremely high.

If the direct effect of the tax were to induce top spenders to save more, it would also affect the spending of others indirectly. Each individual's spending, after all, constitutes part of the frame of reference that influences what others spend. And given the importance of context, the indirect effects of a progressive consumption tax promise to be considerably larger than the direct effects.

The expenditure cascades discussed in chapter 4 have pressured many middle-income families to spend beyond their means. If people at the top were to save more and spend less on mansions, that would shift the frame of reference that influences the housing expenditures of those just below them. So they, too, would spend less on housing, and so on all the way down the income ladder. People at the top would also spend less to celebrate special occasions. They'd spend less on gifts. They'd spend less on jewelry. Those changes, too, would produce similar indirect effects.

By all available evidence, that would be a good thing. The aggregate household savings rate in the United States was negative during both 2005 and 2006. Americans were actually spending more than they earned during full calendar years for the first time since the Great Depression. Low savings rates helped precipitate the financial crisis that brought the global economy to its knees in 2008. For decades, liberals and conservatives alike have agreed that we would all be better off if we all spent less and saved and invested more. But no individual has the power to alter the aggregate savings rate. If we want to increase it, we must act collectively. A progressive consumption tax would be the perfect policy instrument for that purpose.

It would raise needed revenue while simultaneously reducing the incidence of behavior that causes harm to others. A CEO who spent $10 million to stage a coming-of-age party for his daughter may have had no intention of harming others. But his action caused harm nonetheless. By shifting the frame of reference that defines what constitutes a special occasion, it confronted others with a difficult choice. They could either increase their own spending or hold the line, courting the impression that they didn't appreciate the occasion's significance. Many ten-year-olds in middle-income families are now disappointed if their parents don't hire a clown or magician to perform at their birthday parties. And since there's absolutely no evidence that children are happier in the wake of across-the-board increases in spending on parties, it would be bizarre to insist that shifting this particular frame of reference caused no harm to others.

As we'll see in the next chapter, people's interest in not being harmed by the actions of others must of course be weighed against the cost to others of restricting their freedom of action. It's here that the progressive consumption tax really shines. For example, consider a family that is currently spending $10 million a year and is considering a $2 million addition to its mansion. If the top marginal tax rate on consumption were 100 percent, the project would cost $4 million. If the family went ahead with the project exactly as planned, its additional tax payment would reduce the federal deficit by $2 million.

Alternatively, it could scale back, building only a $1 million addition. It would then pay $1 million in additional tax and could deposit $2 million more in savings than if it had built the original plan. The federal deficit would fall by $1 million, and the additional savings would stimulate investment, promoting growth. Either way, no real sacrifice would be required of the wealthy family, because if all wealthy families had gone ahead with their original plans, the result would have been merely to redefine what constitutes acceptable housing.

The important point is that the utility from consumption at extremely high levels is almost purely positional. A tax that encourages top earners to save more and spend less thus has virtually no direct negative effect on those who face the tax. On the contrary, as noted in chapter 4, an across-the-board reduction in the growth of the largest mansions might well leave top earners feeling happier than they'd have been on the current trajectory. Tending to a big mansion is a hassle.

Libertarians of all people should be positively disposed to using taxes, rather than prescriptive regulation, to curb the impact of behavior that causes harm to others. The tax approach doesn't forbid someone from doing what he wants; it merely makes doing it more expensive. The advantage of using taxes to curb positional externalities is thus exactly analogous to the advantage of using effluent fees to curb environmental pollution.

In the environmental domain, firms for which pollution reduction is most expensive may find it in their interest to continue to pollute even after the imposition of an effluent tax. Similarly, those families for whom consumption reductions would be especially difficult may respond to higher tax rates by expending additional effort in order to maintain their previous spending levels. But in both the environmental and consumption domains, the harm we're trying to prevent depends more on overall activity levels than on the activity levels of particular individuals or firms. And just as the imposition of effluent charges mitigates pollution damage by leading most firms to curtail pollution, a progressive consumption tax would mitigate the costs of positional externalities by increasing the incentive to save.

Despite the gaps in current knowledge about positional concerns, recent experience provides some insight into how switching to a steeply progressive consumption tax might affect social welfare. Compared to the current income tax, such a tax would reduce high-end consumption and increase public spending. If affluent consumers are generally rational, private spending reductions would be concentrated in the categories they consider least urgent. Political imperfections notwithstanding, governments would spend at least some of the resulting tax revenue on the public services that voters value most. The practical question, then, is whether the loss from cutting the least urgent high-end private consumption categories would outweigh the gain from increasing the most highly valued public services. To be sure, it's possible to imagine a society so poor in private consumption and so rich in public consumption that such a switch would reduce welfare. But what about societies with high levels of private consumption and low levels of public services, like the United States in recent years?

In the absence of detailed empirical evidence, a plausible conjecture is that the first expenditures that high-end consumers would reduce in response to a steeply progressive consumption tax are the same ones they have recently been increasing most rapidly in response to their growing incomes. As discussed in chapter 4, some of the most spectacular increases in high-end consumption in recent years have occurred in housing and the events families use to mark special occasions. By all accounts, such expenditures are hyperpositional.

Facing high marginal tax rates on consumption, the wealthiest families would surely spend less on parties for their children. If they did, the standards that define a special occasion in their circle would shift accordingly. Could anyone argue with a straight face that these changes would constitute a significant welfare loss for the children involved?

What about the welfare impact of the public services made possible by additional revenue from a steeply progressive consumption tax? Even allowing for the fact that some of the extra revenue would be spent wastefully, much of the rest would pay for useful things. For example, we could repair unsafe bridges like the one on Interstate 35 that collapsed into the Mississippi River in downtown Minneapolis on August 1, 2007, killing 13 people and injuring 145. We could inspect the cargo containers that currently enter the nation's ports without scrutiny.

Limited empirical knowledge does not always prevent us from drawing reasonable inferences about the likely welfare effects of specific tax policy changes. Most economists would agree that the welfare cost to wealthy families of having smaller and less expensive mansions would be smaller than their benefit from having safer roads and improved security. If so, the benefit of those upgrades to the nonwealthy would be pure gravy.

These observations provide reasons beyond those I will discuss in chapter 10 to question the traditional assumption that tax policy confronts us with an agonizing trade-off between equity and efficiency. If context shapes spending patterns in the ways suggested by available evidence, higher marginal tax rates on top earners would appear justified not only on grounds of equity, but also on grounds of narrow economic efficiency.

A Political Pipe Dream?

I have been advocating the progressive consumption tax for many years. When my liberal friends hear me talk about it, they often say it sounds like a promising idea, but they are usually quick to add that it's politically unthinkable. Given the strength of the antitax, antigovernment rhetorical framework that shapes political discourse in the United States, it's easy to share their pessimism. But at some point, refusal to consider fundamental tax reform will cease to be a viable option. We can continue to borrow and cut back essential public services for a while longer. But not forever. And when the moment of reckoning comes, there are good reasons to view the progressive consumption tax as a promising candidate for adoption.

A version of this tax was actually introduced in the U.S. Senate in 1995 under the bipartisan sponsorship of Sam Nunn (D, GA) and Pete Domenici (R, NM). Other budget battles kept their bill from reaching the top of the agenda, but others have continued to tout similar proposals in the years since. Shortly after I published an article advocating adoption of the progressive consumption tax in 1997,[10] I received a warm letter from Milton Friedman, who, until his death in 2006, was the patron saint of small-government conservatism in the United States. The federal budget was on the verge of running large surpluses then, and Friedman wrote that he didn't share my view that the government should be raising more revenue. But he went on to add that if the government did need additional revenue, the progressive consumption tax would be far and away the best way to raise it. He enclosed a reprint of an article he himself had published in the 1943 volume of the *American Economic Review* in which he advocated this tax as the best way to pay for the war effort.[11]

Many other conservatives have advocated a flat tax or value-added tax, which are essentially national sales taxes. But because the rich save much larger shares of their incomes than the poor, such taxes are extremely regressive. Taxing all consumption at a uniform rate would actually put more disposable income into the hands of the nation's top earners, which would exacerbate the expenditure cascades described in chapter 4. Those cascades are launched by increased spending at the top. Steering resources to more productive uses will require fairly high marginal consumption tax rates on the biggest spenders. That's possible under a progressive consumption tax but not under a value-added tax.

The economist Laurence Seidman has proposed that a good first step toward the adoption of a progressive consumption tax would be to retain the current income tax for now while supplementing it with a progressive consumption surtax.[12] Under his proposal, families with adjusted gross incomes less than $1 million would be completely exempt from the surtax. Those with higher incomes would document their annual savings and calculate their annual consumption expenditure as the difference between their annual income and that amount. A progressive surtax would then be levied only on their consumption in excess of $500,000.[13] Over time, the income tax could be completely transformed into a progressive consumption tax by gradually lowering the threshold for the surtax.

An added attraction of Seidman's proposal is that it would create a temporary spending boom for a sluggish economy that could really use it. The key step would be to pass the surtax right away, but delay its implementation until the economy was once again operating near full employment. Mere announcement that the tax was coming would spur a flood of additional high-end spending as wealthy families rushed to build mansion additions and stage lavish parties before the tax took effect. Granted, that might not be the best way to stimulate additional spending. But it would clearly be better than standing idly by while total spending remains far too low to support full employment.

In the long run, a progressive consumption tax would gradually shift the composition of final spending away from consumption toward investment, causing productivity to grow more rapidly. In the event of an economic downturn, a temporary suspension or reduction of the tax would be a powerful stimulus tool, since consumers would benefit only if they increased their spending right away. In contrast, temporary income tax cuts tend to be a weak stimulus tool, because fearful consumers often save them.

Movement libertarians can of course be expected to denounce the progressive consumption tax in the same harsh terms they reserve for other taxes. Theft! Social engineering! Frank thinks the bureaucrats in Washington know how to spend our money more wisely than we do! Class warfare!

But mature adults understand that we must tax something. Right now we tax savings, which discourages productive investment. We tax payrolls, which discourages job creation. Instead, why not tax things that we would otherwise have too much of?

SIX

Perpetrators and Victims

I N ALMOST EVERY COUNTRY IN EUROPE, individual behavior is more heavily regulated than in the United States. And in the United States, behavior is more heavily regulated now than it was a century ago. Both comparisons are rooted in differences in population density. There have always been many more people per square mile in Europe than in the United States, where population density is much higher now than it was in frontier days. With higher density, people collide with one another more often.

Society is not only more densely populated now, but also much more highly interactive, in part because of higher density. These trends will continue, and with them will come additional demands for regulation. The societies that respond more intelligently to those demands will be more likely to prosper.

But until we understand the market failures that prompt demands for regulation, we're unlikely to adopt the best remedies. Liberals have always seen market failure as rooted in natural or artificial barriers to perfect competition. But greater population density does not cause monopoly in product markets. Nor does it undermine competition in labor markets. Nor, finally, does it render consumers less rational or well informed. The positive link between regulation and population density thus provides no support for the traditional liberal view.

That same link, however, is squarely consistent with Darwin's insight that individual and group interests often diverge sharply. When they do, opportunities for causing harm to others clearly increase with population density.

Darwin himself wasn't much concerned with how to narrow the wedge between individual and group interests. Most animal species, after all, have only extremely limited capacity to act collectively. Humans are of course a conspicuous exception. Even the earliest hunter-gatherer groups employed social norms extensively to constrain the self-interested behavior of their members.[1] Yet we remain in the dark ages in terms of our understanding of how best to limit behavior that causes harm to others.

It may be only a slight exaggeration to say that every human act that harms someone else provokes a corresponding demand for additional regulation. But preventing all activities that harm others is obviously not an option. John Stuart Mill's harm principle must be understood as saying that the only legitimate reason for government to limit someone's freedom is to prevent *undue* harm to others. We permit harmful behavior all the time. Unkind remarks, for example, cause harm to others, yet we permit them within limits because the harm from curtailing free speech would be even greater. Similarly, a firm is permitted to cut its price and thereby harm its rivals, perhaps even drive them out of business, because failure to allow this would cause even greater harm to consumers. For the harm principle to make any sense at all, it must be understood to mean that the legitimacy of a restriction must be decided by weighing its cost to those being restricted against the harm others would suffer if the behavior weren't restricted.

The Pivotal Contribution of Ronald Coase

Ronald Coase (rhymes with "rose") won the Nobel Prize in economics in 1991 largely on the strength of his contribution to our way of thinking about this delicate balancing act. An economist born and educated in England, Coase spent the latter part of his career on the faculty of the University of Chicago Law School, where he was revered by that university's free-market enthusiasts as the world's foremost authority on behavior that causes harm to others.

Movement libertarians are reluctant to acknowledge that such behavior is ever a proper concern of regulators. But more serious libertarians, who are well represented among the University of Chicago's distinguished faculty, have always recognized the need to grapple with the implications of harmful behavior.[2] They saw Coase as their champion because they believed his framework provided the most cogent arguments for limiting the reach of regulators. In one sense they were right. But in another sense, they were profoundly mistaken.

On the first point, Coase showed that, under certain restrictive conditions, private parties could resolve many problems on their own that were once thought to require detailed intervention by regulators.[3] But although Coase deeply appreciated the ingenuity and elegance of many market solutions, he was no ideologue. Many of his disciples simply ignored his clear acknowledgment that practical obstacles often prevent private parties from negotiating efficient contracts. In such cases, he recognized, government intervention could often improve matters.

His core insight first appeared in the context of a brief example in a 1959 paper entitled "The Federal Communications Commission."[4] Then as now, broadcast rights worth millions of dollars were awarded free of charge to private entrepreneurs by regulators at the Federal Communications Commission. Coase argued that much better use would be made of those rights if they were instead sold to the highest bidders, who would put them to the highest-valued uses.

One of the issues that had prompted broadcast regulation in the first place was that the exercise of broadcast rights often caused harm to others. Signals broadcast on one frequency often interfered with those broadcast on closely adjacent frequencies. Coase's insight was that if negotiations between broadcasters were practical, they could resolve such problems satisfactorily on their own.

His now-famous example likened the problem of broadcast interference to one adjudicated in a lawsuit filed by a doctor whose practice was disturbed by noise from an adjacent factory. The facts of the case as Coase summarized them were as follows:

> A confectioner had used certain premises for his business for a great many years. When a doctor came and occupied a neighboring property, the working of the confectioner's machinery caused the doctor no harm until, some eight years later, he built a consulting room at the end of his garden, right against the confectioner's premises. Then it was found that noise and vibrations caused by the machinery disturbed the doctor in his work. The doctor then brought an action and succeeded in securing an injunction preventing the confectioner from using his machinery. What the courts had, in fact, to decide was whether the doctor had the right to impose additional costs on the confectioner through compelling him to install new machinery, or move to a new location, or whether the confectioner had the right to impose additional costs on the doctor through compelling him to do his consulting somewhere else on his premises or at another location.[5]

Before Coase, it was common for policy discussions of activities that cause harm to others to be couched in terms of perpetrators and victims. A factory that created noise was a perpetrator, and an adjacent physician whose practice suffered as a result was a victim. Coase's insight was that externalities like noise or smoke are purely reciprocal phenomena. The factory's noise harms the doctor, yes; but to invoke the doctor's injury as grounds for prohibiting the noise would harm the factory owner.

It was surely not the factory owner's intent to harm the doctor. Nor was it the doctor's intent to impede the workings of the factory. Their proximity to one another and the nature of their specific activities created a mutual problem to be solved. Both the factory owner and the doctor, Coase argued, have a shared interest in finding the least costly solution to it. He concluded that unless it were impractical for them to negotiate with one another, they'd always be able to resolve it efficiently, regardless of whether the government held the factory owner liable for noise damages.

Suppose, for example, that if the doctor did nothing, the noise would cause his practice $20,000 in damage, but that he could avoid noise damage altogether by moving to a different location, which would cost him $10,000. Suppose also that the factory owner could eliminate the noise by installing soundproofing on his machinery at a cost of $5,000. Since soundproofing is cheaper, it's a better way to solve the noise problem than for the doctor to incur the expense of moving. Coase pointed out that if the doctor and factory owner could negotiate with one another at negligible cost, they should be able to reach an agreement calling for the installation of soundproofing, whether or not the government held the factory owner liable for noise damage.

The first part of that claim was obvious. Thus, suppose government made the factory owner liable for noise damage, meaning that if he continued to produce noise, he'd have to pay the doctor $20,000 to compensate for the damage. The owner's best response would then be to install soundproofing, since that would cost him only $5,000 and would eliminate the need to compensate the doctor.

It was the second part of Coase's claim that caught most readers off guard. He pointed out that if the government did *not* make the factory owner liable for noise damage, the doctor's best option would then be to offer to pay the factory owner to install soundproofing. His next-best alternative, after all, would be to bear the $10,000 cost of moving to escape the noise.

The doctor's payment to the factory owner would have to be large enough to cover the $5,000 cost of the soundproofing, or else the factory owner would refuse to install it (since he is not liable for noise damage). And the payment demanded by the factory owner could not exceed $10,000, because in that case the doctor could solve the noise problem more cheaply by moving.

In short, Coase argued, both parties would have a strong incentive to implement the efficient solution to the problem, irrespective of whether the law held the factory owner responsible for noise damage. Coase was quite explicit that this conclusion rested on the assumption that it was practical for the affected parties to negotiate with one another. Thus, he wrote, "Once the legal rights of the parties are established, negotiation is possible to modify the arrangements envisaged in the legal ruling, if the likelihood of being able to do so makes it worthwhile to incur the costs involved in negotiation."[6]

When "The Federal Communications Commission" appeared in 1959, it provoked little discussion. Many of those who did react to it—including, notably, Milton Friedman, George Stigler, and other prominent free-market enthusiasts at the University of Chicago—believed that Coase was simply mistaken. Even in a hypothetical world in which contracts could be negotiated at zero cost, they argued, production decisions would surely be affected by whether the law held people liable for damages they inflicted on others. Coase acknowledged that the wealth levels of the doctor and the factory owner would be affected by liability rules, but he insisted that their decision about how to solve the problem would not be.

Never ones to shrink from debate, a group of University of Chicago economists invited Coase, who was then teaching at the University of Virginia, to Chicago to discuss his ideas with them. Twenty economists and Ronald Coase met for dinner at the home of Aaron Director, who was then editor of the *Journal of Law and Economics,* in which Coase's paper had appeared. Years later, Stigler offered this recollection of the evening's conversation: "Milton Friedman did most of the talking, as usual. He also did much of the thinking, as usual. In the course of two hours of argument the vote went from twenty against and one for Coase to twenty-one for Coase. What an exhilarating event! I lamented afterward that we had not had the clairvoyance to tape it."[7]

Coase was persuaded to write a much more detailed exposition of his insight, which was published in the *Journal of Law and Economics* the following year as "The Problem of Social Cost."[8] That paper quickly became and remains the most widely cited economics paper ever published.[9] But despite the incredible volume of attention it has received, scholars haven't yet grasped its full significance.

What no one disputes is that the paper quickly provoked a firestorm of criticism. Scholars on the left were upset because they interpreted Coase to be saying that government had no essential role to play in regulating pollution or other activities that cause harm to others (beyond seeing to it that property rights were clearly defined and enforced). Others complained that Coase's analysis seemed oblivious to the moral framework underlying the earlier perpetrators-and-victims approach to such activities. (The doctor didn't harm anyone! Why should *he* have to pay for the soundproofing?) But neither of these objections withstands scrutiny.

Barriers to Negotiation

Consider first the charge that Coase had written government out of the picture. Again, his claim that an efficient solution would be achieved irrespective of whether polluters were held liable for damages was quite explicitly predicated on an assumption that anyone familiar with his earlier work would know he believed to be unrealistic. Coase's first significant paper, "The Nature of the Firm," published in 1937, was in fact inspired by his observation that practical difficulties often prevented people from negotiating efficient contracts with one another.[10] This paper was based on field research he had conducted in 1932, when as an undergraduate he received a fellowship to travel to the United States to observe the operations of large American corporations. The specific question he tackled in the 1937 paper was, why do firms exist in the first place? Why, he wanted to know, weren't all business transactions carried out directly between independent contractors? His answer—which, like many big ideas, seems painfully obvious in hindsight—was that the latter approach would necessitate a host of complex and costly transactions.

If you wanted to buy a car, for example, you'd have to negotiate contracts with numerous miners to extract iron ore from the earth, more contracts with others to process the ore into steel, still more contracts to mold the steel into the desired shapes, and so on. Even if the buyer dealt with the most efficient suppliers in each instance, the number and complexity of the required contracts would make the ultimate price of the car prohibitively high. The whole process could be dramatically streamlined, he argued, by forming organizations in which employees simply did the bidding of supervisors.

In the wake of the 1937 paper's publication, a new field in economics emerged and prospered. Called transaction cost economics, it tries to explain organizational forms and behavior as implicit or explicit consequences of attempts to economize on transaction costs.[11]

In the light of his intellectual history, there is no question that Coase was well aware of practical impediments that often make it prohibitively costly for private parties to negotiate agreements. His intended message simply cannot have been that government has no useful role to play in the regulation of activities that cause harm to others. On the contrary, the deeper message of his 1960 paper was that when negotiation is impractical—as it typically will be—the assignment of liability will often change how problems get solved. In Coase's view, then, the structure of legal responsibility really matters. But it matters in a way that earlier writers had not appreciated. The prevailing view had been that perpetrators should always be held responsible for the damage they cause. Coase challenged that logic at its core. His view was that government should assign the burden of adjusting to externalities to the party for whom that burden would be least costly.

Referring to the earlier example, if the doctor and the factory owner cannot negotiate, the government should hold the factory liable for noise damage if—as under the hypothetical cost values assumed—it would be less costly for the factory to reduce its noise than it would be for the doctor to move to a more sheltered location. But if the reverse were true, then the government should not hold the factory liable. That posture, Coase reasoned, would induce the doctor to relocate, which would be the efficient solution under the circumstances.

Is Cost-Benefit Analysis Immoral?

What about the objection that Coase's analysis ignored the underlying moral framework governing activities that cause harm to others? What many of Coase's critics still fail to perceive clearly is that his formulation of the problem reveals a fundamental flaw in the traditional moral framework. That framework, again, viewed the factory owner as the perpetrator and the doc-tor as the victim. It assumed, without explaining why, that the doctor has a right to conduct his practice undisturbed by noise, and that the government has a duty to enforce that right.

Coase's analysis raises the question of why the doctor's position should be privileged in this situation. Suppose, for example, that the cost figures assumed earlier were reversed—that is, suppose the doctor could solve the noise problem by moving at a cost of $5,000 and that the factory owner could soundproof his machines at a cost of $10,000. The least costly solution to the problem would then be for the doctor to move. And if negotiation is impractical, Coase's analysis would recommend not holding the factory owner liable for noise damage, in which case the doctor would have an incentive to solve the problem on his own by moving.

Would it be better to hold the factory owner liable in this case? If we did and if negotiation were practical, we'd still get the efficient solution, because the factory owner would have an incentive to pay the doctor to move, thereby to avoid having to incur the $10,000 cost of soundproofing. But such negotiated settlements are typically impractical. So if we make the fac-tory owner liable, his best option would be to spend $10,000 to install soundproofing, because his alternative would be to pay $20,000 to compen-sate the doctor for noise damage. Yes, the noise problem still gets solved, but at twice the cost of solving it by relocating the doctor.

Although intuition might seem to favor calling the factory owner the per-petrator in this case, Coase's analysis makes clear that there is no logical basis for that claim. If the doctor had arrived first, he might have acted on the assumption that he could continue to operate his practice undisturbed by noise. And if it could be shown that being able to act on such an assump-tion helped facilitate productive patterns of investment, that might argue for holding late-arriving noisemakers liable for damage.[12] But as Coase's exam-ple made clear, the factory owner happened to have been first on the scene in this case.

Alternatively, some might worry that the cost of solving the problem would be too big a burden for the doctor to bear. But *someone* must bear the cost of solving the problem, no matter what. Nothing in the example suggested that the factory owner was wealthier and hence better able to do so. Perhaps the Latina wheelchair-bound factory owner was barely able to keep her business afloat and employed fifty hard-working, churchgoing, nondrinking, salt-of-the-earth employees, each the sole support of a wife and two kids and a dog and a cat. And perhaps the single playboy dermatologist had an incredibly lucrative practice polishing up the complexions of the idle wives of plutocrats and played golf three afternoons a week.

In the absence of any such countervailing considerations, we must consider the possibility that the traditional perpetrators-and-victims moral framework was simply misguided or question-begging. That is, we must consider the possibility that the most sensible way to define rights in situations like these is, as Coase suggested, to mimic as closely as possible the solutions people would have negotiated on their own if negotiations had been practical. Those solutions would always place the burden of adjusting to externalities on the party for whom that burden was least costly. Sometimes that would entail assigning liability to the party whom most would describe as the perpetrator. But not always.

There is a measure of irony in the fact that Ronald Coase quickly emerged as the reigning intellectual hero of free-market conservatives on all matters related to activities that cause harm to others. Their embrace of Coase stems largely from the perception that his framework helped expand the range of problems believed to be soluble without regulatory intervention. That perception is accurate as far as it goes. But again, Coase was never an ideologue. His framework is rooted in strictly pragmatic concerns.

Libertarians often speak of fundamental human rights and freedoms that trump pragmatic concerns. But defending any given right entails both costs and benefits.[13] Coase's approach emphasizes that in the end, questions regarding which specific rights to defend are quintessentially practical ones.

Coase might conclude, under certain circumstances, that doctors should have a right to operate free from noise from their neighbors. But if so, it would not be because he thought there was a sacred right to a noise-free environment in all cases. Rather, it would be because he believed that it would be cheaper for people to curb the noise they emit than for affected parties to avoid noise on their own.

Because most moral questions involve actions that cause harm to others, Coase's framework has something to say about such questions. If his academic appointment had been in a department of moral philosophy, he'd have been classified as a consequentialist—someone who believes the right course of action is the option that produces the best overall consequences.[14] Their antagonists, the deontologists, concede that consequences matter, but insist that there are also certain bedrock moral principles that must be followed irrespective of consequences.

To the extent that libertarians think it self-evident that people have a right to be free from interference by government regulation—except for laws that prohibit theft, assault, and other egregious forms of direct harm to others—most of them fall squarely in the deontologists' camp. Yet the Coase framework that so many of them embrace is uncompromisingly consequentialist. It demands an explanation of why such a broad right to be left alone leads to the best consequences overall. And as we'll see, that's a formidable hurdle.

Deontologists face other hurdles, such as how to explain where the bedrock moral principles they invoke come from. But they often manage to score telling debate points by constructing examples in which the action with the best overall consequences seems clearly impermissible to most observers.

A perennial favorite describes a botanist who wanders into a jungle village where ten innocent people are about to be shot.[15] He is told that nine of them will be spared if he himself will shoot the tenth. What should the botanist do? The consequentialist framework seems to suggest that shooting the innocent man would be the right choice, because doing so would result in a net saving of nine lives. Yet most normal sentient beings are loath to endorse that conclusion. Deontologists insist that such examples demonstrate the bankruptcy of consequentialist moral reasoning.

Consequentialists and deontologists have been at each other's throats for millennia. Nothing I say here could possibly settle the issues that divide them.

But because I will advocate policy claims that follow from Coase's consequentialist framework, it's important to emphasize that the two frameworks
are less squarely in conflict than may often appear.

An Illustrative Example

A concrete example helps highlight some of the factors that exaggerate the
scope of disagreement between the two types of moral reasoning. It's an
example of the type that deontologists often employ to demonstrate the
moral bankruptcy of the consequentialist position. Set in Atlanta, Georgia,
during the mid-1960s, the question it poses is, "Should interracial couples be
prohibited from holding hands in public?" Although most young Americans today find it difficult to believe, there were then laws on the books in
some states that prohibited people of different races from marrying. Those
laws were declared unconstitutional by a 9-0 vote of the Supreme Court in a
landmark 1967 civil rights case.[16] But Atlanta in the mid-1960s was still an
environment in which interracial couples were a rare sight, and also one in
which a substantial proportion of the majority white population would
experience significant agitation at the sight of such couples holding hands in
public. In that environment, there were few who would benefit from having
the right in question and many who would be offended by the exercise of it.
The apparent implication is that the option with the best consequences overall would be to prohibit interracial handholding. Because most people would
find such a prohibition morally reprehensible, however, deontologists conclude that we must reject the consequentialist framework for thinking about
moral questions.

The problem could easily be reframed as a numerical example of the type
Coase favored. We might imagine, for instance, that if the city's 100 interracial couples were each willing to pay $100 a week for the right to hold
hands in public, then the combined benefit to them of being able to do so
would total $10,000 per week, and that if a million of the city's whites would
be willing to pay $1 a week to avoid the sight of interracial handholding, the
weekly cost of granting that right would be $1,000,000. If it were possible

for the two groups to negotiate, each of the million whites could chip in, say, $0.10 a week, for a total of $100,000, which would finance a payment of $1,000 a week to each interracial couple that was prevented from holding hands. Compared to the option of no prohibition, each interracial couple would be $900 a week better off than before (the $1,000 payment they receive minus the $100 loss they suffer from not being able to hold hands in public), and each offended white would be $0.90 a week better off (the $1 value each assigns to avoiding the sight of interracial handholding minus the $0.10 each contributes to the compensation payments).

The Coase framework thus seems to say that if it had been practical for the affected parties to negotiate, they'd have agreed to implement the ban on interracial handholding and carried out the indicated compensation payments. Under the circumstances, negotiation would of course be impractical. In such cases, the Coase framework says that the law should place the burden of adjusting to the externality on the party for whom it would be least costly. And since the cumulative monetary damage to interracial couples from not being able to hold hands in public ($10,000) is smaller than the cumulative cost of the sight of handholding to offended whites ($1,000,000), the Coase framework still seems to imply that the right thing to do is to prohibit interracial handholding.

Such examples surely do help explain why consequentialist moral reasoning remains suspect in the eyes of many. But before rejecting the Coase framework, those who share my view that a prohibition on interracial handholding would be wrong should consider the possibility that the framework was simply applied incorrectly in the example.

As described, the analysis completely ignores the fact that people adapt over time in dramatically different ways to different forms of real or imagined injuries. The cumulative amount that white residents of Atlanta in the 1960s would have been willing to pay to avoid the sight of interracial handholding probably did outweigh the cumulative amount that the small number of interracial couples would have been willing to pay for the right to hold hands. But as interracial relationships have become more common during the intervening years, attitudes have changed dramatically, and in ways that were completely predictable at the time.

I was an undergraduate in Atlanta in the 1960s. Many of my college friends were staunchly opposed to interracial relationships of any kind. But my own children, who have never lived in the South, report that they experience no emotional reaction whatsoever to interracial handholding, which has always been a common sight in the environment in which they grew up. As anyone who had experienced life outside the South would have been able to predict, the sense of injury experienced by Southern whites would diminish sharply over time as they adapted to the changing environment.

In contrast, there are many other forms of injury that not only fail to decay over time but actually become more severe. The damage caused by exposure to background noise is a case in point. Not only do people fail to adapt to living in noisy environments, the physiological stress they suffer actually increases with continued exposure.[17] The time profile of injury experienced by someone prohibited from holding hands with the person of his choosing would almost certainly exhibit a similar pattern. Not only would he fail to adapt to the fact that he was denied a right routinely granted to others, his sense of injury would grow over time.

Activities that cause harm to others are inherently reciprocal. If interracial handholding occurs, some may feel injured. If interracial handholding is prevented, others will surely be injured. The Coase framework says the best response in such cases is the one that minimizes total harm. Proper application of that framework requires an assessment not just of the injuries different parties feel, or claim to feel, in the current moment but also of their capacities to avoid those injuries or adapt to them over time. In short, the Coase framework, properly applied, would never have ruled against interracial handholding in the first place.

Which Rights Should We Defend?

Rights to behave in certain ways don't arise out of thin air. Defending any given right creates benefits for those who value it. But it also generates costs —not just for those tasked with enforcing the right, but also for those whose behavior is restricted by it.

As even deontologists concede, costs and benefits matter in moral decisions. And society's decision about which rights to enforce clearly has a moral dimension. It isn't my claim that the Coase framework is the uniquely correct way of thinking about such decisions. But to the extent that we can agree that the costs and benefits of the alternatives we face matter to at least some extent, I hope we can agree that the Coase framework might often facilitate clearer thinking about the relevant trade-offs.

Many libertarians and conservatives have of course long since embraced the Coase framework. As a moment's reflection makes clear, however, that embrace severely constrains their ability to evade the logical implications of John Stuart Mill's harm principle. Many libertarians seem inclined to embrace the harm principle when doing so provides them with additional ammunition against a regulation they don't favor. When the principle seems to support a regulation they don't like, however, they're often quick to reject it, insisting that it's trumped in that instance by some prior right to act in the way they wish to. But the latter tactic forces them to confront the question of where that right comes from.

The Coase framework they embrace says that society should define and enforce rights in such a way as to mimic the agreements people would reach on their own if open negotiation between them were practical. In this framework, a harmful act is one whose consequences someone would be willing to sacrifice real resources to avoid. Harm thus conceived is not confined to physical violence or theft of property. It also includes the various forms of indirect harm discussed in preceding chapters, such as the harm experienced by a sprinter whose rivals consume performance-enhancing drugs.

If libertarians want to stick with their current mix of policy prescriptions, then, they must confront some difficult choices. To continue to reject Mill's harm principle when it suits them, they must assert that they have the right to take actions that impose substantial, easily measured harm on others even when the actions are of little benefit to themselves. Because such a right would be impossible to defend within the Coase framework, that choice would require them to reject Coase outright. But think what a difficult position that would be for an honest libertarian to defend! If you really care about freedom, how can you reject a framework that defines rights for the explicit purpose of mimicking as closely as possible the outcomes completely free people would have agreed to among themselves?

For the sake of discussion, I'm going to adopt the position of a libertarian who refuses to abandon Coase and try to explore further where that approach to rights leads us. Now, it's one thing to agree in principle that costs and benefits matter in deciding which rights to defend. But it's quite another matter to agree on how to measure the relevant costs and benefits. Few questions have spawned more disagreement among social theorists than that of how to weigh the competing claims of people whose interests are in conflict. In the next chapter, I'll argue that the Coase framework provides useful guidance for thinking about this question as well.

SEVEN

Efficiency Rules

THE DEVELOPMENT OF MONEY was a critical step that facilitated the division and specialization of labor, a process that enabled per-capita income to grow thousandsfold during the past several centuries. Money has also been indispensable as a unit of account for deciding which of two competing interests should prevail.

Thus, in Ronald Coase's example of the factory owner whose machinery disrupted the neighboring doctor's practice, the best solution to the problem was easily identified by comparing the factory owner's monetary cost of soundproofing his machines to the doctor's monetary cost of moving to a quiet location. The incomes of the two parties were completely irrelevant for that comparison, although their incomes would clearly be affected by how the law chose to assign responsibility for noise damage.

How Income Differences Affect the Cost-Benefit Test

But sometimes the incomes of parties affected by harmful activities play a direct role in determining the least costly solution to the problem. Suppose, for example, that Sarah likes to play her violin at night, which disturbs her neighbor Sam. Should the law restrain Sarah's playing? To keep the discussion simple, let's suppose that legislators are considering only two options—banning music after 10:00 PM on weeknights or banning it after 11:00 PM. To decide which alternative would ameliorate the problem at lower cost, legislators would need two pieces of information: (1) the value to Sarah of being able to continue playing until 11:00 rather than having to stop an hour earlier and (2) the value to Sam of having Sara stop playing at 10:00 rather than an hour later.

Sarah would obviously like to be able to continue playing until 11:00, but how strongly does she feel about it? To most economists, the answer to this question is simple in principle, if not always easy to come up with in practice. It's the largest amount she'd be willing to pay to maintain her right to play until 11:00. Economists would answer the question of how much Sam values the right to have quiet starting at 10:00 in a similar way. It's the largest amount he'd be willing to pay to secure that right. Economists realize, of course, that if the two parties were simply asked how much they were willing to pay, they'd have clear incentives to overstate their responses if they knew that the timing of the noise ordinance depended on them. So as a practical matter, economists often try to infer how much the respective parties would be willing to pay from indirect behavioral evidence—perhaps by comparing property values in otherwise similar communities whose noise ordinances kick in at different times.

But practical measurement problems would be the least controversial aspect of any proposal to base the solution to a noise problem on a comparison of the amounts that affected parties are willing to pay to have their way. Far more troubling would be the fact that willingness to pay depends so heavily on ability to pay. How much people would be willing to pay for an extra hour of quiet, or for the right to continue playing music for an extra hour, depends on many things—including their feelings about music, the thickness of their apartment walls, and their work schedules. But willingness to pay also depends heavily on income. Holding all else constant, the more people earn, the more they're willing to pay to have their way.

The upshot is that Coase's approach to solving the noise problem will tend to tilt heavily in favor of the solutions preferred by those who have the most money. Suppose, for example, that Sarah feels extremely strongly about being able to practice until 11:00, but her meager income enables her to pay at most $8 a day for the right to do so. And suppose that Sam is really not much disturbed by Sarah's playing in the evening, but because he is extremely wealthy he'd be willing to pay $15 a day for the right to silence after 10:00. The Coase framework would then hold that the efficient solution to the problem would be to adopt an ordinance that prohibits noise after 10:00 PM. Yet when I polled a class of more than ninety graduate students about what should be done in this example, more than eighty thought the noise curfew should begin at 11:00.

When the 1960 Coase paper first appeared, much of the negative reaction from critics on the left was prompted by the perception that measuring costs and benefits by willingness to pay was morally tone-deaf, a gross violation of the principle that citizens should have equal rights irrespective of their incomes. But despite the intuitively compelling attraction of this statement, it's misguided. As we'll see, it accounts for our repeated failure to implement policies that would benefit all citizens, rich and poor alike.

Most people actually seem willing to accept the fact that willingness to pay determines who gets what in private markets. If a painting is being auctioned, for example, and many people want it, the one who's willing to pay the most gets it. Willingness to pay is also decisive when cost-benefit analysis guides public decisions. But its use in the public sphere is more controversial—so much so that we often reject the recommendations of traditional cost-benefit analyses in major public policy decisions.

All Talk or All Music?

A simple example conveys the flavor of some of the issues at stake. Suppose a community must decide whether to switch the format of its public radio station from all music to all talk. To keep things simple, we'll assume that the two formats cost the same and all voters are indifferent between them except for the following three: One wealthy voter favors the switch and, with equal intensity, two poor voters oppose it. But because of their income differences, the rich voter would be willing to pay $1,000 to see the change enacted, while the poor voters would be willing to pay only $100 each to prevent it. Should the switch be made?

According to standard cost-benefit analysis, the benefit of making the switch is the $1,000 the rich voter would be willing to pay for it. Its cost is $200, the sum of what the two poor voters would be willing to pay to avoid it. The net benefit of making the switch is thus $800. The cost-benefit rule recommends adopting all options whose benefits exceed their costs. This rule thus says unequivocally that the format switch should be made.

Critics object, however, that using the cost-benefit test to resolve such issues offends the aforementioned important democratic value that each citizen's interests are entitled to equal weight in the eyes of the law. In the example just discussed, each interested party was assumed to feel equally strongly about the format switch. So why, critics ask, should the preferences of one wealthy voter trump those of two poor voters?

The question has obvious rhetorical force. There *is* something troubling about the prescription of cost-benefit analysis in such cases. This concern has made many governments reluctant to rely on it. Executive orders issued during the Clinton administration, for example, instructed Federal agency heads to temper the results of cost-benefit analysis by distributional considerations.[1] If we were to completely temper willingness to pay by ability to pay, the cost-benefit test in our radio example would become a simple head count. The proposed switch from all music to all talk would fail by a 2 1 margin.

Is that the right outcome? The question is not whether the prescription of cost-benefit analysis is troubling in some way, but whether some alternative decision rule would yield a better outcome.

One obvious consequence of abandoning cost-benefit analysis in this example is that failure to switch formats results in a net loss of $800—the difference between the $1,000 benefit forgone by the rich voter and the $200 in combined losses avoided by the two poor voters. That loss could easily be avoided. For example, the switch could be made conditional on the rich voter's payment of additional taxes of, say, $500, which could then be used to reduce the taxes of each poor voter by $250. Relative to the status quo, this move would improve the welfare of each voter.

The rich voter may complain about having to pay extra taxes. But from her perspective, the alternative would be even worse. The $1,000 benefit she gets from the format switch is more than enough to compensate her for the additional levy. Similarly, although the two poor voters will not be pleased about losing their preferred all-music format, the alternative would be worse for them, too. By their own testimony, each is more than adequately compensated for the format change by the $250 tax reduction. Without the income transfer, all parties lose.

Movement libertarians—not to mention a multitude of others—object that the government cannot legitimately impose such transfers. ("It's your money, and the government has no right to take if from you and give it to the poor!") But although this objection is commonly attacked on equity grounds, it's perhaps more transparently vulnerable on efficiency grounds.

In a democratic society, the interests of poor voters will receive attention one way or another. As in the example just discussed, ruling out income transfers often means that those interests will be addressed in other, more costly ways. Permitting such transfers, by contrast, creates the possibility of crafting policies that will advance the economic interests of rich and poor alike. Yet we cannot identify or implement those policies unless we're free to rely much more fully than we do now on willingness to pay; and this freedom can often be purchased only at the expense of a greater willingness to employ income transfers.

Willingness to pay, as noted, is more widely accepted as a basis for who gets what in the private sector than in the public sector. Yet even in the private sector, reliance on willingness to pay sometimes offends cherished values. But here, too, the central question must be not whether willingness to pay results in the best possible allocation, but rather whether some practical alternative could yield a better one. As the following example will make clear, willingness to pay has much to commend it, even when it leads to outcomes that offend in some ways.

Who Should Get the Rare Clock?

Imagine an antique shop with a 1905 Stickley grandfather clock on display in its storefront window. Two potential buyers want it: Susan, a fourth grade teacher who's an aficionado of early twentieth-century grandfather clocks, and Malcolm, a wealthy personal injury lawyer who has no particular interest in clocks from that era or any other. Susan regularly attends seminars on antiques and has always dreamed of finding a Stickley in her price range. Malcolm happened to be in the neighborhood purely by chance when he saw the clock and thought it might look good in his office waiting room. Susan, a single mother of two who earns $28,000 a year, would be willing to pay up to $5,000 to own this clock. From her perspective, this is a large sum indeed, one that clearly bespeaks her eagerness to own it. Malcolm earns $950,000 a year. Even though he doesn't care very much about the clock, he'd nonetheless be willing to pay $10,000 to have it. And in a market system, Malcolm's greater willingness to pay assures that he'll get it.

Many people, including even many fans of the free-enterprise system, harbor strong intuitions that this can't be the best outcome. After all, the clock promises an enduring stream of deep satisfaction for Susan, but would appear largely wasted on Malcolm. Despite these misgivings, many might nonetheless accept the market outcome, because they see no practical way to make use of informal information about intensity of preference of the sort assumed in the example. For instance, it would hardly be practical to allocate goods and services on the basis of what people *say* about how desperately they wish to own them.

Yet a much less equivocal defense of willingness to pay can be offered even in this example. Granted, Susan cares more about this clock than Malcolm does. But if we take at face value what the two say about how much they'd be willing to pay for the clock, it really would *not* be better for her to own it. The reason is that she also has more urgent uses than Malcolm for virtually everything else that money might buy. Because Malcolm earns so much more than she does, the marginal dollar he spends in each arena addresses a less urgent need than the same dollar would for Susan. Being able to move to a house in a safer neighborhood or in a better school district, for example, would make more of a difference in Susan's case than in Malcolm's—not because Malcolm doesn't care about those issues, but because he already lives in a safe neighborhood with good schools. If Susan were given the clock, her best option—according to her own valuation of it—would be to sell it to Malcolm.[2] He's willing, after all, to pay more than the clock's $5,000 value to Susan. By saying she'd pay up to $5,000 for the clock, Susan is saying that the clock is extremely important to her, *but not more important than the other things she could buy with the same $5,000.*

Suppose Malcolm ends up buying the clock for $8,000. Susan might feel bitterly disappointed about not having felt able to buy it. But by her own assessment, she'd have felt even more disappointed about not having the other things that $8,000 would buy. If we credit their statements about how much they're willing to pay for the clock, then it *must* be better for both parties—Malcolm *and* Susan—if Malcolm ends up with it. And since they're the only two interested parties, that should settle the matter.

That doesn't mean that this is the best outcome anyone might imagine. It's hardly far-fetched, for example, to suppose that the world would be better if the distribution of purchasing power were somewhat less skewed. If, for example, teachers earned $75,000 a year and personal injury lawyers earned $200,000, Susan might have outbid Malcolm for the clock, since Malcolm cared so much less about it than she did. But given that the income distribution is what it is, the best available outcome is for Malcolm to get the clock.

As this example illustrates, the size of the economic pie is maximized when scarce goods are allocated on the basis of willingness to pay, notwithstanding the fact that using that criterion may offend in some way. If we allocate on some basis other than willingness to pay, it will always be possible, as in the clock and radio examples, to find a rearrangement that benefits every party. The underlying principle is that when the economic pie grows larger, everyone can have a larger slice. Rich and poor thus have a shared interest in making the economic pie as large as possible, and that means relying on willingness to pay for allocation decisions.

Who Should Wait When a Flight Is Oversold?

The attractiveness of willingness to pay becomes even more transparent in the context of the question of how to allocate seats on overbooked commercial airline flights. It's common practice for commercial air carriers to issue more reservations for specific flights than those flights can accommodate. By so doing, they limit the number of empty seats that result when passengers fail to claim their reservations. Although overbooking thus helps keep fares down, there is also an obvious downside—namely that on a small proportion of flights, more passengers actually show up than there are seats on the plane.

Suppose, for instance, that 260 people have shown up for a flight from New York to Los Angeles with only 250 seats. Among the 260 are John, the second passenger to arrive at the gate, and Eric, the 255th. John is an office custodian on his way to visit his gravely ill mother in Los Angeles. If he misses this flight, he'll have to wait ten hours for the next available one. He'd be willing to pay $350 to avoid missing his flight. Eric was one of the last passengers to arrive, not because he was careless, but because his connecting flight into New York was delayed. He's a Microsoft vice president on his way to vacation in Hawaii. Although he can get there via an alternative routing through Seattle with only one hour's delay, he'd be willing to pay $1,000 to avoid missing the flight. Of these two, who should miss the flight?

Prior to 1979, this question would have been decided on a first-come, first-served basis. John would have gotten to go, and Eric would have had to wait. Unlike the earlier example of the grandfather clock, this outcome would probably strike most observers as a good thing, at least insofar as John's reasons for arriving on time seem more pressing than Eric's.

The problem is that a first-come, first-served approach does not always yield intuitively pleasing results, and it may not have yielded the best result even in this case. Eric might just as easily have been the second passenger to arrive, for example, and John the 255th. Given the many random factors that can delay the arrival of connecting flights, there is no reason to presume that those who arrive first at the gate have the most pressing needs to claim their seats.

Because first-come, first-served does not allocate scarce seats in accordance with willingness to pay, it fails to maximize the size of the economic pie. It forces some people to wait who would be willing to pay a lot for the right to arrive on time, while permitting others to fly even though they wouldn't be willing to pay much to avoid waiting. For this reason, the Civil Aeronautics Board (CAB, the federal agency that regulated the commercial airline industry until 1984) proposed that first-come, first-served be abandoned in favor of an alternative procedure based on willingness to pay.

The CAB's specific proposal was to require carriers with oversold flights to offer cash payments, free tickets, or other compensation to induce volunteers to relinquish their seats. All passengers holding confirmed reservations had the right to remain on the flight under the proposal, which called for carriers to keep raising the compensation offer until enough volunteers stepped forward.

When a federal agency proposes a regulation of this sort, the public and other affected parties have an interval of time, usually sixty days, to comment on it. Shortly after the CAB announced its proposal, a passionate brief was filed by the Aviation Consumer Action Project (ACAP), a group founded by Ralph Nader in Washington, D.C. ACAP's ostensible mission is to protect airline passengers from being exploited by air carriers. In its filing, it objected that if the CAB adopted its proposal, the burden of waiting for the next available flight would fall disproportionately on the poor. As in other arenas, ACAP feared, the rich would be empowered to buy their way out of the hassles of life, while the poor were forced to endure them.

ACAP's objection initially struck a resonant chord in some listeners. On more careful reflection, however, most people seem to recognize it as silly. The problem is that rejecting the auction procedure meant sticking with the status quo, which often had even less desirable consequences for the poor. Suppose, for example, that John, the custodian on his way to visit his ailing mother, had been the 255th passenger to arrive, not the second. Under the CAB auction procedure, he'd have had the right to remain on the flight if he chose; or he could have relinquished his seat by accepting the compensation payment offered by the airline. But under first-come, first-served, he'd have been forced to miss his flight.

Under the auction proposal, the airline would need to recruit ten volunteers. Imagine that John had refused the airline's initial offer of $200, which elicited only three volunteers. When the airline upped its offer to $300, one more volunteer stepped forward, but John still remained behind. Finally, when the carrier offered $400, John and five others (Eric, the Microsoft vice president, not among them) agreed to wait, clearing the flight to leave. Now imagine that just as John was about to accept the cash payment of $400, ACAP officials arrived with a court injunction blocking the auction. Under the circumstances, John could have been forgiven for wondering how, exactly, ACAP was protecting his interests by denying him the option of volunteering. He didn't have to volunteer; it was just an option. He volunteered because, in his judgment, the $400 offer was greater than the value he placed on retaining his original seat. Otherwise, he'd have refused.

I've discussed this example with hundreds of people over the years and have not yet encountered anyone who's willing to say that the CAB should have withdrawn its proposal in response to the ACAP objection. The auction is efficient because it allocates seats on the basis of willingness to pay. Using willingness to pay means that poor people who have pressing needs will sometimes wait for the next flight, while rich people who don't have pressing needs will continue their journeys uninterrupted. But those who volunteer receive a payment that helps them meet other needs that they consider even more pressing. John will be late to visit his mother, but he will also be able to do other valuable things with the extra $400.

The decision of whether to volunteer might be a difficult one for some people. But the CAB decided that it would be better to allow people to make that choice for themselves, rather than follow ACAP's advice to withhold the option. As before, the important question isn't whether willingness to pay results in a perfect outcome, but whether an alternative exists that would be better.

To reject the ACAP objection is not to deny the difficulty of being poor. Nor does the example imply that willingness to pay must be the ultimate arbiter of every allocation problem. My focus here is on the distribution of ordinary goods and services: What kinds of programs should a public radio station broadcast? Who should get an antique clock? Who should wait for the next flight? And so on.

The CAB's volunteer auction proposal was just one of several mechanisms the agency might have proposed for allocating seats on the basis of willingness to pay. For example, it could have proposed that carriers award seats to those passengers willing to bid the most to retain them. No less than the original proposal, this alternative would have allocated available seats on the basis of willingness to pay. But had the CAB proposed requiring passengers to bid for the right to remain on the flight, the proposal never would have been adopted.

The CAB was by no means alone among federal agencies in its sensitivity to such distributional concerns. Even in the face of lax campaign finance laws, low-income voters have considerable voice in the political process. They and those who speak for them will oppose any policy that gives short shrift to their interests. Whether they have the political power actually to block specific policies will of course depend on circumstance.

Apart from the ACAP objection, the CAB's volunteer auction proposal attracted no significant opposition from the poor or their advocates. An important reason was that it granted low-income passengers a right with real economic value—namely the right to hold onto their seats unless they volunteered to relinquish them for compensation. Had the proposal not granted that basic right, it would surely have been rejected. The first-come, first-served system would have persisted, leaving passengers rich and poor worse off than they are under the current volunteer auction system.

ACAP was incorrect to assert that the poor would always be the ones left waiting under the auction proposal. Poor passengers with pressing needs to arrive on time often refrain from volunteering, while more prosperous passengers in no particular hurry often step forward. Yet low-income passengers are surely more likely to volunteer than high-income passengers. But when they do step forward, it's presumably because the cash compensation or free ticket is more valuable to them than the time they'd have saved by not volunteering.

Liberal Hostility to Cost-Benefit Analysis

As the preceding example clearly demonstrates, the monetary values people assign to the options they face provide extremely valuable guidance for how limited resources can best be allocated. Given whatever inequities may exist in the distribution of income at any moment, a public policy that allocates resources on any basis that ignores willingness to pay can always be transformed to produce better results for everyone.

Skepticism about markets in general, together with legitimate concerns about the high and rising inequality that characterizes market reward systems, have made many liberal commentators hostile to the use of unweighted willingness-to-pay measures in public policy decisions. And because the principles at work in the CAB example are completely general, this hostility has proven costly to the very same low-income constituents whose cause these commentators profess to champion. With careful attention to design details, virtually every public policy decision that does not reflect what people are willing to pay for the alternatives at issue can be transformed to produce a better outcome for everyone involved. Those who resist such changes would do well to imagine themselves in the role of Ralph Nader waving a court injunction that would block a low-income passenger from volunteering to accept compensation for agreeing to take a later flight.

Why Efficient Policies Are Often Impossible without Income Transfers

Conservatives, through their opposition to income transfers, have been an even bigger obstacle to the adoption of efficient public policies. That's because any democracy that does not transfer income from rich to poor almost always ends up attending to the interests of the poor in other, far more costly ways.

The earlier example involving the public radio format choice illustrates the basic idea. Recall that the switch from an all-music to an all-talk format would create $1,000 in benefits for a rich voter but cause $100 in harm to each of two poor voters. The poor voters have the power to vote down the switch. But because the switch would generate greater benefits than costs, it's not in their interest to exercise that power. It would be better for everyone if the poor allowed the switch in return for an income transfer. Without the ability to make such transfers, the proposed switch fails, leaving both rich and poor voters worse off than if it had occurred.

Such instances are far from isolated. The energy crisis of 1979, for example, led President Jimmy Carter to propose a tax on gasoline of up to $0.50 per gallon. The idea was to use the price system to discourage gasoline consumption, thereby to reduce America's dependence on foreign oil. An immediate objection to proposals of this sort is that they impose unacceptable hardship on poor families. Anticipating this objection, however, Carter simultaneously called for a reduction in the payroll tax, financed by revenue from the gasoline tax. Since the payroll tax is highly regressive, cutting it would mitigate the hardship imposed on low-income families by the gasoline tax.

Carter's proposal was rejected in the end, partly because many of its critics mistakenly believed that the payroll tax rebate would undo the incentive to conserve. (What these critics failed to see was that even though the payroll tax rebate might *enable* people to purchase as much gasoline as before, the higher after-tax price of gasoline would give them a powerful incentive not to.) But another important reason for the Carter proposal's failure was its call for income transfers to the poor. Ronald Reagan's election was then still more than a year away, but congressional hostility to income redistribution was already on the rise.

The ultimate effect of failure to enact Carter's proposal was to reduce the economic well-being of rich and poor alike. Instead of curbing gasoline consumption through the price system, as Carter had proposed, we extended price controls to protect the poor against higher prices. The results were costly to everyone: long lines at gas stations, valuable journeys postponed, and so on. Had Carter's proposal been adopted, the higher gasoline prices would have been a small burden for rich citizens to bear in return for not having had to wait in line. Poor citizens would have avoided lines as well, and the payroll tax reduction would have cushioned the sting of higher gas prices.

Again and again, the pattern is the same. Because we can't or won't redistribute through the tax system, we're forced to attend to the interests of the poor in other, more costly ways. The poor can't afford a decent place to live? The most efficient remedy would be to increase the Earned Income Tax Credit (EITC), one of the few income-transfer programs that Ronald Reagan endorsed. But conservatives in Congress have grown increasingly hostile to the EITC in recent years. If we can't transfer income directly, the alternative is usually a more costly one, such as rent controls.

Struggling farmers can't make ends meet? The most efficient solution would be to transfer income to them directly. But with that option closed, we turn to other, far more costly measures, such as price supports for agricultural products. Poor people can't afford telephone service or pay their gas and electric bills? Again, the most efficient response would be income transfers, but instead we require "lifeline" utility rates that encourage inefficient use patterns and lead to higher rates for other customers.

Another consequence of our unwillingness to transfer income is the exemption of older vehicles from pollution regulations. Although cars fifteen years or older constitute only a small fraction of those driven in Los Angeles, these cars nonetheless account for most of the smog in the Los Angeles basin. They're exempt from pollution regulation because of legislators' concern that failure to exempt them would impose unacceptable costs on the mostly poor motorists who drive them.

The problem of polluting older vehicles could be eliminated relatively cheaply by transferring enough income to the poor to enable them to purchase used cars of more recent vintage. That strategy would enable us to reduce emissions of hydrocarbons and nitrous oxide at a cost of roughly $15 per pound.[3] Because it has exempted these vehicles, however, the California legislature has mandated the development of electric vehicles, for which the cost of removing these compounds is some $900 per pound. Here, too, our reluctance to transfer income has proven costly to rich and poor alike.

Economists have estimated that we could save billions of dollars in highway construction costs and wasteful traffic delays if we adopted a simple system of congestion pricing.[4] Using variants of existing technology (for instance, the E-ZPass system currently in use on many turnpikes and bridges in the Northeast), cars could be equipped with small electronic receivers that would register road-use fees that varied with traffic congestion. Thus a motorist who drove across Manhattan during the midday rush might incur $10.00 in extra tolls levied automatically through this receiver.

The clear obstacle to adopting this system is the specter of the burden it would impose on poor motorists forced to venture out into heavy traffic. Never mind that the revenue and other savings from the new system would be much more than enough to support income transfers sufficient to cushion the blow. Unless we're able to make the necessary transfers, congestion pricing will never be adopted. We will continue to incur highway construction and congestion costs that could easily have been avoided.

These are hardly isolated examples. Rather, they're part of a pervasive pattern in which our reluctance to transfer income to the poor leads us to address their concerns in other ways. Refusal to redistribute income through the tax system does not alter the fact that the interests of the poor will receive attention in a democratic society. It merely constrains us to attend to those interests in more costly ways.

Some Interesting Exceptions

Although failure to address distributional concerns often prevents implementation of efficient policies, there have been at least some instances in which policy makers have employed direct income transfers to pave the way for such policies. An instructive case in point was the New York State Public Service Commission's proposed imposition of a $0.10 charge for each directory assistance call placed from a private telephone. (At the time, such calls were available free of charge to telephone subscribers.) The commission's motive for making this proposal was that free calling privileges forced telephone companies to employ hundreds of extra operators to look up numbers that most callers could have easily looked up for themselves.

The commission's proposal drew the inevitable firestorm of protests. Sociology professors and others testified at commission hearings that essential community communications patterns would be seriously disrupted if callers lacked access to free directory assistance. As it became increasingly clear that the proposal was headed for failure, commission Chairman Alfred Kahn proposed the following simple amendment. The $0.10-per-call charge for directory assistance would still be added, but with the money saved by reassigning former directory assistance operators to other, more useful tasks, each subscriber would also receive a $0.30 credit on his or her monthly bill. Callers who made an average of fewer than three directory assistance calls per month would thus have lower total phone bills than before. With this amendment, the commission's proposal was enacted virtually without opposition.

The trivial sums at stake in this example demonstrate the power of distributional concerns in the public policy arena. Even if directory assistance calls had continued to be free, few families would have made more than ten of them in any month; and it's hard to see how an additional expenditure of $1 per month could be viewed as a significant threat to the living standard of even the poorest families. The example also shows that opposition to efficient policies can be overcome if cash transfers or their functional equivalent are an available policy instrument.

The agricultural arena provides another example of the use of direct income transfers to facilitate efficient policy change. The background problem was the chronic economic pressure imposed on American family farmers by their inability to keep pace with the rapid productivity growth in corporate agriculture. By greatly expanding agricultural production, modern agribusiness had driven crop prices so low that many family farmers could not make ends meet. Concern for the plight of these farmers periodically prompted Congress to increase the levels at which it supports agricultural prices. Crop price supports induced farmers to spend billions of dollars on hired labor, machinery, seed, fertilizer, insecticides, and other inputs to produce crops that consumers didn't want to buy at the supported prices. Government had to purchase the surplus and then watch much of it go to waste after extended and costly storage. If Congress's goal had been to design the most inefficient possible program for aiding family farmers, it could hardly have done better.

But the U.S. Department of Agriculture also administers at least one other program that attacks farm poverty in a much more efficient way. I refer to the department's Conservation Reserve Program (CRP), under which farmers receive cash payments for retiring some of their current acreage from cultivation. This program provides additional income to struggling family farmers without incurring the waste of producing crops that no one wants to buy.

Despite the fact that the CRP is far more efficient than price supports, it remains controversial. Indeed, it's easy to see why critics might complain about a program that pays farmers for not producing something. The attraction of the program becomes clear, however, if the alternative is to pay them premium prices to produce crops that go to waste. In any event, the example illustrates that opposition to income transfers does not *always* prevent us from switching from an inefficient policy to a less wasteful one. In so doing, however, it raises the question of why we're not able to do this more often.

Other Barriers to the Adoption of Efficient Policies?

If we can negotiate efficient solutions in some cases, why do we avoid cost-benefit logic in others? One difficulty might be that since virtually every issue up for public decision has at least some distributional implications, case-by-case compensation might simply be impractical. Perhaps it's reasonable to hope for efficient solutions in only those cases that lend themselves to simple compensation arrangements—such as the volunteer auction solution for oversold flights or the monthly rebate palliative for the directory assistance charge. But many issues clearly do not lend themselves to such arrangements.

Yet efficient solutions are often elusive even in cases for which transfer remedies could be easily administered. If rent controls are inefficient, for example, why don't cities use vouchers to buy people out of their rent control leases? Tenants could relocate to smaller apartments at the market rate and be compensated by receiving the equivalent of a cash transfer in the form of a voucher.

By the same token, why don't we use auctions to determine the siting of prisons and other unattractive public facilities? Each community could submit a sealed bid indicating the minimum amount it would be willing to accept in return for agreeing to host the facility. The low bidder would get the facility and could be compensated with a cash payment equal, say, to the second-lowest bid.[5] This payment could be financed by a tax levied on other communities in proportion to the bids they submitted, a measure that would give communities a strong incentive to keep their bids honest.

As the preceding discussion suggests, there seem to be at least two barriers to achieving efficient solutions through the use of cost-benefit analysis in the public domain. One is that many people—movement libertarians most prominently among them—are opposed to government redistribution as a matter of principle. The other is that, given the myriad of cases that must be decided on an almost daily basis, case-by-case distributional remedies may simply be impractical to administer.

As compelling as each of these two barriers may seem, neither can withstand careful scrutiny. Consider first the claim that income transfers are illegitimate as a matter of principle ("It's your money . . ."). The principle at stake here is the claim that since the individual has earned her income through fair, voluntary exchange in the marketplace, she is entitled to do with it as she pleases. Taken literally, however, this argument is unpersuasive, for it implies that the government ought to have no power to tax at all. As noted in chapter 1, such a government would be unable to field an army, and its citizens would sooner or later find themselves paying taxes to a foreign invader's government.

The "It's your money . . ." principle fails for another important practical reason. Proponents of this principle presumably favor it because they believe that it would be better for people to have direct control over the largest possible share of the resources that they themselves have helped to produce. Yet this principle hardly seems worth fighting for if, as I have argued, its implementation actually reduces the amount of resources over which people have control. Again, democracies must choose between transferring resources to low-income people directly or responding to their interests in other, more costly ways.

What about the second barrier to efficiency, the fact that it may just not be possible to work out case-by-case compensating transfers for each of the myriad public policy decisions we confront every day? The answer is that we can employ cost-benefit analysis without taking this cumbersome step at all. My point is not that compensation is unnecessary, but rather that it need not occur on a case-by-case basis. Critics of cost-benefit analysis are correct that using willingness-to-pay measures virtually assures a mix of public programs that are slanted in favor of the preferences of high-income persons—for the simple reason that high-income persons are *able* to pay more.

But rather than abandon cost-benefit analysis, we have a better alternative. We can employ willingness-to-pay measures without apology, and use the welfare and tax systems to compensate low-income families for the resulting injury. Again, this compensation need not—indeed cannot—occur on a case-by-case basis. Rather, low-income persons could simply be granted concessions through the tax system reflecting their expected loss from the implementation of cost-benefit analysis based on willingness to pay. Such concessions would be in addition to the welfare and tax breaks required by other factors, which are our subject in the next chapter.

EIGHT

"It's Your Money . . ."

IN HIS *The Second Treatise of Civil Government,* the seventeenth-century British philosopher John Locke wrote that "every man has a property in his own person. This nobody has any right to but himself. The labour of his body, and the work of his hands, we may say, are properly his."

These words made Locke an intellectual hero of movement libertarians, who continue to view all taxation as theft. Although more serious libertarians grudgingly concede the need for at least some taxation, there is no denying that Locke's words have had enormous rhetorical force far beyond libertarian circles. If you make something more valuable by applying your own talent and effort to it, the added value *feels* like it's yours. By what right might government lay claim to it?

The notion that people have a natural right to the fruits of their own labor has gained considerable strength in the decades since Ronald Reagan began advocating it forcefully in his speeches. Former House Ways and Means Committee Chairman Bill Archer (R, TX) echoed Reagan's language in defense of a proposal to reduce taxes on high-income households in the late 1980s: "It's a matter of principle," he wrote, "to return excess tax money in Washington to the families and workers who sent it here." And as George W. Bush memorably put it when speaking in defense of his proposed $1.3 trillion in income tax cuts targeted largely to America's wealthiest families, "It's your money. You paid for it." If an American politician today proposes a tax on anything, his opponents will immediately lambaste him for believing that "the bureaucrats in Washington know how to spend your money more wisely than you do."

The Myth of Ownership

On closer examination, the intuition that people have a moral right to keep all of their pretax income quickly crumbles. The high incomes of people in modern industrial democracies are not a consequence of their efforts alone. They're in large measure the result of vast current and past public investments in infrastructure, education, and institutions for defining and enforcing private property rights. It's easy to lose sight of the central role such investments continue to play in our prosperity.

Decades ago I had an opportunity to observe firsthand what life was like in an environment that had not benefited from investments of this sort. Fresh out of college, I served for two years as a Peace Corps volunteer math and science teacher in a small village in Nepal, which was then, and remains, one of the poorest countries on the planet.

As was the custom among Peace Corps volunteers there, I hired a cook. His name was Birkhaman Rai. He'd come to Nepal a few years earlier from a remote Himalayan village in neighboring Bhutan, and although he'd never spent a day in school, he was by far the most resourceful and multitalented person I've ever met.

In addition to being a skilled cook and a shrewd negotiator in the marketplace, he could butcher a goat and repair thatched roofs. He could plaster walls and fix broken alarm clocks. He was an able tinsmith and a remarkably skilled carpenter. When a pair of my favorite shoes wore out, he repaired them as well as any professional cobbler might have. He quickly became the village authority on home remedies.

Because he hadn't learned to read and write, I never managed to keep in touch with him during the years after I left. But because Nepal is still almost as bereft of infrastructure as when I lived there, the several hundred dollars a year I was able to pay Birkhaman from my Peace Corps living allowance was in all likelihood the high-water mark in his lifetime income stream.

If he'd been born in the United States, there's a good possibility he'd have long since become a wealthy man. At the very least, someone with his skills and determination would have earned hundreds of times as much as he ever managed to earn in Nepal.

Each year as the April 15 tax filing deadline draws near, wealthy libertarians mount the stump in high dudgeon to denounce the government for seizing money that is rightfully theirs. They might do well to reflect briefly on the fact that no matter how talented and industrious they are, they wouldn't have had any significant wealth to seize in the first place if they'd grown up in a country like Nepal or Somalia. The infrastructure that made their wealth possible was paid for by taxes. Much of that wealth is thus an unearned return on investments made by others.

The philosophers Liam Murphy and Thomas Nagel have examined the "myth of ownership" encouraged by "It's your money . . ." rhetoric, arguing that it deflects us from considering important questions we should be asking about our entire system of laws and social institutions.[1] Thus, they write,

> The question, *How much of "our money" may the government take in taxes?* is logically incoherent, because the legal system, including the tax system, determines what "our money" is. The real moral issue is how the legal system that governs property rights should be designed, and with what goals. What kinds of markets will best promote investment and productivity? Which goods, at what level, should be provided by collective public decision and which goods by private individual choice? Should all citizens be guaranteed a minimum level of economic protection? To what extent should equal opportunity be publicly supported? Are large social and economic inequalities morally objectionable, and if they are, what may legitimately be done to discourage them?[2]

It's of course impossible to discuss such questions without talking about who should be paying what kinds of taxes. Yet public conversations among elected officials about taxes of any kind are typically stopped in their tracks by "It's your money . . ." incantations from the right. Our inability to pursue these conversations has made us all poorer.

Social Engineering!

For more than a century there was intense debate about whether people would be more likely to thrive under a centrally planned and managed economy or under one that relegated most economic decisions to decentralized private markets. That debate is over. Whatever the shortcomings of a decentralized market system might be, the experience of the collective economies of the former Soviet Union has persuaded most neutral observers that some variant of a market system must figure prominently in any successful economic program.

In practice, of course, even the least regulated market economy has a large public sector. In addition to maintaining the legal framework under which private firms and consumers operate, it produces public goods like roads, education, police and fire protection, and national defense. The tax system must pay for those goods.

A tax on any activity not only generates revenue, it also discourages the activity. Taxes on useful activities, such as those on savings or job creation, make the economic pie smaller. In contrast, taxes on activities that harm others, such as those on pollution or congestion, make the economic pie larger. In chapter 11, I'll consider in detail how we might shift away from taxes on useful activities toward those on activities that cause harm to others.

Because shifting taxes in that way would make the economic pie larger, making it possible for everyone to have a larger slice than before, this should be a relatively uncontroversial step. Yet taking it would inevitably provoke howls of protest from movement libertarians. "Social engineering!" they'd scream in unison, by which they'd mean attempts to "control our behavior, steer our choices, and change the way we live our lives." Gasoline taxes aimed at discouraging dependence on foreign oil, for example, invariably elicit this accusation.

But as noted in chapter 1, it's an empty complaint, because virtually every law and regulation constitutes social engineering. Laws against homicide and theft control our behavior, steer our choices, and change the way we live our lives, so they're social engineering, as are noise ordinances, speed limits, even stop signs and traffic lights. The only alternative to social engineering is complete anarchy. Taxes are a far cheaper and less coercive way to curtail harmful behavior than are laws or prescriptive regulations. That's because taxes concentrate harm reduction in the hands of those who can alter their behavior most easily, a point about which I'll say more in chapter 11.

Here we'll take up a much more controversial dimension of tax policy—namely its effects, both intended and unintended, on the distribution of after-tax incomes. What constitutes a just distribution of income, and what responsibility, if any, does the government have to promote one? Few questions have received more attention from philosophers, economists, legal scholars, and others.[3] Those questions, however, are well beyond the scope of our discussion here. Rather, my focus will be on the claim, often pressed by libertarians and political conservatives, that deliberate income redistribution is illegitimate under any circumstances. This claim, it turns out, is difficult to defend no matter what beliefs one might hold about the broader questions just mentioned.

As we saw in the preceding chapter, for example, refusing to transfer income from rich to poor often causes democracies to address the interests of low-income voters in other, less efficient, ways, to the detriment of rich and poor alike. It's one thing to claim a right to keep 100 percent of your pretax income. Exercising that right, however, makes little sense in cases in which doing so makes you and everyone else poorer. But there are other, more telling, problems with the libertarian objection to redistributive taxation.

Efficient Provision of Public Goods

An important practical worry is that reluctance to transfer income will often make it impossible to supply public goods that high-income citizens value and would be happy to pay for. As in the case of private goods, people's willingness to pay for public goods generally increases with their income. The wealthy tend to assign greater value to public goods than the poor do, not because the wealthy have different tastes, but because they have more money.

A society consisting only of the wealthy would choose to provide more and better public goods than one consisting only of the poor. But when people of all income levels live together in a single society, the very nature of public goods requires that their quantity and quality be the same for every-one. Society must decide how much people of different income levels should be taxed to pay for those public goods. Some simple numerical examples help illustrate why progressive taxation is often a practical step that benefits people all along the income scale.

Suppose two citizens, Rand and Paul, own adjacent summer cottages on a lake. Because of a recent invasion of zebra mussels, each must add chlorine to his water system each week to prevent it from becoming clogged by the tiny mollusks. A manufacturer has introduced a new filtration device that eliminates the nuisance of weekly chlorination. The cost of the device, which has the capacity to serve both houses, is $1,000. Both owners feel equally strongly about having the filter. But Rand, who earns twice as much as Paul, is willing to pay up to $900 to have it, whereas its value to Paul is only $300.

Neither will purchase the filter individually, because its separate value to each is below its selling price. But because the two together value it at $1,200, it would be worthwhile for them to share its use. If they were to do so, their total economic surplus (their combined benefit from the filter, minus its cost) would be $200. And when the economic pie grows larger, it must always be possible for each party to enjoy a larger slice than before.

Since it's efficient for Rand and Paul to share the filter, we might expect them to quickly reach agreement to purchase it. Unfortunately, however, the joint purchase and sharing of facilities is often easier proposed than accom-plished. As Ronald Coase clearly recognized, people typically must incur costs merely to discuss joint purchases. With only two people involved, these costs might not be prohibitive. But if hundreds or thousands were in-volved, communication costs could easily make the transaction impossible.

With large numbers of people, the so-called free-rider problem also emerges. If a project will either succeed or fail independently of any one per-son's contribution to it, everyone has an incentive to hold back—or "free ride"—in the hope that others will contribute. Finally, even when only few people are involved, reaching agreement on what constitutes a fair sharing of the total expense may be difficult. For example, Rand and Paul might be reluctant to disclose the true amounts they'd be willing to pay for the filter for the same reason you might be reluctant to tell a merchant the most you'd be willing to pay for an Oriental rug.

Such practical concerns may lead us to empower government to buy public goods on our behalf. But even that step does not eliminate the need to reach political agreement on how to pay for them.

Suppose Rand and Paul could ask the government to help broker their water-filter purchase. And suppose the government's tax policy must follow a "nondiscrimination" rule that prohibits charging any citizen more than his or her neighbor for a public good.

If public goods can be provided only if a majority of citizens approve of them, a government bound by these rules would not be able to provide the filter. Because it would have to rely on a head tax (one levied in equal amounts on every citizen), it would need to raise $500 from Rand and $500 from Paul to cover the filter's price. But since it's worth only $300 to Paul, he'd vote against the project, thus denying it a majority. So a democratic government could not provide the filter if it had to rely on a head tax.

The point illustrated by this example applies whenever the valuation of a public good differs significantly across taxpayers, as it almost always will whenever people earn significantly different incomes. An equal-tax rule under these circumstances would make it impossible to provide many worthwhile public goods.

Now suppose that government can impose a progressive tax on income. If Rand, who earns twice as much as Paul, were a libertarian, he'd complain bitterly about the injustice of his being taxed so much more heavily than Paul. On a moment's reflection, however, he'd realize that this objection would kill the project. He'd be better off to let the government levy a tax of $750 on him and one of $250 on Paul. Under this levy, Rand gets a filter whose use is worth $900 to him for a payment of only $750. So by abandoning his opposition to progressive taxation, he gets to enjoy an additional economic surplus of $150. Paul, for his part, gets a filter worth $300 to him for a payment of only $250, so he enjoys an additional economic surplus of $50.

The absurdity of demanding that every citizen contribute an equal absolute amount, or even an equal proportion of his income, to pay for collectively consumed goods is cast into even sharper relief by imagining what would happen if married couples were subject to similar constraints. Suppose, for example, that Julie earns $2 million a year while her husband Bruce earns only $20,000. Given her income, Julie as an individual would want to spend much more than Bruce on housing, travel, entertainment, and the many other items they consume jointly. But if each member of the couple were forced to contribute an equal amount toward the purchase of such items, they'd be constrained to live in a small house; send their children to substandard schools; skimp on vacations, entertainment, and dining out; and so on. It's therefore easy to see why Julie might find it attractive to pay considerably more than 50 percent for things that she and Bruce consume jointly.

The justifications for progressive income taxation implicit in the examples just discussed were rooted in strictly practical concerns. Progressive taxation was an instrument that helped both rich and poor achieve their goals more fully. It had nothing to do with moral concerns about fairness or equity. The latter concerns have of course always been at the heart of liberals' case for progressive taxation. And it has been these concerns that many libertarians and conservatives have rejected as illegitimate. But the distinction between moral concerns and strictly pragmatic ones is often less clear than many believe.

A Libertarian Rationale for Progressive Taxation

Again it's Ronald Coase whose insights help uncover a productive new way of thinking about an old problem. Rank in any hierarchy is, like the externalities that were the focus of his work, a reciprocal phenomenon. That is, no person can occupy a position of high rank in any group unless others in that same group occupy positions of low rank. The pursuit of high-ranked positions in any group thus gives rise to a positional externality. If those who desire such positions are to achieve what they wish, others must bear the cost of occupying the low-ranked positions without which high rank wouldn't be possible. In these simple observations, as we'll see, lie the seeds of a libertarian theory of progressive taxation.

To sketch this theory in broad outline, let's begin with a thought experiment that is stacked heavily in favor of libertarian sensibilities. Imagine that you and 999 others have just emerged from an ark after an epic flood that has destroyed all existing social arrangements. Your task is to form a new society with others of your own choosing. If others want to structure society in ways that offend you, you needn't join them. Nor, however, can you force others to join you in a society they don't favor. In short, membership in the new societies that form under this thought experiment is strictly by mutual consent.

At the outset, every society that forms is entitled to a proportional share of the land and other property that survived the flood. For example, if you and 99 others agreed to form a separate society, you'd constitute 10 percent of the world's population, so you'd start out with 10 percent of all existing land and other property. Not all property in each society's initial allocation is equally desirable. Part of the task of forming a society is thus to agree on rules that determine how property will be allocated among the members of that society.

Talent and temperament are assumed to be perfectly observable. Once you and others agree to form a society, you're free to earn as much as your efforts and abilities permit, but you must also comply with whatever tax laws and other regulations your society agrees to adopt.

As a moment's reflection makes clear, important outcomes hinge on the identities of those who agree to join you in forming a society. If most of them were highly productive, for example, your society would be able to purchase more and better public goods than would be possible in a society consisting only of unproductive people. But there would also be a downside if most of your fellow citizens were far more productive than you.

Suppose, for example, that you and most others would enjoy having a house with a view. Not all home sites have views, unfortunately, and in the likely event that your society adopts something like a market mechanism for allocating land and other property, it's all but certain that the least productive members of society won't be able to afford a house with a view.

Perhaps having a view is of no concern. But you probably do care about being able to send your children to good schools, ones that will prepare them to compete effectively for admission to a good university or to be considered favorably for a desirable job. But again, a good school is an inherently relative concept. It's one that compares favorably with other schools in the same environment.

In virtually every country, the best schools tend to serve the most expensive neighborhoods. In some places, that's because property taxes provide a large component of school budgets. But even when expenditure per pupil is the same in every school, the best schools tend to be those in the most expensive neighborhoods. One reason is that a major component of a school's quality is the quality of its students, and the children of the most successful parents enjoy significant learning advantages both before and after they begin school. The schools that serve these students would thus offer better learning environments, even if their budgets were the same as in other schools.

If your children's education matters to you, then, you'll need to bid for a house in a good school district in whatever society you elect to join. If we again assume that private markets will be the main allocation mechanism adopted by most societies, your prospects of being able to send your children to a relatively good school would be much diminished if you joined a society in which most others were significantly more productive than you.

The upshot is that your choice of which society to join must take into account where you'd rank on the productivity scale vis-à-vis your fellow citizens. The best outcome, of course, would be to be one of the most productive members of a highly productive society, for that way you'd enjoy the advantages of both absolute and relative wealth. But for most people, that's simply not an option. As the average productivity of the others in any society rises, your rank within that society declines. Conversely, as the average productivity of the others you join declines, your rank in that society rises.

Any advantages that might accrue from living in a society with higher average productivity will thus be offset in part by the fact that in such a society, your rank on the income scale will be lower. If all else were equal, of course, most people would prefer to occupy positions of high social rank than positions of low social rank. And if the advantages of high social rank could be had for free, everyone would choose it. But it's mathematically impossible for everyone in every society to enjoy a position of high rank. So the question becomes, why would anyone agree to join a group in which he'd be a low-ranked member?

If people were determined to avoid positions of low social rank, they could form separate societies with people who were exactly as productive as themselves. The most able people could form one society of equals, the next-most-able a second society of equals, and so on. No one would have low social rank in these societies, but this solution would also pass up some obvious possibilities for mutually beneficial exchange. Who, for example, would sweep the streets in the society consisting of only the most talented people? Who'd perform brain surgery in the society consisting of only the least talented?

Even apart from such practical difficulties, pure stratification would eliminate another potentially important gain from exchange, one that arises whenever some people care more than others about rank. If the value of high rank for some people exceeds the corresponding cost of low rank for others, groups of mixed ability can form in which everyone fares better than each would as a member of a separate society of equals.

Suppose, for example, that if Rand were permitted to keep the full fruits of his own labor, he could produce and earn $10,000 a week, and that the corresponding figure for Paul would be only $5,000. And suppose that each would be willing to pay up to 30 percent of his income to occupy a position of high rank in society, because that way he'd be able to purchase a house with a view, or one that would enable him to send his children to good schools. Imagine, too, that each would be willing to accept compensation of as little as 30 percent of his income for agreeing to occupy a position of low rank. Let's suppose, in other words, that Rand would be just as happy earning $7,000 a week in a society in which he enjoyed high rank as he'd be in a society of equals in which he earned $10,000, or as he'd be if he earned $13,000 in a society in which he was the least productive member. He wouldn't be able to afford a house with a view in the latter society, but there would be other attractive things he could buy with his extra money. Paul, for his part, would be just as happy earning $6,500 a week in a society in which he occupied a position of low rank as he'd be in a society in which he and all others earned $5,000.

Under these circumstances, both Rand and Paul can do better by working together than by joining others whose abilities exactly match their own. If the two men join together, their total weekly earnings will be $15,000 (the sum of what they produce separately). If Rand claimed $8,000 of that total and Paul claimed the remaining $7,000, then Rand would enjoy an economic surplus of $1,000 a week and Paul would enjoy a surplus of $500 a week relative to the alternative of joining others of like ability and being paid the respective values of what they produced.

What if Rand didn't care about occupying a position of high social rank? His best bet would then be to join a group consisting of others more productive than himself who do care about rank. His presence as a low-ranked member of that group would be an asset that makes the value of high rank in the group available to others, for which he'd be compensated accordingly.

My claim, then, is that in an environment constructed for the specific purpose of shielding libertarian sensibilities from any possibility of coercion, the voluntary societies that formed would all feature progressive income taxation. The degree of progressivity that would emerge in this thought experiment would depend on how much some were willing to pay for positions of high social rank and on how much others were willing to accept for agreeing to occupy positions of low rank. Those are empirical questions, about which I'll have more to say in a moment. For now, note that no libertarian would have grounds for complaint about living under such a tax system. The key point is that if progressive taxation were not permitted, the result would be societies completely stratified by ability, which would be a less attractive arrangement for every person.

The rationale for progressive taxation suggested by this thought experiment doesn't explicitly invoke concerns about fairness or justice. Rather, each society's tax structure emerged as a straightforward consequence of self-serving exchange among free and independent individuals.

But if we can agree that high-ranked positions in a social hierarchy are valuable, the interpretation suggested by the thought experiment is completely compatible with conventional discourse about fairness and justice. Again, the only way some can occupy positions of high social rank is for others to occupy positions of low social rank. In any society of mixed ability that lacked progressive taxation, then, people of high rank would be enjoying a valuable asset completely free of charge. That asset's value wouldn't exist except for the fact that others bore the costs associated with the low-ranked positions that made high rank possible. As the terms *fairness* and *justice* are conventionally understood, there is nothing mysterious about saying that it would be unfair or unjust for some to profit free of charge from costs borne by others without compensation.

The Implicit Market for High Rank in the Labor Market

Although the thought experiment may seem fanciful, a close approximation of it actually plays out in the competitive labor markets we see all around us. In the United States and most other democracies, no one can be forced to work for a firm against his wishes. We can also safely assume that if all other relevant factors were equal, most people would prefer to occupy a high-ranked position vis-à-vis their co-workers than a low-ranked position. These two assumptions imply a clear prediction—namely that it would be impossible for work groups of mixed ability to form and remain stable unless pay were transferred from the most productive members in each group to the least productive. (The underlying argument is exactly analogous to the one that drives the thought experiment just discussed.)

To test this prediction, we can compare pay patterns within work groups to the patterns predicted by conventional labor market theories, which assume that rank doesn't matter. According to those theories, workers are paid the market value of what they produce. In actual markets, pay does rise with productivity, but not by much. The most productive carpenter in a framing crew, for example, might produce twice as much as his least productive colleague, but he is rarely paid even 30 percent more.

The observed distribution of wages within any work group is thus typically much more compressed than the corresponding distribution of individual productivity. To see this pattern first-hand, consider groups of co-workers who perform similar tasks in your own organization. (If you're a junior associate in a large law firm, for example, consider the other junior associates in your group.) In one case, suppose your two most productive colleagues leave the job; in the other, suppose the three least productive leave. Which group's departure would cause a greater loss of value? Most people answer without hesitation that losing the top two would hurt more.

If so, conventional labor market theory holds that their combined salaries should be higher than the combined salaries of the bottom three. Yet the typical pattern is the reverse: any three workers in a group performing similar tasks earn substantially more than any other two. The typical pattern, in short, is that the more productive members of a group performing similar tasks are paid less than the value of what they produce, while the least productive workers are paid more than the value of what they produce.

My claim is that this pattern reflects the workings of an implicit market for high-ranked positions within work groups. If that claim is correct, it suggests a simple answer to the otherwise vexing question of why the seemingly underpaid most productive members in each work group aren't quickly bid away by rival employers. Although their current pay falls short of what conventional models predict, they're receiving something else they greatly value. By their willingness to remain, they're implicitly saying that the high rank they enjoy is more than enough to offset the corresponding sacrifice in pay. By the same token, although their less productive co-workers may find it onerous to be near the bottom of the ladder, their decision to remain on board suggests that they're adequately compensated for that fact by their premium wages.

In effect, then, private labor markets serve up an implicit progressive tax in the schemes that govern the distribution of pay within every work group. Because labor contracts are voluntary under United States law, it would be bizarre for a libertarian to object that these transfers violate anyone's rights.

How Much Is High Rank Worth?

How big are the implicit income transfers from high-ranked workers to their low-ranked colleagues? Or, to put this question another way, by how much does the most productive worker's value to her employer exceed the amount she is paid? Because production is often a complex team activity, individual differences in productivity tend to be exceedingly difficult to measure. Yet circumstances sometimes permit us to place reasonable bounds on differences in individual contributions to an employer's bottom line.

An example from my own university illustrates how we might proceed in a specific case. The two main missions of my colleagues on the faculty are to teach and conduct research. Contributions in each domain are complex and multidimensional. Even so, it's possible to place at least crude lower bounds on the extent to which the overall values of individual contributions differ.

For example, although total research productivity is exceptionally difficult to measure, one dimension of it is fairly easily quantified in monetary terms—namely the grants and other financial support that researchers are able to generate from sources outside the university. When a faculty member receives a research grant from a government agency or private foundation, the funds are typically allocated into two categories, direct costs and indirect costs. Money in the direct cost portion of the budget is meant to cover laboratory equipment, supplies, and other direct expenses incurred while carrying out the funded research. In contrast, the indirect cost portion of the grant budget is for helping to defray the costs of maintaining the university's infrastructure—libraries, utilities, IT networks, administrative and other support staff, snow removal, and so on.

The important point, for present purposes, is that the expenses covered by the indirect cost portion of grant budgets are largely fixed. The fact that a professor receives a grant thus does not cause any increase in the university president's salary, library expenses, snow removal costs, or other overhead expenses. It follows, then, that if a newly hired professor brought with her a stream of grants with an average indirect cost contribution of $1 million per year, the university's annual budget would improve by exactly that amount. That is, the university's budget surplus would be $1 million a year larger than if the professor had remained at a rival university.

Because the labor market for high-quality faculty is extremely competitive, universities compete vigorously with one another to attract any faculty member who consistently generates unusually large contributions to indirect costs. Under conventional theories of competitive labor markets, which make no allowance for concerns about rank, such contributions would be reflected dollar-for-dollar in salaries. Those models predict that a faculty member who reliably brought in $1 million in annual indirect cost recovery would be paid $1 million more than an otherwise identical faculty member who brought in no indirect cost money. (For example, if a university that was trying to recruit the star grant-getter offered a salary premium smaller than $1 million, her current university's clear incentive would be to match the offer.)

When we go to the numbers, however, we see that salaries are nowhere near that responsive to this particular measure of productivity. In one Cornell University science department, for example, each long-run average increase of $1 in overhead cost recovery increased the responsible faculty member's salary by only $0.09.[4]

If the professors whose grants generated the biggest indirect cost contributions were less productive than their colleagues in other ways, the apparent insensitivity of their salaries to indirect cost contributions might be an illusion. That is, the biggest grant-getters might not receive their apparent due in salary because they're inferior teachers, or because they make less valuable contributions to the university's mission in other ways. That's a plausible concern, since teaching and research obviously make competing claims on a professor's limited time and energy.

Evidence suggests, however, that the biggest grant recipients are also more productive than their colleagues along other important dimensions. Grants tend to be awarded in part on the basis of a researcher's academic reputation, for example, so those who bring in the most grant money are also contributing more than others to the university's prestige, independently of the grants they receive. Evidence also suggests that more productive researchers tend to be slightly more effective teachers, on average.[5] The upshot is that individual differences in indirect cost recovery almost certainly understate the corresponding differences in overall productivity. Yet only a tiny fraction of indirect cost recovery differences are reflected in salaries.

This pattern is widespread. In every occupation for which data facilitate the relevant comparisons, the most productive workers in any unit are paid substantially less than the value they contribute, while the least productive workers are paid substantially more.[6] Other factors might of course contribute to the observed discrepancies. But even when such factors can be ruled out, substantial wage compression remains.[7] That's precisely the pattern we'd predict if people assign considerable value to high-ranked positions within work groups.

Because such positions cannot exist unless others agree to occupy the corresponding low-ranked positions, high rank commands a steep implicit price. In effect, each employer administers an implicit income redistribution scheme that taxes the most productive workers in each group and transfers additional pay to the least productive.

Those who especially value high rank are more likely to accept the implicit wage penalty that comes with being one of the most productive workers in a group with relatively low average productivity. In contrast, those who care least about high rank will tend to gravitate to low-ranked positions in groups of high average productivity, for which they receive an implicit wage premium. And the best option available to those with intermediate concerns about rank is a middle-ranked position in a group of average productivity, where their pay roughly matches the value of what they produce.

There is thus, in effect, an implicit market for high local rank that functions much like the analogous implicit markets for job characteristics like safety and autonomy. Those who especially value safety tend to gravitate to the safest jobs and suffer a wage penalty sufficient to cover the cost of additional safety measures. Those who especially value autonomy tend to gravitate to the jobs that offer the most freedom, and they too experience a concomitant wage penalty. And those who especially value high rank tend to choose jobs that offer it, willingly accepting the often-substantial wage penalties.

Like the implicit markets for other desirable job characteristics, the implicit market for high-ranked positions operates largely beyond the conscious awareness of firms and workers. The facilitating taxes and transfers occur without any of the affected parties having to engage in difficult or costly negotiations. Firms simply post their pay schedules and people then decide which jobs best suit them. The implicit market for high-ranked positions in work groups is one of the relatively rare examples in which transaction costs do not prevent people from working out efficient solutions to externalities on their own.

Social Comparisons outside the Workplace

Groups of co-workers aren't the only social hierarchy that matters. People also care about how their incomes compare with those of others outside the workplace. One study, for example, found that a married woman whose sister did not work outside the home was from 16 to 25 percent more likely to seek employment if her sister's husband earned more than her own husband.[8] Neighbors' incomes matter.[9] Friends' incomes matter. Indeed, because the spending of others shapes the frame of reference that governs consumption standards generally, there's almost no one in the community whose income is irrelevant.

The implicit market for high-ranked positions in work groups does nothing to help deal with positional externalities that arise outside the workplace. On the contrary, that market actually exacerbates the strength of such externalities facing those who occupy high-ranked positions in work groups, who have had to sacrifice a significant portion of what they otherwise could have earned.

And unfortunately for everyone, it's considerably more difficult to negotiate solutions to positional externalities with strangers in the community than it is to resolve them within the confines of private work groups. Again, there are virtually no complex agreements that need to be negotiated in order to compensate for positional externalities within work groups. Firms merely need post wage schedules that are relatively compressed with respect to productivity differences, and allow workers to choose the package that best suits them. In contrast, the task of negotiating similar compensation agreements with others outside the workplace would be enormously costly and difficult.

Ronald Coase is the free-market conservative's reigning authority on all questions regarding activities that cause harm to others. His central insight was not that government has no role to play in helping curb the damage from behavior that causes harm to others. Rather, it was that when transaction costs make it impractical for people to negotiate solutions to such problems on their own, government should create laws and define property rights to encourage behaviors that mimic what people would have agreed to if negotiation had been practical.

My claim is that tax systems that transfer income from rich to poor are a case in point.[10] They mimic the implicit transfers we observe in virtually every private labor contract, transfers that reflect the costs and benefits of different rungs on the social ladder. Such tax systems facilitate the formation of more stable and diverse societies.

Since High Social Rank Imposes Costs on Others, Why Should It Be Free?

In describing the details of our thought experiment, I tried to construct an environment in which it would be impossible to violate the rights of someone with even the most extreme libertarian sensibilities. Someone who wanted to ride his motorcycle without a helmet, for example, could never be forced to join a society that would strip him of that right. Nor could he be forced to join a society that would tax him against his wishes.

The surprising conclusion of the exercise is that even in such an environment, libertarians would find no reason not to join a society that taxed the rich to pay for income transfers to the poor. If they cared enough about having high social rank, they'd agree to be taxed rather than to be excluded from a society in which they'd enjoy high rank. And if they didn't care about having high social rank, they'd find it advantageous to join a society in which their low social rank boosted their after-tax income.

It's no surprise, perhaps, that many wealthy libertarians might feel entitled to enjoy their high-ranked position in the social order as a matter of right. But if transaction costs were low enough to permit societies to form and dissolve at will, they couldn't claim that right free of charge. They'd have to bargain for it. And as evidence from the analogous process of bargaining for high-ranked positions in work groups makes clear, those positions do not come cheap.

A wealthy person might prefer to pay for only one of the three steaks he'd just taken from his butcher's cooler, but that doesn't entitle him to do so. A wealthy person might also prefer to occupy a high-ranked position in the social order free of charge. But he's not entitled to that privilege, either.

Opportunities Beckon

Attempts to remedy market failure have been a central, if often implicit, focus of human societies from the beginning. Unfortunately, many of those attempts have been compromised by misguided perceptions at both ends of the political spectrum.

Regulatory remedies traditionally embraced by liberals spring from a perception that market failure stems mainly from exploitation by powerful economic elites. Their counterparts on the right object that markets are highly competitive, insisting that Adam Smith's invisible hand makes regulation unnecessary. But although markets are in fact extremely competitive, conservatives' faith in the invisible hand is overblown.

As Darwin saw clearly, the fact that unfettered competition in nature often fails to promote the common good has nothing to do with monopoly exploitation. Rather, it's a simple consequence of an often sharp divergence between individual and group interests. Nonhuman animal species couldn't do much about that, and despite their superior communication skills, early humans didn't fare much better. But since the dawn of the industrial age, human societies have made dramatic progress. The explosive material advances of that era have been almost entirely a consequence of new institutional arrangements that narrow the wedge between individual and group interests.

Yet enormously valuable opportunities remain unexploited. The "It's your money . . ." rhetoric that has dominated recent political discourse has made it impossible even to discuss tax and expenditure policy changes that would create large benefits for everyone. In this chapter, I've argued that confusion about distributional issues has been an important reason for our failure to seize these opportunities.

The bad news is that opposing parties in the distributional debate embrace their respective positions with such messianic fervor. As we've seen, however, alternative ways of framing this debate hold promise. More egalitarian distributions of resources can be defended not just in abstract moral terms, but also in terms of mutual advantage. And as I'll argue in the next chapter, additional progress will be more likely if we can abandon ill-founded views about the relationship between success and merit. The good news is that because current arrangements are so egregiously inefficient, there's enormous room for improvement.

NINE

Success and Luck

PEOPLE OFTEN SPEAK ABOUT THE EMOTIONAL BRAIN and the rational brain as if there really were two independent people housed within us— one driven by reason, the other by emotion. But neuroscientists stress that the brain's emotional circuits and cognitive circuits are richly interdependent.[1]

In exceptional circumstances, strong emotional reactions can occur even in the absence of significant cognitive processing. This happens, for example, at the sight of a snake-like object, which can provoke fear before the image even reaches the cognitive circuits of the brain.[2] More generally, however, our emotional reactions to events depend critically on how we frame and interpret them cognitively.

To know whether someone's behavior constitutes a violation that merits an angry response, for example, we must first know a lot about the context in which the behavior occurred and the rules that apply in that context. In familiar settings, our emotional reactions to events are generally well calibrated. But misdirected emotional reactions are not uncommon, especially when we find ourselves in unfamiliar cultural settings.

A vivid case in point occurred during the sabbatical year my family and I spent in Paris. My youngest son, Hayden, was a fifth-grader in a French school in the city that year. One afternoon, he came home in a state of high indignation. He explained that he'd been given an *avertissement*—a school disciplinary notice—for something he hadn't done. The charge against him had been filed by a playground supervisor who said that a student had shouted an obscenity at him. The supervisor was unable to identify the specific offender, so he filed charges against all the children who were playing nearby, a group that included Hayden.

Insisting that he'd never said a word to the supervisor, Hayden wanted us to demand a hearing to set the record straight. I asked some friends for advice and was told that there was virtually no chance the school would conduct an investigation. I also learned, however, that there was no consequence from receiving an *avertissement* unless a student had already accumulated three previous ones during the same school year.

I explained to Hayden that the French system of school justice seemed to be a little different from the one we were used to at home. Rather than invest a lot of time and effort to uncover the specific facts surrounding every potential infraction, the French had adopted an alternative approach that produced roughly similar results. I explained that even a full-blown investigation might reach an erroneous conclusion, and that although the odds of making a mistake were obviously higher in the absence of an investigation, it was still very likely that a student who had managed to accumulate four *avertissements* in a single school year would be guilty in at least one instance. What struck me at the time was how quickly my son's sense of outrage evaporated when he considered this alternative way of thinking about the problem.

The cognitive frames within which we view taxes have similarly powerful effects on our emotional reactions to them. If we think of being taxed as akin to some unknown person confiscating something that rightfully belongs to us, it's almost impossible not to react angrily. But taxes are more plausibly viewed through a different lens. As discussed in the preceding chapter, for example, the high average income levels of modern industrial nations would not be possible in the absence of extensive public investments paid for by taxes. That realization begins to chip away at the cognitive frame necessary to support an uncritically angry reaction to being taxed.

But even among those who grant the legitimacy of taxation, there often remains a stubborn perception that they personally are overtaxed. This perception naturally tends to be concentrated among those with the highest pretax incomes, who pay dramatically more than others in taxes. Notwithstanding populist complaints about the myriad tax loopholes available to the wealthy, the top 10 percent of earners in the United States accounted for more than 71 percent of all federal income taxes paid in 2007, while the top 1 percent accounted for more than 40 percent.[3]

Success and Merit

In his address to the Democratic National Convention in 1988, Texas Agricultural Commissioner Jim Hightower described George H. W. Bush as a man who "was born on third base and thought he'd hit a triple."[4] But given the conspicuous role that his family's background had played in his career, Mr. Bush had to have been aware that good fortune had smiled on him. Typically, it's the self-made man who's the more fitting target of Hightower's remark. He *knows* how hard he worked. He vividly remembers every sacrifice he made. And far more than most wealthy heirs, he's likely to be blissfully unaware of good luck's pivotal role in his success.

If people tend to overlook the role of good luck in their own success, they also tend to overlook the role of bad luck in others' failures. People sometimes file for bankruptcy because they failed to work hard and spent recklessly. But in the United States, many more bankruptcies occur when people fall seriously ill or lose their jobs, and with them their health insurance. Such mitigating factors are conspicuously absent from much social commentary about poverty. Witness, for example, the sentiments expressed by a commenter on Instapundit, a conservative blog hosted by University of Tennessee law professor Glenn Reynolds:

A reason for the "wealth or income gap": Smart people keep on doing things that are smart and make them money while stupid people keep on doing things that are stupid and keep them from achieving.

People who get an education, stay off of drugs, apply themselves, and save and wisely invest their earnings do a lot better than people who drop out of school, become substance abusers, and buy fancy cars and houses that they can't afford, only to lose them.

We don't have an income gap. We have a stupid gap.[5]

Reynolds anointed these remarks the "Comment of the Day" on the high-traffic site.

People who work hard and stay focused are of course more likely than others to succeed. Yet as economists have become increasingly aware, success depends far more on the vagaries of chance than most people once imagined. And so does economic failure.

One of my central themes in this book is that as individuals we often face incentives that lead us to undermine the common good, and that to counteract these incentives, taxes are generally a far more efficient and less intrusive instrument than direct regulation. But advocating new taxes in the United States has often been described as politically unthinkable, largely because of prevailing cognitive frames that portray taxation as a violation of individual liberty. The thorough overhaul of tax policy that the country desperately needs will not happen until new cognitive frames begin to crowd out those that have supported that perception.

Attempts to reframe this debate will yield slow progress at best. But because our current tax structure is so profoundly wasteful, they're worth making. A useful first step is to examine more closely the relationship between success and luck.

Contrary to what many parents tell their children, talent and hard work are neither necessary nor sufficient for economic success. Most successful people are of course both prodigiously talented and extremely hardworking. Yet some people enjoy spectacular success despite having neither attribute. (Participants in reality TV shows? Lip-synching members of boy bands? Money managers who bet clients' retirement savings on subprime securities and got out before the market crashed?)

Far more numerous, however, are highly talented people who have worked extremely hard, yet have achieved only modest earnings. There are thousands of them for every person who strikes it rich. The biggest winners tend to be people who are talented, ambitious, hardworking, *and* extremely lucky.

Bill Gates: Lucky Stiff?

Consider Microsoft co-founder Bill Gates, for many years the wealthiest man on earth and still one of the top three. He was born in 1955 to a well-to-do Seattle family, attended private schools, and began programming computers at the age of 13. His Seattle high school had a computer club, an extreme rarity at the time, and he also enjoyed extensive access to the computer labs at the University of Washington.

That background—coupled with his intelligence, ambition, and capacity to work hard—enabled him to form a start-up software company with his high school friend and Harvard classmate, Paul Allen. Microsoft became a going concern long before the rest of us ever heard about it, but its founders surely had no idea when they named their company in 1976 what a spectacular future lay in store for it.

The sequence of events that made that future possible began when IBM approached Microsoft to inquire about developing an operating system for the personal computer it was planning to introduce. As Leonard Mlodinow recounts the story in a 1990 book, Gates initially told IBM that Microsoft couldn't take on the project.[6] He suggested that IBM instead contact Gary Kildall, whose firm, Digital Research, had already developed a personal computer operating system called CP/M.

But Kildall's wife, who managed Digital Research, was reluctant to sign the nondisclosure agreement that IBM required, so those talks broke off. Jack Sams of IBM then went back to Gates to discuss other possibilities. Both Sams and Gates knew about another operating system that might be available. It was QDOS, the "quick and dirty operating system" that had been written in six weeks by Tim Paterson of Seattle Computer Products, using Kildall's CP/M manual as his starting point. Paterson had apparently modified QDOS sufficiently to establish a plausible legal claim to ownership.

In Mlodinow's account, Gates then asked Sams what proved to be the multibillion-dollar question: "Do you want to get . . . [QDOS], or do you want me to?" Not seeming to grasp the economic implications of the question, Sams reportedly responded, "By all means, you get it."

Gates then negotiated Microsoft's purchase of QDOS for roughly $50,000, modified it further, and renamed it MS-DOS, for Microsoft disk operating system. But his biggest stroke of luck came when IBM, apparently pessimistic about the personal computer's prospects for success, permitted Microsoft to retain ownership of the operating system, each copy of which it could then license for a modest royalty fee. It was that last step that sealed Microsoft's meteoric rise.

If it or any one of the other events in the sequence had not occurred—if Gates's high school had not had a computer club, if Kildall's wife had been willing to sign IBM's nondisclosure agreement, if Paterson had negotiated with Microsoft more attentively—Bill Gates almost certainly never would have succeeded on such a grand scale.

To their credit, the Gates family seems well aware of how fortunate they have been. When Gates himself was later asked how many other teens had backgrounds similar to his before heading off to college, he said, "If there were 50 in the world, I'd be stunned. I had a better exposure to software development at a young age than I think anyone did in that period of time, and all because of an incredibly lucky series of events."[7] In recent years, Gates and his wife have donated more than $30 billion to endow the Bill and Melinda Gates Foundation, which has done much to eradicate human suffering around the globe. And Gates's father, Bill Gates, Sr., has long been a forceful critic of proposals to eliminate the estate tax.

Luck in Sports

The importance of each chance event supporting Bill Gates's success may seem obvious in hindsight. But many other success stories rest on chance events that seem insignificant even when called to our attention. Consider the sequence that leads ultimately to a successful career as a professional athlete. In hockey, for example, Malcolm Gladwell points out that some 40 percent of all players in the premier professional leagues around the world were born in January, February, or March, while only 10 percent were born in October, November, or December.[8] The reason for this striking disparity, he argues, is that January 1 was the traditional cutoff birth date for participation in youth hockey leagues almost everywhere.

Players born early in the year were thus the oldest members of their team at each successive stage. On average, they were slightly bigger, stronger, faster, and more experienced than their teammates born in later months. Because they were more likely to excel at each stage, they were more likely to be chosen for elite traveling teams and for all-star teams. They were more likely to be funneled into the programs with the best facilities and the best coaching, more likely to receive athletic scholarships, and so on.

Why It Sometimes Helps to Deny the Role of Luck

Gladwell's point is not that being born in January guarantees that a Pee Wee hockey hopeful will grow up to play in the NHL. Rather, it's that even such a simple accident as the timing of his birthday can profoundly alter his odds of success.

Of course, the fact that hard work and skill do not guarantee success has seldom discouraged successful people from ascribing their own success to skill and hard work. Because most successful people are both highly skillful and extremely hardworking, and since they'd have been much less likely to succeed without those qualities, the attraction of the narrative is palpable. But why are some people more skillful than others in the first place? And why do some people work so much harder than others? On closer examination, it quickly becomes apparent that even those qualities entail heavy elements of luck.

Debate continues about the extent to which personal traits are attributable to environmental and genetic factors. But whatever the true weights may be, in combination those factors explain virtually everything. Someone is smart either because she was born with genes that made her smart, or because she was raised in a nurturing, stimulating environment that fostered her intellectual development, or—almost certainly—because of some combination of those two factors.

The same is true of someone with an unusually strong capacity and inclination to work hard. That aspect of her character may be partly genetic, and it may be partly a result of the particular circumstances of her upbringing. But whatever the true weights might be, there can be no doubt that someone possessed of these qualities enjoys a substantial advantage in life.

On what grounds might people born with good genes and raised in nurturing families claim moral credit for their talent and industriousness? The plain fact is that they were just lucky. Even though having those qualities does not guarantee their success, it makes their odds vastly higher than those for people born without talent and raised in unsupportive environments.

Again, to observe that the link between success and luck is far stronger than many think is not to deny that working harder makes you more likely to succeed. Nor is it to deny that working hard is often experienced as, well, *hard*. The story is told of a man who on meeting a renowned violinist at a cocktail party said, "I'd give anything to be able to play as beautifully as you do." "Would you be willing," the virtuoso asked, "to practice eight hours every day?"

The psychologist K. Anders Ericsson, an expert on professional expertise, estimates that roughly ten thousand hours of dedicated practice time is required for achieving genuine expertise at many skills.[9] Those hours needn't be all toil and drudgery. The Beatles, for example, logged more than ten thousand hours polishing their skills in dive bars in Hamburg, Germany, before becoming an overnight success in their native England; and as various biographies recount their experience, they quite enjoyed their time in Hamburg. Bill Gates spent more than ten thousand hours—many of them focused, happy hours—programming his computer as a teenager.

More typically, however, many of the ten thousand hours that eventually become the foundation of expertise are ones people would have been all too delighted to spend doing something else. As Ericsson and his co-authors note, truly effective practice time is actually quite demanding:

You need a particular kind of practice—*deliberate practice*—to develop expertise. When most people practice, they focus on the things they already know how to do. Deliberate practice is different. It entails considerable, specific, and sustained efforts to do something you *can't* do well—or even at all. Research across domains shows that it is only by working at what you can't do that you turn into the expert you want to become.[10]

In short, getting really good at something is difficult. It demands considerable patience and determination. And when trying to summon that determination, it's probably not useful to think of your willingness to work hard as having been predetermined by chance events. Someone who thinks in those terms may be more tempted than others to sit back and watch fate take its course. In contrast, someone who thinks to himself "good people work hard and I'm a good person" may be more likely to summon the will to stay focused on a difficult task.

So it's probably a useful psychological tendency to exaggerate the extent to which we can claim moral credit for the traits that make our own success more likely. But the utility of that psychological tendency doesn't alter the fact that someone with the inclination and capacity to work hard has been extremely lucky in this life.

How Winner-Take-All Markets Amplify Small Differences

Differences in talent and effort obviously help explain why some earn much more than others. But there is a second important dimension of the problem —namely the way labor markets translate such differences into differences in pretax incomes.

In textbook models of competitive labor markets, workers are paid the value of what they add to their employer's bottom line. Everyday intuitions about how pay varies with performance follow the narrative suggested by these models reasonably well. If a firm sells bricks, for example, then a worker who produces 101 bricks an hour would be paid 1 percent more than another who produces only 100. But as the economist Philip Cook and I argued in our 1995 book, there are many labor markets in which the relationship between pay and ability has never followed this simple pattern.[11]

One of the most conspicuous examples is the market for corporate executives. CEOs of the largest U.S. companies earned forty-two times as much as the average worker as recently as 1980, but by 2001 they were earning more than five hundred times as much,[12] even though there was no evidence suggesting that CEOs had become smarter or more hardworking than they used to be. Because the factors that have caused this explosive growth in earnings are similar to those at work in most other high-end labor markets, it's instructive to review them in some detail. A close look at this market also provides an opportunity to weigh competing claims by Adam Smith and Charles Darwin about why unbridled competition often delivers outcomes that many find objectionable.

Many commentators on the left argue that the staggering growth in executive pay constitutes evidence of a breakdown in competitive market forces. Industrial behemoths conspire to drive out their rivals, we're told, so they can extort ever higher payments from captive customers. Executives pack their boards with cronies, who reward them with exorbitant salaries and bonuses.

To be sure, such abuses occur. But they're no worse now than they've always been. On the contrary, improved communications and falling transportation costs have almost certainly made them less serious. Executive hiring committees may not be perfectly informed, but they have more information than they used to, and this makes reputation a more effective predictor of performance. Similarly, increased vigilance from institutional shareholders and growing threats of hostile takeovers have placed additional constraints on executive pay abuse.

Despite these advances, corporate governance remains imperfect. But although there will always be cases in which mediocre executive performances are rewarded with high salaries, those who fail to deliver generally get the axe more quickly than in the past. Philip Cook and I argued that top salaries have been growing sharply in virtually every labor market because of two factors—technological forces that greatly amplify small increments in performance and increased competition for the services of top performers.[13]

Pay by relative performance is one defining condition of what we call a winner-take-all market. A second is that rewards tend to be concentrated in the hands of a few top performers, with small differences in talent or effort often giving rise to enormous differences in incomes. Both features show up in Sherwin Rosen's description of the market for classical musicians:

> The market for classical music has never been larger than it is now, yet the number of full-time soloists on any given instrument is on the order of only a few hundred (and much smaller for instruments other than voice, violin, and piano). Performers of the first rank comprise a limited handful out of these small totals and have very large incomes. There are also known to be substantial differences between [their incomes and the incomes of] those in the second rank, even though most consumers would have difficulty detecting more than minor differences in a "blind" hearing.[14]

The enormous leverage of the most talented musicians was made possible by the development of breathtakingly lifelike recording and playback technologies. Now that most music we listen to is prerecorded, the world's best soprano can be literally everywhere at once. And since it costs no more to stamp out compact discs from her master recording than from the master recording of any other singer, millions of us are each willing to pay a few cents extra to hear her rather than other singers who are only marginally less able. The upshot is that the best soprano lands a seven-figure recording contract while only marginally less gifted performers struggle to get by.

The same logic holds in the market for leaders of large organizations. The trustees who recruited David J. Skorton as Cornell University's twelfth president in 2007 knew that his most important responsibility would be to head the university's $4 billion capital campaign, which was then just getting under way. The hiring committee identified several candidates they felt would succeed in reaching that goal. They eventually decided, however, that none could have handled the task nearly as well as Skorton.

Having seen him in that role for the past several years, I find it easy to see why. Skorton, a man of great humor, warmth and charm, is a distinguished research cardiologist and an accomplished jazz musician. Alumni adore him. If his compellingly articulated vision of the university's future persuades them to donate only 3 percent more than the next-best candidate would have, he will have boosted the university's endowment by more than $100 million.

I don't know how much Dr. Skorton is paid. But many social critics expressed shock and outrage when it was reported that annual salaries of presidents of some private universities had passed the $1 million threshold several years ago. Leaders of David Skorton's stature are in short supply, however—and because they're so valuable, the real surprise is that they're not paid even more.

Vastly larger sums are at stake in many private companies. Consider a company with $10 billion in annual earnings that has narrowed its CEO search to two finalists. If one would make just a handful of better decisions each year than the other, the company's annual earnings might easily be 3 percent   or $300 million—higher under the better candidate's leadership. So if the top contenders for the CEO position are distinguishable with respect to the quality of the decisions they're likely to make in office, then the competitively determined salary of the best candidate can be dramatically higher than that for the second best, even when the estimated difference in their talents is small.

Decision leverage in the executive suite—always high in the largest companies—has grown sharply in recent decades. Perhaps the most important reason for this is the information revolution, which—together with falling transportation and tariff costs, recent developments in manufacturing technologies, and other factors—transformed many local and regional markets into national and global ones. A firm that produced the best tire in northern Ohio was once assured of being a player in at least its regional tire market, but sophisticated consumers now choose from among only a handful of the best tire producers worldwide. Corporate performance has always depended strongly on the efforts of a handful of people at the top, but because of the broader scope of today's markets, the leaders of the surviving companies have much greater leverage than their earlier counterparts did.

In competitive markets, greater leverage means higher pay. As the economists Xavier Gabaix and Augustin Landier argue in a 2008 paper, for example, executive pay in a competitive market should vary in direct proportion to the market capitalization of the company.[15] They found that CEO compensation in their sample of large companies grew sixfold between 1980 and 2003, roughly the same as the market-cap growth of these businesses.

Deregulation, which provides not only new market opportunities but also new competitive threats, has further enhanced the value of executive talent in the airline, trucking, banking, brokerage, and other industries in the United States. Adding to that has been the increased threat of outside takeovers resulting from the introduction of derivative securities and other new sources of financial capital. These developments have increased the potential gains from superior performance and also the potential damage from poor performance, making it all the more important to have the most talented players in key positions. For all these reasons, the economic value of top executive talent has been growing.

But increasing decision leverage alone cannot account for the observed growth in executive pay in the United States. After all, CEOs in America's largest companies have always had enormous decision leverage, yet barely two decades have passed since the first multimillion-dollar compensation packages appeared. Moreover, globalization has increased the leverage of executives not just in the United States but also in Germany and Japan, where executive compensation has grown in recent years but remains modest by U.S. standards. So the mere fact that a top CEO contributes millions to a company's bottom line does not by itself ensure a commensurate salary.

Before there can be large and concentrated rewards in any winner-take-all market, not only must the top performers generate high value, but there must also be effective competition for their services. In many markets, however, a variety of formal and informal rules traditionally prevented such competition.

Most major sports leagues, for example, once maintained restrictive agreements that prevented team owners from bidding for one another's most talented players. In the wake of the successful challenge of baseball's reserve clause in 1976, however, these agreements have toppled one by one. By now, players have won at least limited free agency rights in all the major professional team sports. In each case, gaining these rights was followed by sharp increases in player compensation.[16]

Unlike the owners of professional sports teams, the owners of business were never subject to formal sanctions against bidding for one another's most talented employees. But informal norms often seemed to have virtually the same effect. Under these norms, it was once the almost universal practice to promote business executives from within. In most cases, there were only a few plausible internal candidates. Executive pay setting was thus a bilateral negotiation between the firm and the chosen internal candidate. That candidate had nowhere else to go, and the firm had no other viable candidates to consider. Under the circumstances, firms were able to retain top executives for less than one-tenth of today's salaries.

The anti-raiding norms of business have all but completely unraveled. Perhaps the most celebrated case in point was IBM's decision to hire Louis V. Gerstner, Jr., a respected corporate turnaround specialist who had produced record earnings at RJR Nabisco but had absolutely no experience in the computer industry. In earlier times, such cross-industry hires would have been almost unthinkable. But IBM's gamble paid off handsomely. Gerstner led the then-struggling computer giant to its dramatic turnaround of the 1990s.[17]

This new spot market for executive talent has affected executive salaries in much the same way that free agency affected the salaries of professional athletes in recent decades. In our earlier study of CEOs hired by roughly eight hundred of the largest U.S. manufacturing and service companies, Philip Cook and I found a 50 percent increase in the proportion of outside hires between 1970 and 1992.[18] That trend effectively broke the implicit reserve clause that once bound executives to their companies.

Although more than half of newly appointed CEOs are still insiders,[19] the game has now fundamentally changed. In the United States, leaving for an outside post has become an increasingly available option for the best performers. To hang onto its most valued senior officers, a firm must now pay them enough to keep them from jumping ship. Elimination of the reserve clause in baseball was an essential precondition for the explosive growth in the salaries of top players in recent years. Increased mobility has played a similar role in the market for top executives.

In short, the argument that skyrocketing executive pay is evidence of a breakdown of competitive forces does not withstand scrutiny. A conspicuous exception is the financial services industry, whose lavish campaign contributions appear to have purchased favorable regulatory treatment that has substantially insulated firms from effective competition.[20] But most of the spectacular pay increases of recent years are in fact a consequence of strengthening market forces.

Winner-take-all markets are nothing new, of course. What has changed is the pace at which technology has been extending the power and reach of the planet's most gifted performers. More than five hundred years ago, the printing press enabled a relatively few talented storytellers to displace millions of village raconteurs. More recently, the electronic newswire has allowed a small number of syndicated columnists to displace a host of local journalists. And the proliferation of personal computers has enabled a handful of software developers to replace thousands of local tax accountants. As a result of such changes, competitive labor markets now amplify individual differences in talent and effort into unprecedentedly large differences in pay. And since even differences in talent and effort stem in part from chance events over which we have little control, the upshot is that the relationship between luck and success is substantially stronger now than at any point in human history.

An enlightened libertarian might abandon the claim that all taxation was theft in favor of the less extreme claim that people have the right to after-tax incomes that closely mimic patterns in their pretax earnings. The latter claim might seem intuitively reasonable in a world in which someone who had 1 percent more talent, or who expended 1 percent more effort, earned 1 percent more income. But it has much less appeal in a world in which such tiny differences often translate into hundred- or thousandfold differences in earnings. And it's the latter world we live in.

Beliefs Matter

Ideas have consequences. Inspired by the "It's your money . . ." cognitive frame, the George W. Bush administration substantially reduced income taxes on the highest earners. To help reduce the resulting federal budget deficits, officials tried to cut whatever government expenditures they could. But government programs have constituents. The programs that end up getting cut are not necessarily the ones that deliver the least value. More often, they're the ones least visible to the public, or the ones whose constituents are least able to push back.

Among the programs cut during the Bush administration was the Energy Department's program to help lock down loose nuclear materials in the former Soviet Union.[21] Those materials are stored in poorly fortified facilities staffed by soldiers who drink too much and are not always paid on time. Terrorists are desperately seeking to acquire nuclear materials. Under the circumstances, it's not difficult to imagine them succeeding.

Viewed from the vantage point of someone at any station along the income scale, cutting that program was a bad decision. But such choices are all too common under our prevailing decision framework.

It costs money to round up poorly guarded nuclear materials in the former Soviet Union. If we want it to happen, we've got to pay for it, which means we must decide whom to tax. For reasons having nothing to do with social justice, I will argue in coming chapters that it would serve the interests of rich and poor alike to raise most of the additional revenue we need from those with higher incomes. But that won't happen unless we can adopt a new framework for thinking about taxes. Evidence on why people earn such different pretax incomes is clearly relevant for thinking about that framework.

The prevailing framework presumes that people have a natural right to keep the full bounty their talents and efforts command in the labor market. Given the extent to which incomes rest on public investment financed by taxes, that presumption has never made much sense. It's further undercut by accumulating evidence on the profound extent to which the labor market success of even highly talented, hardworking people depends strongly on random events. And although there may be substantial psychological utility in the common tendency to claim moral credit for one's own success, the fact remains that even talent and the capacity for hard work are themselves heavily dependent on factors over which we have limited control.

Marian Hossa, who played right wing for the Chicago Blackhawks during the team's 2009–2010 Stanley Cup championship season, earned a salary of $8 million that year. Mr. Hossa, who was born on January 12, 1979, undoubtedly worked extremely hard to achieve his hockey success. I've never met him and have no idea how he feels about his current tax burden. But it's easy to imagine that simply knowing about the link between early birthdays and hockey success might incline him to feel slightly less resentful about it.

TEN

The Great Trade-Off?

SOCIALISMDOESNTWORK.COM, A WEBSITE that bills itself as "the ulti-mate guide to why socialism causes more poverty, inequality, and injustice," greets visitors with the following version of Aesop's sixth-century BC fable of the goose that laid the golden eggs:

> A man and his wife had the good fortune to possess a goose which laid a golden egg every day. Lucky though they were, they soon began to think they were not getting rich fast enough, and, imagining the bird must be made of gold inside, they decided to kill it. Then, they thought, they could obtain the whole store of precious metal at once; however, upon cutting the goose open, they found its innards to be like that of any other goose.[1]

This tale is a perennial favorite of movement libertarians, who invoke it to remind those who favor a more progressive tax system that such a system would impoverish everyone. Former Fed Chairman Alan Greenspan, who describes himself as a libertarian, echoed this view when he wrote that "All taxes are a drag on economic growth. It's only a matter of degree."[2]

But it's not just libertarians who believe taxes inhibit economic growth. Variations of that view, often called trickle-down theory, have been repeated so often by so many people across the political spectrum that it has acquired an air of settled truth.

It cannot literally be true, of course, that all taxes are a drag on economic growth. As noted earlier, unless we tax something, we can't organize and maintain a civil society and defend ourselves from foreign invaders, much less enjoy robust economic growth.

Without going into more detail about what, exactly, is being taxed, it's impossible even to discuss how taxes affect economic growth. In chapter 11, our focus will be on taxes levied on activities that cause harm to others. Such taxes, as we'll see, not only don't reduce economic growth, they actually enhance it.

Income Taxes and the Incentive to Work

Libertarians and conservatives are surely right that, beyond some point, higher taxes on top incomes would curtail economic growth. If the tax rate were 100 percent, for example, and the government distributed the resulting revenue so that after-tax incomes were the same for everyone, then people would have no incentive to accept paid work at all. And in that case, there wouldn't be any revenue to distribute.

But that's hardly an interesting claim, since it doesn't tell us anything about what would happen if we increased actual tax rates on top earners, which are nowhere close to 100 percent. For trickle-down theory to be of interest, then, it must assert something like this: At the tax rates actually observed in modern industrial countries, further rate hikes on top earners would cause economic growth to decline.

Is that claim correct? Its surface plausibility stems from the time-honored belief that people respond to incentives. Because higher taxes on top earners reduce the reward for effort and risk-taking, it seems reasonable that they'd induce people to work fewer hours and take fewer risks. Both responses would reduce economic growth.

As every economics textbook makes clear, however, a decline in after-tax wages also exerts a second, opposing effect. Because it makes people feel poorer, it provides an incentive to reverse their setback by working longer hours or taking more risks than before. Suppose, for example, that a high roller's goal were to achieve a standard of living that could be maintained on $2,000 a day. If his current after-tax wage were $250 an hour, he'd need to work eight hours daily. But if a rate hike reduced his after-tax wage to $200 an hour, he'd need to work two additional hours, or else sell his Ferrari.

Others might react differently to a tax increase. Because a higher marginal tax rate reduces the opportunity cost of taking additional time off (in terms of forgone after-tax income), it might lead some to work fewer hours than before. Economic theory tells us nothing—absolutely nothing—about of which of these opposing effects might prevail.

If economic theory provides no justification for the trickle-down doctrine, what do the numbers say? Here as well, the doctrine finds little support. One test is suggested by the observation that if lower real wages induce people to work shorter hours, then the opposite should be true when real wages increase. Since 1900, average hourly wages in the United States have risen more than fivefold in inflation-adjusted terms. According to trickle-down theory, then, Americans should be working significantly longer hours now. Yet the current American workweek is only about half what it was in 1900.

Trickle-down theory also predicts shorter workweeks in countries with lower real after-tax pay rates. Yet here, too, the numbers tell a different story. For example, even though CEOs in Japan earn less than one-fifth as much as American CEOs and face substantially higher marginal tax rates, they actually work longer hours than their American counterparts.

Trickle-down theory's emphasis on incentives has led many to predict that greater income inequality should be positively correlated with economic growth rates. The idea here is that greater income disparities should cause people to feel greater pressure to catch up with those ahead of them. As discussed in chapter 4, inequality does indeed affect spending patterns. Yet when researchers examine the data within individual countries over time, they find a negative correlation between growth rates and inequality. During the three decades immediately following World War II, for example, income inequality was low by historical standards, yet growth rates in most industrial countries were extremely high. In contrast, growth rates have been only about half as large during the years since 1973, a period in which income and wealth inequality have been steadily rising in most countries.

The correlation between growth rates and inequality is also negative in cross-national data. Using data from the World Bank and the Organisation for Economic Co-operation and Development for a sample of sixty-five industrial nations, the economists Alberto Alesina and Dani Rodrik found that growth rates were negatively related to the share of national income going to the top 5 percent and top 20 percent of earners. Larger shares for poor and middle-income groups were associated with higher growth rates.[3] Time after time, the pattern is the opposite of the one predicted by trickle-down theory.

The Small Business Fallacy

Another variant of trickle-down theory was invoked by George W. Bush in 2001, and then again by John McCain in 2008, as the two men sought to defend reduced taxes on the nation's top earners. This variant made no assertions about how tax cuts might affect the amount of effort people devote to paid work. Rather, the claim in both cases was that because many wealthy people own small businesses, which account for more than half of all new jobs created in the United States each year, the tax cuts would immediately stimulate additional job creation.

At first glance, the claim might seem plausible, and in fact it drew little criticism when they made it. On closer examination, however, it makes no economic sense at all. It's inconsistent with everything we know about the economic logic that governs business hiring decisions.

The claim rests implicitly on the premise that if business owners could afford to hire additional workers, they would. But whether you can afford to do something tells you nothing about whether you ought to do it. The fact that you can afford a CD by a singer you dislike, for example, does not mean you should buy it. The fact that business owners can afford to hire additional workers is similarly uninformative. What matters is whether hiring them would increase their profits.

The basic hiring criterion, found in every introductory textbook, is straight-forward: If what the additional workers would produce can be sold for at least enough to cover their salaries, they should be hired; otherwise not. If this criterion is met, hiring extra workers makes economic sense, no matter how poor a business owner might be. Conversely, if the criterion isn't satis-fied, hiring makes no sense, even if the owner is richer than Bill Gates. The after-tax personal incomes of business owners are simply irrelevant for hir-ing decisions.

To this objection, defenders of the tax-cut proposals sometimes responded that business owners need money up front to cover the hiring and training costs incurred before new workers can start boosting production. Tax cuts would help them cover those costs. It's a fair point, but it doesn't alter the basic hiring rule.

Owners who used their tax cuts to finance the initial costs of new hiring would be lending money to themselves in the hope of earning future returns. They'd be acting, in effect, as their own bankers. The test for whether such loans make sense is exactly the same as the test for external loans.

A loan from a bank passes the cost-benefit test if the firm's eventual gain from hiring extra workers is enough to cover not only their salaries but also repayment of the loan plus interest. Internal loans must meet the same stan-dard. They're justified only if the firm's gain from hiring extra workers is enough to cover their salaries and repayment of the loan, including the interest that owners sacrificed by not leaving their tax cuts in the bank. In hiring decisions, those implicit costs of internal loans have exactly the same weight as the explicit costs of external loans.

The argument that low tax rates for the owners of small businesses will stimulate them to hire more workers thus flies in the face of bedrock prin-ciples outlined in every introductory economics textbook. Small businesses have been justly praised as the primary engine of job creation in the Ameri-can economy. But that doesn't negate the fact that personal income tax rates should have no bearing on their hiring decisions.

If an extra plumber would bring in an extra $2,000 a week in revenue but would be paid only $1,500 a week in salary, Joe's Plumbing Service would have every incentive to hire him. Yes, a tax cut would put more money into Joe's pocket. But Joe would hire the extra plumber even without one. Conversely, if the extra plumber would bring in less than $1,500 a week, Joe wouldn't hire him no matter how big a tax cut he got.

In sum, neither economic theory nor available empirical evidence provides support for either variant of trickle-down theory. We have no persuasive reasons to believe that higher taxes on top earners would inhibit economic growth. And yet, as noted, this claim is often repeated and seldom questioned.

Why Lower Tax Rates on Top Earners
Often Inhibit Growth

Still more troubling, there are cogent reasons for believing that lower tax rates on top earners may actually hamper the economy's ability to take full advantage of available resources. For example, even though lower tax rates on top earners do not appear to encourage people to work significantly harder, they do appear to alter career choices in unproductive ways.

Prior to the financial crisis that began in 2008, a steadily growing proportion of the nation's best and brightest students each year left school in hopes of becoming Wall Street money managers. In Princeton University's class of 2007, for instance, 45 percent of all employed graduates had taken jobs in the financial services industry.[4] Accounts of these jobs portray them as unattractive along many dimensions.[5] They entail long hours, and many experience them as highly stressful. Others complain that they're not intellectually challenging. But on one point all are agreed: these jobs pay extremely well. The best and the brightest have been seeking employment in the financial services industry in record numbers because people who are successful in that industry earn staggering amounts of money.

According to Institutional Investor's *Alpha* magazine, for example, the hedge fund manager James Simons earned $1.7 billion in 2006, and two other managers earned more than $1 billion. The combined income of the top twenty-five hedge fund managers exceeded $14 billion that year. A year later, hedge fund manager John Paulson earned some $4 billion.

These managers also enjoy remarkably favorable tax treatment, for reasons that no one can seem to explain with a straight face. For example, even though "carried interest"—mainly their 20 percent commission on portfolio gains—has the look and feel of ordinary income, it's taxed at the 15 percent capital gains rate rather than the 35 percent top rate for ordinary income. That provision alone saved Mr. Paulson some $800 million dollars in taxes in 2007.

Congress periodically considers proposals to tax carried interest as ordinary income. To no one's surprise, financial industry lobbyists are always quick to insist that doing so would kill the geese that lay the golden eggs. The deals brokered by their clients often create enormous value, to be sure. Yet the proposed legislation would not block a single transaction worth doing. The same deal that currently augments a hedge fund manager's after-tax income by $1 million would augment it by $765,000 if carried interest were taxed as ordinary income. Can anyone credibly claim that this would make him abandon the deal?

Economic analysis suggests that higher taxes on hedge fund managers would actually boost production in other sectors of the economy by alleviating wasteful overcrowding in the market for aspiring portfolio managers. This market is a prime example of a winner-take-all market—essentially a tournament in which a handful of winners are selected from a much larger field of initial contestants. Such markets tend to attract too many contestants for two reasons.

One is an information bias. Before you can make an intelligent decision about whether to enter a tournament, you need at least some idea of what your odds of winning would be. Yet people's assessments of their relative skill levels are notoriously optimistic. More than 90 percent of workers, for example, consider themselves more productive than their average colleague. A similar proportion of drivers believe that they're more skillful than the average motorist. These biases don't seem to be eradicated by additional education. More than nine out of ten college professors believe themselves to be more productive than their average colleague.[6]

Overconfidence is especially likely to distort career choice because, in addition to the motivational forces that support it, the biggest winners in many tournaments are so conspicuous. For example, NBA stars who earn eight-figure salaries appear on television several nights a week, whereas the thousands who failed to make the league attract little further attention. Similarly, hedge fund managers with ten-figure incomes are far more visible than the legions of contestants who never made the final cut. It's a matter of simple logic that when people overestimate their chances of winning, too many forsake productive occupations in traditional markets to compete in winner-take-all markets.

The Tragedy of the Commons

Potential contestants in winner-take-all markets also confront a problem called the tragedy of the commons, an incentive structure that was first invoked to explain overfishing in ocean waters.[7] The cod, once abundant in the North Atlantic, saw its population decline by more than 95 percent from overharvesting. The incentives that led to this decline were similar to those that produce excessive entry into many winner-take-all markets.

The tragedy of the commons provides a vivid illustration of Darwin's insight that individual and group interests often diverge sharply. A simple numerical example captures the essence of the conflict. Consider one hundred people, each trying to choose between two occupations: fishing for cod in an isolated fishery or working in a factory at an annual salary of $50,000 each. For simplicity, suppose that each views the two alternatives as equally attractive, apart from the matter of pay. So someone will choose fishing only if he can earn at least $50,000 a year in that occupation. Otherwise, he'll choose factory work.

Now imagine that cod in the fishery are initially so abundant that the first fisherman on the scene could earn $100,000 a year. Since that's twice what someone would earn in the factory, others would quickly gravitate to fishing. But with only limited supplies of cod in the fishery, the average catch would steadily decline as the number of fishermen rose. Economic theory predicts that entry into the fishing industry would cease once the annual earnings from fishing had declined to $50,000, at which point people would be indifferent between fishing and factory work. Arbitrarily, let's say that happens when there are forty fishermen (the qualitative point of the example is independent of that number).

With annual earnings of $50,000 apiece, those forty fishermen would earn a total of $2 million a year, and the remaining sixty who chose factory work would earn a total of $3 million. Collectively, then, our one hundred workers would earn $5 million a year. But that's the very same total they'd have earned if all one hundred had chosen factory work! The fishery, potentially an extremely valuable resource, ended up being of no economic value at all. The problem was that individual incentives led too many people to become fishermen, in the process completely dissipating the potential economic surplus from fishing. (That it would have been possible to do better is clear by noting that if only one person had chosen fishing, the collective earnings of the one hundred would have been larger by $50,000, since the lone fisherman would have earned $100,000 while the other ninety-nine would have earned $50,000 as factory workers.)

The tragedy of the commons occurs because of a simple externality. Each potential fisherman cares only about the earnings from the fish he expects to catch. He has no reason to consider the fact that his entry would reduce the number of fish caught by existing fishermen. When the market reaches equilibrium, the last entrant's $50,000 in earnings from fishing is just enough to compensate him for the $50,000 he gave up by not working in the factory. But because his entry also reduced the size of each existing fisherman's catch, the systemwide effect of his entry was actually negative. Individual incentives to enter fishing are thus far too large, and overfishing is the expected result.

The incentives confronting aspiring portfolio managers are exactly analogous. Just as there are only so many fish in the sea, at any given moment there are only so many deals to be struck. Beyond some point, increasing the number of money managers produces much less than proportional increases in total commissions on managed investments. One contestant's good fortune in landing a position in a leading hedge fund is thus largely offset by her rival's failure to land that same position. So here, too, private incentives result in wasteful overcrowding.[8]

The tendency to attract excessive contestants is by no means confined to the financial sector. It's a feature found to some degree in almost every winner-take-all market. As a practical matter, moreover, almost all markets that generate society's highest incomes are winner-take-all markets. There are typically a few highly leveraged positions atop each profession—Grammy-winning recording artists, all-star shortstops, best-selling novelists, Fortune 500 CEOs, major network news anchors, Academy Award–winning actors, popular radio talk show hosts, leading plaintiffs attorneys, and so on. Because these positions are so lucrative, competition to occupy them is invariably intense. There are literally hundreds—in many cases even thousands—of highly capable, ambitious candidates for each opening.

Again, potential contestants in winner-take-all markets tend to overestimate their odds of success and to ignore the fact that their entry into one of these contests would make each existing contestant less likely to succeed. For both reasons, such labor markets tend to attract too many contestants.

In the fishing industry variant of the tragedy of the commons, total earnings rise when people shift from fishing to factory work. Similarly, if the least talented contestants were to forsake Wall Street or some other winner-take-all market for more traditional career paths, there would still be an ample number of talented competitors for each superstar position. So if half the people who are currently jockeying for positions in hedge funds and private equity firms were to leave the financial industry tomorrow, there would still be no shortage of extremely qualified candidates to fill those positions. The resulting gains from having more and better engineers, medical researchers, teachers, and family physicians would more than compensate for any lost value from having fewer contestants in winner-take-all markets. If after-tax incomes in winner-take-all markets were lower, fewer contestants would compete for positions in them. So the desired employment shifts could be encouraged simply by raising tax rates on top earners.

Referring to proposals to eliminate preferential tax treatment for hedge fund and private equity managers, a finance professor at Columbia Business School objected that "Private equity is a very important part of our economy," adding that higher taxes will discourage it.[9] Others have characterized the proposals as envy-driven class warfare.

Both observations, however, miss the essential point. No one denies that the talented people who guide capital to its most highly valued uses perform an important service for society. But the number of profitable deals to be had is not indefinitely expandable. Beyond some point, sending ever larger numbers of our most talented graduates out to prospect for them has a high opportunity cost, yet adds little economic value. Almost without exception, the graduates of Harvard, Princeton, and Yale who flocked to the financial services industry are extremely intelligent and industrious. Had they pursued other careers, some might have helped develop effective treatments for life-threatening diseases. Others might have helped develop more efficient solar panels. Instead, many of them helped market complex derivative securities that sent the nation into the deepest economic downturn since the Great Depression.

In short, making the after-tax rewards in winner-take-all labor markets a little less spectacular would raise the attractiveness of other career paths, ones in which extra talent would yield real gains. The resulting tax revenue would pay for many things that clearly need doing. In an economy in which winner-take-all markets play an increasingly prominent role, the conventional wisdom about the great trade-off between equity and efficiency is turned upside down. In today's environment, higher taxes on top earners may actually promote both goals at once.

Even so, I believe that imposing higher income taxes on top earners would be a bad idea. As explained in chapter 5, a more steeply progressive tax on each household's total consumption expenditure would be far more efficient than the current income tax. My reasons for opposing income taxes are very different from those offered by libertarians and other antitax crusaders, whose slogans have prevented us from having an intelligent conversation about how to reform our highly dysfunctional tax system.

That conversation needs to focus on fundamental questions that transcend the details of any particular tax. How should property rights be designed? What's the optimal balance between private and public goods, and what sorts of institutional arrangements might best promote that balance? How should we pay for public goods? What sorts of duties, if any, do we have toward society's poorest members? What sorts of institutions would best promote environmental sustainability? And so on.

A Mindless Slogan Contest

An informed conversation about tax policy would benefit people on both sides of the political aisle. It would benefit people at every point along the income scale. At every turn, however, antitax and antigovernment slogans have stopped this conversation in its tracks. Almost without exception, these slogans are transparently at odds with existing theories and evidence about human behavior. Yet people continue to utter them with no apparent sense of embarrassment. Indeed, many of them are repeated deferentially even by highly sophisticated, ostensibly neutral commentators. Genuine reform will become possible only when these slogans provoke the widespread scorn they richly merit. So before pressing forward, it's an opportune moment to review some of their deficiencies.

In a contest to determine the most mindless antitax slogan of all, "All taxation is theft" would get my vote. The ostensible point of this slogan is that meddlesome government officials shouldn't be allowed to confiscate economic resources that we have created by dint of our own talent and effort. But there isn't much economic value to confiscate in countries that lack well-defined and enforced systems of property rights and the public infrastructure required for highly developed and specialized markets. None of that could exist unless government had the power to employ mandatory taxation. No informed person would seriously consider living in a society in which government lacked that power—even apart from the concern that such a society would quickly be conquered by an army supported by a neighboring country's mandatory taxation.

A distant second in the mindless slogan contest would be some variant of "It's unjust to tax some people more heavily than others." This slogan fails in multiple ways. All societies benefit from having roads, bridges, police and fire protection, national defense, and a host of other public goods and services. But no society can provide these things without raising the tax revenue to pay for them. As in the case of private goods, higher incomes generally spawn demands for more and better public goods. But any society that was constrained to collect no more in tax revenue from some citizens than others could provide public goods only in the quantities and qualities demanded by its poorest members. Again, no informed person would want to live in such a society.

Another problem with slogans decrying the injustice of progressive taxation is that they rest on a very strange theory of justice. In a libertarian's ideal universe, people would be free to form societies with others of their own choosing and be bound by only those rules that commanded unanimous approval. In such a universe, if people wanted to form a society in which they occupied positions of high social rank, they'd have to persuade others to occupy the corresponding positions of low social rank. And if the implicit market for high-ranked positions within work groups in competitive labor markets is any guide, high-ranked positions in those voluntary societies would carry a steep price. Because such positions are highly valued, and can exist only if others bear the costs associated with the low-ranked positions required for high rank to exist, it's completely consistent with normal English usage to call progressive taxation fair. Yet antitax crusaders insist that people are entitled to occupy high-ranked positions free of charge, just because transaction costs make it impractical to form new voluntary societies at will. That position actually betrays a profound disdain for justice, as the term is conventionally understood.

Another influential antitax slogan has been "Success in the marketplace depends on talent and effort, not luck." To the extent that it encourages people to strive harder for success, this slogan has actually done much good. But it has also done much harm. There are millions of hardworking, talented people who never achieve any significant measure of market success. The more we learn about how modern labor markets function, the clearer it becomes that chance events are often decisive. Even personal talent and the capacity for hard work are themselves heavily influenced by genetic and environmental factors, for which any reasonable person should be reluctant to claim moral credit. Slogans that downplay luck's role in life reinforce the belief that people have a moral right to keep 100 percent of their pretax earnings. And that belief has been unambiguously harmful.

Among all antitax slogans, however, none has caused more profound damage than the one that has been our focus in this chapter: "Taxing the rich kills the geese that lay the golden eggs." Though unsupported by economic theory or empirical evidence, it's less transparently absurd than "All taxation is theft." But for that very reason, it's far more widely believed and has therefore had far more pernicious influence on public policy. For example, it was the foundation for the George W. Bush tax cuts on the wealthiest households, which helped double the national debt during his presidency. Those same cuts, as we saw in chapter 4, also altered spending patterns in damaging ways.

Every American president elected during my lifetime campaigned on a pledge to eliminate wasteful spending in government. A few even made genuine progress toward that goal. Yet total government spending continued to increase throughout each and every one of those presidencies. We should of course continue to attack waste aggressively. But the bulk of the future spending increases we face are nondiscretionary, and our expectations must not be unrealistic.

With the baby boomers retiring, for example, we face a growing gap between Social Security payments and payroll tax receipts for the foreseeable future. Revenue shortfalls in the Medicare program, already large, will grow much faster than Social Security shortfalls because of inevitable cost increases in the medical sector. As experience has shown, these entitlement programs are politically sacrosanct.

There are other compelling candidates for additional public expenditure. Our transportation infrastructure, for example, has been neglected for decades. At some point, we will really have no choice but to repair our roads and bridges. We have no high-speed rail systems, even though many less developed countries are now building them.[10] With soaring energy prices, a smart energy grid has become an increasingly attractive public investment.[11] Many urban areas still lack even rudimentary public transportation systems. We still need to round up those loose nukes in the former Soviet Union. We should reverse earlier funding cuts for scientific research, which has always been an important source of competitive advantage. The list goes on.

We may be able to rationalize our major entitlement programs at the margins, and extract some savings here and there from other cutbacks. But only a fool could pretend that we will be able to do what needs to be done in the years ahead in the absence of substantial additional revenue. Although I believe it would be a bad idea to raise top marginal income tax rates, we must be prepared to consider other ways of taxing society's most prosperous members. As Willie Sutton said when asked why he robbed banks, that's where the money is. If we can't tax the rich, there's no hope of raising the revenue we'll need. But the good news, as we'll see, is that certain taxes can be levied on top earners without harming their interests in any way.

ELEVEN

Taxing Harmful Activities

A TAX ON ANY ACTIVITY NOT ONLY generates revenue, it also discourages the activity. That simple observation constitutes welcome news indeed, for not only do we desperately need additional tax revenue right now, but our economy is also bedeviled by a host of harmful activities. Taxes levied on those activities would kill two birds with one stone, helping to bring government budgets into balance while discouraging activities that cause more harm than good.

Pigouvian Taxes

Before discussing specific examples, it will be useful to flesh out the economic logic behind the claim that the tax approach often leads to better results than attempts to regulate harmful activities directly. The basic argument was first made by the British economist A. C. Pigou, for whom taxes on harmful activities came to be known as Pigouvian taxes.[1]

Imagine two companies, Limpio and Sucio, that are the sole sources of sulfur dioxide (SO_2) pollution in a valley region. Each company has three possible technologies it could employ. In each case, the technologies differ only in terms of their operating costs and the amounts of SO_2 they emit. Those costs and the corresponding levels of SO_2 emissions are as summarized in Table 11.1. Take a moment to look over the pattern of the entries in

TABLE II.I   Operating Costs and SO$_2$ Emissions for Different Production Processes

	Cleanest process (0 tons of SO$_2$/day)	Intermediate process (3 tons of SO$_2$/day)	Dirtiest process (6 tons of SO$_2$/day)
Limpio Corporation's daily operating cost	$100	$40	$10
Sucio Corporation's daily operating cost	$4,500	$1,500	$500

the table, which illustrate some important general properties of different methods for dealing with harm abatement.

Note first, for example, that as you read from right to left across the cost entries, the cleaner production processes are also the more expensive ones. That's a simple consequence of the fact that better filters are more costly than less effective ones. Note also that the cost of removing a given amount of pollution—in this case, each 3-ton daily increment—rises as more pollution is removed. That's because rational economic actors always avail themselves of the most cost-effective options first, and then move on to less attractive ones. For instance, the cost to Limpio of removing the first 3 tons of SO$_2$ from its smokestacks each day is just $30 (the difference between the cost of its dirtiest process and its intermediate one), while its cost of removing the next 3 tons is $60 a day (the cost difference between its cleanest and intermediate processes).

Another important pattern illustrated by the production cost entries is that removing pollution is more costly for some firms than others. Note, for example, that it would cost Sucio $1,000 a day to remove the first 3 tons of SO$_2$, and $3,000 a day to remove the remaining 3 tons—much more in each case than the corresponding cost for Limpio.

Let's assume, plausibly, that it's impractical for those who are damaged by SO$_2$ emissions to negotiate with polluters. A standard assumption in economics is that firms try to maximize their profits, which implies they'll choose the cheapest production method the law allows. In the absence of regulation, then, each company would use its cheapest (and dirtiest) process, which would result in a total of 12 tons of daily SO_2 emissions, 6 from each company.

Why the Optimal Pollution Level Is Generally Not Zero

What level of SO_2 emissions would be optimal for this valley? Many non-economists are quick to say zero, but we cannot answer this question without knowing the costs imposed by SO_2 emissions. Reducing emissions is also costly, after all, and if the damage caused by SO_2 were sufficiently low, the best outcome would be just to tolerate it. But to make the discussion more interesting, let's imagine that SO_2 emissions cause damage at a constant rate of $40 per ton each day. Total damage would thus be $480 per day if each firm used its dirtiest process.

Limpio, as noted, can reduce SO_2 emissions far more cheaply than Sucio. That means the cheapest first step in reducing total damage would be for Limpio to switch from its dirtiest process to its intermediate one. The move would increase daily total production costs by only $30, and since that's smaller than the $120 savings from reduced emission damages, it would clearly be a step worth taking. To reduce damage further, the cheapest next step would be for Limpio to switch from its intermediate to its cleanest process, which would cut emissions by another 3 tons a day and increase daily production costs by $60. Since daily emissions damage would again fall by $120, this step would also be worth taking. But at that point, Limpio will have done all it can.

If we wanted to reduce damage any further, the next step would be for Sucio to switch from its dirtiest to its intermediate process. But taking that step would cost $1,000 a day, far more than the resulting reduction of $120 a day in damages. In this example, Sucio's abatement costs are so high that it has no useful role to play in the cleanup effort. A total of 6 tons a day of SO_2 emissions is the best we can do here.

Many people find it difficult to accept that a nonzero level of pollution could be optimal. But that must be true whenever emissions reduction beyond some point becomes more costly than the corresponding reduction in damages. If someone insists that the optimal level of every pollutant in every environment is zero, ask him why he isn't at home vacuuming his living room at this very moment. Every minute that passes since the last time it was vacuumed, more dust accumulates. If he insists the optimal level of dust is zero, he should vacuum continuously, or hire someone to do so.

But of course that would be silly. Vacuuming consumes valuable time, and a little bit of dust doesn't do much damage. The same logic dictates that zero is also generally not the optimal level of other types of pollutants. An optimal pollution abatement program employs the cheapest abatement methods first, then works its way down the list until the value of additional abatement no longer justifies its cost.

This simple example puts us in a position to see why command-and-control regulation is so inefficient. The historical approach to pollution regulation was to require each and every polluter to reduce its historical pollution level in a base year by the same proportional amount. In the example just considered, if regulators wanted to reduce total SO_2 emissions by half, they'd have required both Limpio and Sucio to switch from their dirtiest process to their intermediate one. That would have achieved the desired total reduction, but the increase in total operating cost would have been $1,030 per day: $1,000 for Sucio and $30 for Limpio. That's $940 more than the $90 it would have cost to achieve the same result by having Limpio switch from its dirtiest process to its cleanest one.

Requiring equal proportional reductions from all polluters is wasteful because it takes no account of the fact that some polluters can reduce pollution far more cheaply than others. Regulators could have achieved the efficient result by simply instructing Limpio to switch to its cleanest process. In general, however, regulators lack detailed knowledge about the kinds of different abatement technologies that are available to individual firms. It's unrealistic to expect them to be able to micromanage the process at that level.

Why the Tax Approach Minimizes Total Cleanup Costs

Regulators can, however, ensure that any given pollution target is achieved in the cheapest possible manner. In the example just discussed, suppose regulators levied a tax of $40 on each ton of SO_2 emitted. Limpio would respond by switching from its dirtiest to its cleanest production process, since doing so would save $240 a day in tax payments but would cost only $90 a day. Sucio, for its part, would continue using its dirtiest production process, since the tax savings it could achieve by switching to cleaner processes would be too small to cover the corresponding cost increases.

Limpio would thus assume the entire burden of the pollution reduction effort, which would be efficient because its abatement costs are so much lower than Sucio's. But because Limpio would be emitting no SO_2, it would also pay no emissions taxes. The tax approach to pollution abatement is thus not only efficient but also equitable.

Compared to the alternative of taking no action to curb emissions, the tax approach increases the economic well-being of society as a whole. The only cost incurred because of the tax was the extra $90 a day Limpio spent in switching to its cleanest production process. And since the total benefit of the tax was the $240 daily reduction in emissions damages, the net benefit to society as a whole was $150 a day. The daily tax payment of $240 made by Sucio was a cost of the policy from Sucio's perspective, but not from the perspective of society as a whole, because the extra revenue meant that other taxes could be reduced by precisely the same amount.

The key to understanding the efficacy of the tax approach is to recognize that the damage done by SO_2 emissions depends on their total concentration in the atmosphere, not on who put them there. Society's interest thus lies in holding down the total cost of any given pollution reduction, not in achieving specific reductions by specific parties. The tax approach minimizes that cost by giving the parties with the lowest abatement costs an incentive to assume most of the cleanup effort.

The optimistic portrait that emerges from this hypothetical example was affirmed in practice when Congress adopted SO_2 permits as part of its amendments to the Clean Air Act in 1990. SO_2 is an important precursor of acid rain, a problem that had grown increasingly costly in the Northeast in the 1970s and 1980s. The new legislation required that firms obtain a permit for each ton of SO_2 they emit into the atmosphere. Total SO_2 emissions were brought down by gradual reductions in the number of permits issued. Since firms were permitted to buy and sell permits at an auction organized by the Chicago Board of Trade, the permit requirement was functionally equivalent to a tax on SO_2. Emitting an extra ton of SO_2 required the permit holder to forgo the revenue it could have received by selling the permit, so the opportunity cost of using a permit is essentially an implicit tax on SO_2.

The program was spectacularly successful, achieving emissions targets well ahead of schedule and at a cost well below what would have been required under command-and-control regulation.[2] Articles about the acid rain problem, which used to appear regularly in the news media, have all but completely disappeared.

Objections to the Tax Approach

Economists had been actively proposing the permit/tax approach to pollution abatement since the dawn of the environmental movement, but environmental groups and other critics on the left were initially hostile to those proposals. One environmentalist, for example, was reported to have asked, "What's next, the L.A. Police Department trying to buy civil rights credits from Wisconsin?"[3] Criticisms like "Economists want to let rich firms pollute to their heart's content!" were common.

The latter criticism betrays a comically naïve view of firm behavior. Firms don't pollute because they derive pleasure from doing so. They do it because removing pollution costs money. Although it took decades for the economists' proposals to be enacted into law, environmental groups are now among the most enthusiastic supporters of the tax approach. Groups like the Sierra Club, for example, have urged their supporters to purchase SO_2 permits and tear them up, thus helping to bring emissions even lower than regulatory targets.

What reasons might libertarians or other free-market conservatives offer for opposing a tax on SO_2? For the moment, let's assume agreement that the framework outlined by the economist Ronald Coase is the right way to think about this question (see chapter 6). Some libertarians may disagree, but as I'll explain in the next chapter, that's a very difficult position for them to defend. Many free-market enthusiasts embraced the Coase framework in the belief that it would help minimize government's regulatory footprint. This belief was grounded on Coase's demonstration that if negotiation among parties affected by harmful activities were practical, they'd have strong incentives to arrive at efficient solutions on their own.

Well and good. But as Coase understood clearly, transaction costs often make it impractical for people to negotiate with one another. And in such cases, efficient solutions may require government intervention. When negotiation is impractical, Coase argued, government should adopt institutional arrangements that guide affected parties to the solutions they'd have negotiated on their own if negotiation had been practical.

With hundreds of different SO_2 sources and millions of different people adversely affected by SO_2, privately negotiated solutions are simply not a practical option. Coase's framework thus suggests that law should place the burden of ameliorating pollution damage on whoever can accomplish it at lowest cost.

Consumers have almost no attractive options for solving this kind of problem. Emitters, in contrast, have a variety of options, such as installing scrubbers in their smokestacks or burning low-sulfur coal. Coase's framework thus suggests that the best remedy for acid rain was to define property rights in such a way that producers would have an incentive to reduce SO_2 emissions. Taxing SO_2 emissions—or equivalently, requiring permits for them —is the most efficient way to solve this problem. It's also the least intrusive.

Such a tax is not theft. It makes goods whose production is accompanied by SO_2 emissions more expensive, yes, but the increase in price is simply a reflection of the costs that those emissions impose on others. The price of any product that generates harmful side effects should reflect their cost, just as it should reflect the cost of the labor and materials used to produce it. Because the tax reduced damage from SO_2 emissions by more than the corresponding increase in production costs, it made the overall value of economic output larger, not smaller. Citizens as a whole were not victims of this tax; they were beneficiaries of it.

Legislators who favor an SO_2 tax do not reveal by that fact that they think the bureaucrats in Washington know how to spend your money more wisely than you do. On the contrary, they understand that when valuable resources, such as the air we breathe, are free, people tend to use them inefficiently. This tax actually makes it possible for you to purchase *more* of the things you value.

If libertarian antitax rhetoric had blocked implementation of this tax, it would have been like Ralph Nader's Aviation Consumer Action Project having succeeded in its effort to block airlines from offering compensation to volunteers who relinquished their seats on overbooked flights. As discussed in chapter 7, using the price system to allocate scarce resources makes the economic pie larger, whether the resources in question are seats on an overbooked flight or air currents with limited capacity to disperse SO_2.

Libertarians would also have no grounds for objection if transfer payments had been necessary to secure legislative approval of a tax on SO_2. Using the price system to allocate scarce resources makes the economic pie larger, but that does not guarantee that everyone will automatically get a larger slice than before. For example, perhaps most of the customers served by Sucio have low incomes, making it difficult for them to bear the higher prices made necessary by that company's SO_2 taxes. Their political opposition to the tax might be eased by including provisions to strengthen the social safety net. The important point is that when a policy change makes the economic pie larger, it's always *possible* for those who benefit from that change to fully compensate those who are harmed by it. As discussed in chapter 7, failure to carry out such compensation has blocked many efficient policy changes, to the detriment of rich and poor alike.

Climate Change and CO_2 Taxes

Essentially the same case can be made for taxing CO_2, growing atmospheric concentrations of which are believed to be a principal contributor to global warming. Critics of proposals to tax CO_2 emphasize that forecasts involving climate change are highly uncertain, a fact they view as arguing against taking action. But uncertainty is a two-edged sword. Climate researchers themselves readily concede that estimates based on their models are extremely uncertain. But that means that although the actual outcome might be much better than their median forecast, it might also be significantly worse.

Organizers of the 2009 climate conference in Copenhagen sought to limit global warming to 3.6°F by the end of the century. But even an increase that small will cause deadly harm, and the most respected climate change models estimate that there is essentially no chance that average temperature will rise by less than that amount if we take no action.

According to recent estimates from the Integrated Global Systems Model at the Massachusetts Institute of Technology, the median forecast is for a climb of 9°F by century's end, in the absence of effective countermeasures.[4] The same model estimates a 10 percent chance of temperature rising by more than 12°F. If that happened, the permafrost would melt, freeing vast quantities of methane into the atmosphere. Methane is fifty times more potent a greenhouse gas than CO_2. Thus, according to the MIT model, we face a roughly one in ten chance of global warming sufficient to extinguish much of life on earth.

Again, forecasts from climate models are highly uncertain. Things might not be as bad as predicted. But they could also be much worse. Should we take action? To respond to that question, we must ask, how much it would cost? The answer, as it turns out, is astonishingly little.

The Intergovernmental Panel on Climate Change estimated that a tax of $80/ton on carbon emissions would be needed by 2030 to achieve climate stability by 2100.[5] A tax that high would raise the price of gasoline by $0.70 a gallon. This figure was determined, however, before the arrival of the more pessimistic MIT estimates. So let's assume a tax of $300 a ton, just to be safe. Under such a tax, the prices of goods would rise in proportion to their carbon footprints—in the case of gasoline, for example, by roughly $2.60 a gallon.

As we saw in 2008, a sudden price increase of that magnitude could indeed be painful. But if phased in gradually, it would cause much less harm. Facing steadily increasing fuel prices, for example, manufacturers would scramble to develop more efficient vehicles. Many Europeans now pay $4 a gallon more for gas than Americans do. But precisely because of that fact, European automakers have pioneered development of many of the world's most fuel-efficient cars. Europeans actually spend less on gas than Americans do, yet they seem no less happy with their rides.

If a family traded in its aging Ford Bronco (15 mpg) for a Ford Focus wagon (32 mpg), it would spend less on gas than before, even if it drove just as much. The tax could be phased in slowly, to give people time to adjust. People would also move closer to work, form car pools, choose less distant vacation destinations, and so on. Some of the revenue from the tax could be used to send checks to low-income families to ease the burden of higher gas prices. Portions of it could help pay down debt and rebuild crumbling infrastructure, or reduce other taxes.

In 2009 the House of Representatives actually passed an energy bill that included a comprehensive carbon cap-and-trade system, the functional equivalent of a carbon tax. Although many Republican legislators had long advocated cap-and-trade legislation as a framework for mitigating environmental externalities, the movement libertarian/Tea Party wing of the Republican Party has come out foursquare against such policies, denouncing them as social engineering.

Of course they're social engineering! The reason for this tax is that because we're currently allowed to discharge CO_2 into the atmosphere for free, we spew out far too much of it, threatening gross harm to everyone. Yet today it's difficult to find even a single Republican candidate for national office who publicly supports cap and trade. And Republicans now have more than enough votes in the Senate to prevent energy legislation from even coming to a vote in that chamber.

The logic they offer in support of their position would be comical if the stakes weren't so high. James Inhofe, a Republican senator from Oklahoma, has said that "the claim that global warming is caused by man-made emissions is simply untrue and not based on sound science."[6] It's a preposterous misstatement. Only a tiny minority of scientists working in the climate arena would even pretend to agree with it, and virtually all of them have been heavily funded by the energy industry. The vast majority of climate scientists believe that unchecked greenhouse gas emissions will continue to cause average surface temperatures to rise substantially. The only uncertainty is about how much. The risk of catastrophic climate change could be eliminated by a simple change in tax policy. Yet the antitax zealots are poised to prevent that from happening. Movement libertarians are a small minority, but their slogans have wreaked havoc far out of proportion to their number.

Congestion Fees

Exactly analogous logic applies to taxes on other activities that cause harm to others. When you enter a congested roadway, for example, you cause harm to others by making them take longer to get where they're going. Libertarians and other free-market conservatives have no grounds for objecting to congestion taxes like the daily fee of $14 that was imposed on cars entering central London on weekdays beginning in February 2003. As a direct consequence of that fee, traffic fell by a third and travel times on some bus lines fell by half. CO_2 emissions fell by 20 percent, and there were substantial declines as well in emissions of particulates and nitrogen oxides, the main components of urban smog.[7]

As in the example of the SO_2 tax discussed earlier, people for whom being unable to drive in central London would have been most costly responded by paying the fee and continuing to drive. Others rescheduled their trips during off-peak times or took public transportation. The aggregate value of reduced congestion and pollution was far larger than the cost of the accommodations people made. And revenue from the fee meant that the government would need to collect less revenue from other taxes. We must tax something, and it's far better to tax harmful activities than useful ones.

In 2007, New York City Mayor Michael Bloomberg proposed a similar congestion fee for motorists who enter Manhattan south of 86th Street on weekdays. Cars would face a daily charge of $8 between 6 AM and 6 PM, and the proposed fee for commercial trucks was $21. Although the mayor's proposal would have produced net benefits comparable to those of the London plan, critics immediately denounced it as unfair to the poor. New York City councilman Lewis A. Fidler, for example, said "It creates a city of haves and have-nots," adding that the bill says "those who can afford it may come and those who cannot afford it may not."[8]

Although the mayor's proposal won tentative approval from the New York City Council, such objections persuaded legislators in Albany to block it. Yet critics' concerns could have been addressed easily. In light of high bridge tolls and parking fees, very few poor people were commuting by car into Manhattan in the first place. Most were already taking public transportation. Occasionally, however, a low-income worker must drive into the city in order to take a child or parent to the doctor or run some other errand. Had Mayor Bloomberg been less concerned about political pushback from the right, he might have been willing to consider amending his proposal to include ten free vouchers every year for every low-income motorist who works in the city. Most of those vouchers probably would have ended up being sold to others on Craigslist, and the offer would have gone a long way toward eliminating opposition to the proposal.

But any such amendment would have provoked howls of protest from movement libertarians and other free-market conservatives. "Government has no right to tax me and give my money to the poor!" Such slogans have been astonishingly effective. All too often, however, they have served only to block policies that would make life better for everyone.

Taxing Vehicles by Weight

Mill's harm principle also suggests the legitimacy of taxing vehicles by weight. For many years, American motorists purchased sports utility vehicles in steadily growing numbers, many in the belief that these vehicles were safer than sedans. The truth, however, is more complex. Other things equal, when two vehicles collide head on, occupants of the heavier vehicle are more likely to survive. In a head-on collision between a 7,200-pound Ford Excursion and a 2,500-pound Honda Civic, for example, you definitely want to be in the Ford. Yet because of their weight and high center of gravity, large SUVs typically handle poorly, which makes them less likely to avoid collisions in the first place, and more likely to roll over during evasive maneuvers. Overall, the occupant of a typical SUV is less safe than the occupant of a typical sedan.[9]

But in terms of which type of vehicle poses a bigger risk to others, it's no contest: the SUV is the hands-down winner. The heavier a vehicle is, the more likely it is to cause deaths and serious injuries to the occupants of other vehicles.

As in the SO_2 example, there is no prospect that people might negotiate private solutions to this particular externality. If the government's challenge is to define property rights to mimic as closely as possible the outcomes that people would have agreed to on their own if negotiation had been practical, the simplest solution would be a tax on vehicle weight. Such a tax would induce motorists to consider the risks they impose on others when choosing which vehicle to buy. Under current arrangements, they have no incentive to take those risks into account at all. Another advantage of having such a tax would be that current tax rates on beneficial activities could be lower. On what grounds could anyone insist that taxing vehicles by weight would deprive motorists of a right they ought to enjoy?

Tobacco Taxes

Taxes on tobacco also reduce harm and are attractive for similar reasons. Smoking is indisputably harmful to those who smoke, and there's persuasive evidence that second-hand smoke causes significant harm to others. Most smokers, in fact, say they wish they had never started. The most reliable predictor of whether someone will take up the habit is the proportion of her friends who smoke. Cigarette company lobbyists cite evidence of that fact in support of their claim that higher tobacco taxes won't reduce smoking rates.

A heavily addicted adult smoker would indeed be unlikely to stop smoking only because of a steep tax on cigarettes. But most people who smoke took up the habit when they were teenagers. And because most teenagers have limited disposable incomes, cigarette taxes have much more impact on their decisions.

More important, peer effects cut both ways. If taxes discourage a teenager from smoking, that teen's peer group will have a smaller proportion of smokers in it. And that, in turn, will discourage still others from smoking, and so on. Studies have actually found that smokers themselves are happier in states with higher tobacco taxes.[10] Most smokers would like to quit their habit, and they seem to understand that their goal will be much easier to achieve in an environment with fewer smokers and higher-priced cigarettes. Higher taxes help create such environments.

Being a smoker causes harm to others, not just by exposing them to second-hand smoke but also by making others more likely to become smokers themselves. A world without cigarette taxes would be a world with many more smokers. If your children grew up in such a world, they'd be much more likely to become smokers. They'd be more likely to get lung cancer. They'd be more likely to suffer from emphysema, more likely to suffer from heart disease. They'd be more likely to die in a house fire. Why would parents want their children to grow up in a world like that, rather than in one in which cigarette taxes not only make such outcomes less likely but also permit lower taxes on useful activities?

Alcohol Taxes

The arguments regarding taxation of alcohol are somewhat more complex. Unlike most smokers, most people who consume alcoholic beverages do so with no apparent signs of regret. Most drinkers are also not significantly more likely to cause harm to others than people who don't drink at all. In the United States, harmful effects from alcohol consumption are caused almost entirely by the 5 percent of drinkers who consume more than 40 percent of all alcohol consumed.[11] Many members of this group harm others in multiple ways. They neglect and abuse family members; they injure and kill others in automobile accidents; they physically assault others; and so on.

Opponents of higher alcohol taxes often complain that the behavior of long-term heavy drinkers would not be much affected by such taxes. But available evidence suggests otherwise. It's true that many drinkers continue to consume alcohol to excess long past the point at which it has begun to take a heavy toll on their careers and marriages. Such people wouldn't want to cut back their alcohol intake just because the after-tax price of drinking went up. But as economists have long emphasized, choice is about scarcity. People often ignore increases in the prices of goods that account for only a small share of their total expenditures. If the price of salt were to double, for example, most people would consume the same amount of it as before. But long-term heavy drinkers spend a substantial share of their incomes on drink—in part simply because they drink so much, but also in part because their heavy drinking causes them to earn less. They simply cannot afford to ignore steep increases in the price of alcohol.

The challenge confronting any attempt to examine how alcohol taxes affect problem drinkers is that sales data tell us nothing about who bought and consumed the alcohol. The economist Philip Cook came up with an ingenious way to circumvent this problem.[12] His strategy was based on the observations that long-term heavy drinkers are responsible for a large proportion of all alcohol-related traffic accidents and also account for an overwhelming proportion of all deaths from cirrhosis of the liver. His core finding: in the wake of a significant increase in a state's alcohol taxes, there were striking reductions in the number of both alcohol-related traffic accidents and deaths from cirrhosis of the liver, but there were no such changes in neighboring states that did not raise alcohol taxes. Although most heavy drinkers with liver disease know that the surest path to recovery is by reducing their alcohol intake, that knowledge alone is seldom enough to change their behavior. Yet many respond quickly to a change in price incentives.

Another objection to alcohol taxation is that it's unfair to punish the majority who drink responsibly to curb the behavior of a small minority who drink irresponsibly. But the fact that heavy drinkers consume the lion's share of all alcohol purchased means that any tax on alcohol would fall disproportionately on them. The resulting revenue would make it possible for income tax rates to be lower by more than enough to offset alcohol taxes paid by moderate and light drinkers.

Taxing Activities That Cause Indirect Harm

The harmful activities I've discussed so far in this chapter have all been ones in which one person's action harms others in ways they have no practical ways to avoid on their own. You can take all reasonable care as a driver, for example, yet still be at risk of being hit by an SUV that runs a stop sign. The examples so far have also been ones in which the activity in question causes direct, physical harm to others. Regulating such activities is thus legitimate even under a fairly restrictive reading of Mill's harm principle, as discussed in chapter 1.

The harms caused by many of the consumption activities discussed in chapter 5 are also ones that victims would have great difficulty avoiding on their own. But those activities typically do not cause physical harm directly. Compared to tax remedies for activities that cause direct physical harm, many libertarians may feel uncomfortable embracing tax remedies for problems caused by shifting social frames of reference. But in the next chapter I will press the case that the distinction between physical and nonphysical harm should not be decisive. The real issue is how costly it is to avoid the adverse consequences of others' behavior. When others borrow more heavily to increase their bids for houses in good school districts, for example, you have no good options. You can either borrow more yourself, and suffer the attendant financial risk, or else refrain from borrowing and be forced to send your children to lower-quality schools.

Bicycle and Motorcycle Helmet Rules

A more challenging hybrid case is the example of bicycle and motorcycle helmet rules. When one of my sons was 14, he took a serious spill on his bike, landing violently on his head and shoulder. Fortunately, he suffered only a mild concussion and a broken collarbone. But the emergency room doctor who treated him told me he probably would have been killed had he not been wearing his helmet, the right side of which was completely shattered when he struck the ground.

The main reason he was wearing a helmet was that New York State has a law requiring them for all bicyclists under the age of 16. Some parents object to this law, saying that it should be their responsibility, not the state's, to prescribe safety standards for their children.

But even before my son's accident, I and many other parents I know were grateful for the requirement. Many boys display their willingness to incur risks as a badge of honor, and those who wear helmets in the absence of a requirement are often derided by their peers. In an ideal world, parents would successfully condition their children to ignore such pressures. But we don't live in an ideal world. What is clear, in any event, is that if helmets were not required, substantially fewer children would wear them, notwithstanding the best efforts of their parents.

Does New York State's helmet requirement meet John Stuart Mill's test? That is, does it restrict someone's behavior in order to prevent undue harm to others? That the requirement prevents enormous harm is beyond dispute. Except for it, many more children, perhaps including my son, would be dead today. Quite apart from the loss of their own lives is the loss suffered by parents and others who care about these children. Even without precise estimates of the magnitude of those losses, surely no one can doubt their immensity. The question then is whether the considerable harm prevented by the helmet requirement outweighs the harm experienced by those who are forced to wear them.

Of course, many people who are subject to the requirement would have worn a helmet anyway. Even so, many of them are quietly grateful for the requirement, because they find it socially less awkward to wear one when almost everyone else does. For the same reason, many others who would not have worn helmets without a requirement are pleased about being required to do so. For these groups, the requirement causes no harm at all, just as a helmet rule causes no harm to most hockey players. But inevitably there will also be a minority who are offended by the mandate, and the harm suffered by this group must be weighed against the harm prevented.

As discussed in chapter 7, strict application of Mill's harm principle would require defensible estimates of the dollar equivalent magnitudes of the harms on both sides of the equation. The New York State legislature passed its helmet law in the absence of such estimates, perhaps because most lawmakers thought that the obvious harm it would prevent vastly outweighed any possible harm it might cause.

Libertarians who oppose the helmet rule should be prepared to argue that the annoyance of those who would be offended by it constitutes greater harm than the pain and suffering that the requirement prevents. Few libertarians, however, seem prepared to argue in these terms. Instead, they appear content merely to assert that helmet rules should not be permitted, because the state doesn't have the right to tell people how to conduct their lives. But unless they're willing to abandon Mill's principle completely, that simply won't do. If libertarians have the power to block the majority's desire to implement a helmet rule for children, they have the power to inflict enormous harm on parents and others. By what right might they claim such an entitlement?

Some libertarians will object that the example is unfair, that of course the state should have the right to enact helmet requirements for children, who, after all, often lack the necessary judgment and experience to make prudent decisions about risky behavior. It's a reasonable objection. But evidence suggests that nothing magical happens when a child morphs into an adult. Myopia, naïve optimism, and vulnerability to social pressure may diminish with chronological age, but these traits are still present in ample measure in most adults. And like children, the typical adult has many others who love him, people who will suffer greatly if he is seriously injured or killed.

During a sabbatical year in Paris, I had a conversation with a colleague who biked to the office daily through forty-five minutes of heavy traffic. Although bicycle accidents are common in Paris, this intelligent, emotionally mature woman never wore a helmet. I told her about my son's accident and urged her to consider wearing one. When she demurred, I teasingly suggested that her reluctance was rooted in her fear of looking unfashionable. She protested vigorously, and I believe truthfully, that she had little interest in fashion. A few weeks later, however, she sheepishly admitted that she'd tried on some helmets over the weekend and just couldn't imagine herself appearing in public with one. Little wonder. I can't recall seeing even one female cyclist wearing a helmet during the entire year I spent in Paris. To be the only one would indeed be socially awkward.

Nor can I imagine the French passing a law requiring helmets (although neither could I have imagined their recent passage of a law banning smoking in bars and restaurants). But libertarians who accept Mill's harm principle cannot categorically oppose such laws, even when they apply to adults. Because the social environment profoundly affects individual decisions, many individuals find it extremely costly to escape the effect of what others do. Some people will be harmed whether we require helmets or not. In such cases, our shared interest is in minimizing total harm.

Over the violent objections of libertarians, many states have passed laws requiring even adult motorcyclists to wear helmets. My son who suffered the bicycle injury is an adult now. He is not a motorcyclist, but if he were I would be grateful that New York is among the states with a helmet requirement. But too often missing from public debates about such requirements are forceful advocates for alternative strategies that would be less costly to the people who are most deeply offended by outright prohibitions.

The decision by even mature adults about whether to wear helmets is often sensitive to the proportion of other people who wear them. In environments in which helmet wearing is rare—an environment, for example, like the one confronting my former colleague in Paris—someone who wears one can stand out like a sore thumb. And it's a plain fact that stable environments exist in which few wear helmets, even though most might prefer that they and others wear them. We also know that not wearing helmets can cause grievous harm, not only to the persons injured but also to those who care about them. Requiring helmets might thus bring about a reduction in total harm that would dwarf the harm caused by the requirement to those who don't want to wear helmets under any circumstances.

Yet the libertarian objection to such a requirement has obvious force. Anyone who wants to wear a helmet is free to do so. Without denying that the prospect of being embarrassed by standing out from the crowd could discourage someone from wearing one, the impulse is to say that's her problem. Perhaps she should think harder about what's really important and do her best to get over her concern about what others might think. If the alternative were to force others to wear helmets who don't want to, it would be *those* people who'd be left with no recourse. Still, there is something troubling about a situation in which most people aren't wearing helmets, and know they won't unless others do, and yet wish most people including themselves were wearing one.

Fortunately, however, an absolute helmet requirement is not the only way to deal with this problem. We could adopt a flexible helmet requirement from which anyone could purchase an exemption for a modest fee. By paying, say, $300 a year, someone could buy a decal from the Department of Motor Vehicles that could be affixed to the bike's license plate, serving notice to police that the rider of that particular bike was exempt from the helmet requirement.

The logic of this approach runs exactly parallel to the logic that made taxing SO_2 attractive. Just as removing SO_2 is more costly for some firms than others, having to wear a helmet is more costly for some people than others. Just as the damage from SO_2 depends on the total amount of it discharged into the air, the social pressure that dissuades people from wearing helmets depends on the proportion of riders who ride without one. And in each case, the efficient solution will be one that induces those who can adjust most easily to take the necessary remedial actions. Just as a tax on SO_2 induces firms whose abatement costs are low to adopt cleaner technologies, a tax on riding without a helmet would most encourage helmet wearing by those who object least strongly to them.

If libertarians still aren't comfortable with this tax, they might consider that it not only reduces harm but also raises revenue that could be used to pay for useful public services. It would thus enable tax rates on useful activities to be lower. A tax on riding without a helmet would mean we could reduce the payroll tax, which discourages job creation, or reduce the tax on income, which discourages savings.

A Slippery Slope?

I conclude with an example involving perhaps the most controversial tax proposals of recent years. These would be proposals to tax sugared soft drinks, which have been identified as an important causal factor in the obesity epidemic. Over the vociferous objections of libertarians and others, such a tax was recently enacted by the city of Washington, D.C. The Senate Finance Committee considered and rejected a similar tax during its search for ways to pay for the Obama administration's health care reform legislation. And former New York Governor David Paterson unsuccessfully proposed such a tax as he desperately sought additional revenue to bridge the state's huge budget deficit.

Critics of soda taxes regard them as the ultimate intrusion by the nanny state. The case for them is indeed different from the case for taxes on behavior that causes harm to others. People who become obese from drinking too many sodas fortified with high-fructose corn syrup are also more likely to suffer from diabetes and heart disease. They're more likely to have their feet amputated. They're more likely to die prematurely. But these are primarily costs that the soda drinker imposes on his future self, not others. To be sure, medical complications from excessive corn syrup consumption often require treatment at public expense. But much of this expense is in lieu of similar end-of-life medical expenses that would be incurred if the soda drinkers had lived a normal lifespan. And as many economists have pointed out, premature deaths actually spare the government billions of dollars in Social Security payments.

In short, taxing sugared drinks is closer to a pure form of paternalism than taxing behaviors that pose direct threats to others. Yet there can be little doubt that soda taxes would change behavior in ways that would please many taxpayers themselves. As discussed in chapter 2, for example, evidence suggests a persistent human tendency to place too much emphasis on immediate costs and benefits, and too little on those that occur with uncertainty or delay. Most people who consume sugared soft drinks do so because they taste good, not because they want their future selves to be obese. Years later, if a tax had led them to reduce their consumption of these beverages, few would look back on that fact with regret.

From a behavioral perspective, the future self is in many respects a more separate person from the current self than a perfect stranger is. Suppose, for example, that the *immediate* consequence of drinking sugared sodas were to require amputation of a perfect stranger's foot because of diabetes-impaired circulation. If that causal connection were clear, almost no one would drink too many sugared sodas. But concern to avoid harm restrains behavior much less forcefully when the victim is the distant future self and the damage is uncertain.

Arguing against soda taxes, the economist Greg Mankiw worries that to approve them would be to embark on a slippery slope. Thus, he wrote, "Taxing soda may encourage better nutrition and benefit our future selves. But so could taxing candy, ice cream and fried foods. Subsidizing broccoli, gym memberships and dental floss comes next. Taxing mindless television shows and subsidizing serious literature cannot be far behind."[13]

It's a legitimate concern. But we're forced to go part way down slippery slopes all the time. It's a concern we can set to one side until we have traveled further down this particular slope. Consuming large quantities of soda laced with high-fructose corn syrup clearly causes substantial harm. And as long as we're continuing to tax saving, job creation, and other beneficial activities, the case for replacing such taxes with taxes on harmful activities is compelling.

TWELVE

The Libertarian's Objections Reconsidered

DIFFERENT PEOPLE HAVE DIFFERENT VISIONS of the good life. Although almost everyone values personal autonomy, for example, libertarians value it far more than most. Even the staunchest libertarian, however, chooses to sacrifice many valuable options every day in pursuit of others. If you're a salaried employee, you must adhere to someone else's schedule and do many things you may not feel like doing. Even if you're in business for yourself, your time is never completely your own. But you accept that fact, because the resulting income enables you to pursue a host of other valuable options.

In short, complete autonomy is an unattainable limiting case. The challenge for libertarians, as for others, is to achieve the most highly valued mix of options.

The direct effect of paying a tax—any tax—is to reduce your autonomy, because you can no longer use the same money for other things you want to do. That fact alone, however, does not mean that the tax diminishes the total value of your options. That would depend on a host of factors—most notably, on how the value of what's purchased with the tax compares with the value of what you'd have bought with the same money. Notwithstanding the rhetorical force of "it's your money . . ." slogans to the contrary, many public services deliver high value. And as we saw in the preceding chapter, many taxes confer the added benefit of discouraging activities that cause more harm than good.

As noted repeatedly, the primary source of our political paralysis in recent decades has been a collection of slogans that completely misrepresent the true nature of the actual choices we face. Although such slogans have come from diverse sources, many of the most damaging ones have come from antigovernment activists who insist that the state has no legitimate right to limit individual freedom in any way. Yet no rational person would want to live in a country in which people enjoyed complete freedom to do as they please.

My aim in this chapter will be to explore what sorts of state-imposed limitations on personal autonomy a rational libertarian ought to be willing to accept. By "rational libertarian" I have in mind a person who values personal autonomy intensely and ranks available options according to how well they fulfill her goals. I make no presumption about what those goals might be. A libertarian's only aim, for example, might be to consume as much as possible, or amass the biggest fortune. But she might also want to assist others in need, or become a spiritual healer, or enter politics. The specific question then is, "If all options were open, what kind of society would a rational libertarian choose to join?"

The "rational" qualifier is important. Some people are content to reject arrangements that best serve their goals, on the grounds that they violate some abstract principle. The arguments I'll advance in this chapter will not persuade such people. But I believe they should persuade rational libertarians that the social institutions that would best promote their goals would closely resemble those we see in most modern industrial democracies. Many of those same institutions would of course be completely impermissible under libertarian dogma.

Coase Revisited

The framework suggested by the economist Ronald Coase, discussed at length in chapter 6, provides a useful way of thinking about the issues at hand. To recapitulate briefly, Coase began with the observation that activities that cause harm to others are reciprocal in nature. Tom may emit smoke that harms Sam, for example, but in most cases, harming Sam wasn't Tom's intent. He was just trying to achieve his goals in the cheapest way possible. If we prevent Tom from emitting smoke, we harm Tom. Coase's revolutionary insight was that Tom and Sam have a shared interest in minimizing the total harm suffered by both parties.

As discussed in chapter 6, careful study of Coase's work leaves no doubt that he believed that practical barriers often prevent parties from negotiating private solutions to externalities. But the first step in his analysis was to ask how events would unfold in the absence of such barriers. What would happen, he asked, if there were no costs of negotiating, no costs of writing or enforcing contracts, and no other roadblocks that could prevent people from discussing how to solve their problems?

Coase argued that under such conditions, people would always implement efficient solutions. If the cost to Tom of removing the smoke were less than the harm to Sam, for example, he'd remove it, whether the law required him to or not. If the law did not hold Tom liable for damages, he'd be free to pollute with impunity. But rather than see that happen, it would be in Sam's interest to pay Tom to remove the smoke.

Alternatively, if it were less costly for Sam to escape the damage by moving upwind, then he'd move. If the law held Tom liable for smoke damage, Sam could stay put and be reimbursed for whatever injury he suffered. But in that case, it would be cheaper for Tom to pay Sam to move.

The important point is that failure to agree to the most efficient solution would leave each party worse off. The Coase framework casts in sharp relief an underappreciated link between efficiency and autonomy. Because this link is important, it will facilitate discussion to state it explicitly:

Personal autonomy will always be compromised unless all problems stemming from activities that cause harm to others are resolved efficiently.

An Illustrative Example

A simple example demonstrates why this must be so, and in the process helps clarify what it means to solve a problem efficiently. Suppose that Tom and Sam are considering whether to share a two-bedroom apartment that rents for $3,000 a month. Their alternative is for each to rent a one-bedroom apartment for $2,000 a month. Rent aside, they'd be indifferent between the two options except for the fact that Tom is a smoker and Sam dislikes being exposed to smoke. If they lived in separate apartments, this problem would not arise. So the question is whether the rent savings from sharing an apartment would be sufficient to compensate for the smoke problem.

To answer that question, we'll need to know how strongly Tom feels about being able to smoke and how strongly Sam feels about living in a smoke-free environment. As discussed in chapter 7, the best available metric for assessing the strength of such feelings is the amount they'd be willing to pay for what they want. Let's suppose that Tom would be willing to pay $800 a month rather than abstain from smoking at home and that living in a smoke-free environment is worth $1,600 a month to Sam. (For the sake of simplicity, I'll take these assessments at face value, ignoring the possibility that Tom might welcome an incentive to give up smoking.)

The two men confront a standard cost-benefit problem. By sharing a two-bedroom apartment, their $3,000 in total monthly rent would be $1,000 lower than the combined rent they'd pay for separate one-bedroom apartments. The benefit of living together is thus $1,000 a month. What's the cost? Since being able to smoke in the apartment is worth only $800 a month to Tom but would cause $1,600 a month in damage to Sam, the efficient solution if they share living space would be for Tom not to smoke at home. His cost of making that accommodation is $800 a month, the amount he'd be willing to pay to continue smoking. So the cost of sharing living space is $800 a month.

Since the benefit of living together is $1,000 a month and the cost is only $800, they'll have an additional economic surplus of $200 to divide if they share the two-bedroom apartment under an agreement that prevents Tom from smoking at home. If they decide to split that surplus equally, they'll apportion the rent so that each man ends up $100 a month better off than he'd have been by living alone.

Since Sam is indifferent between living alone and living together, except for the smoke problem, he'd be $100 a month better off in the two-bedroom apartment if his share of the rent were $1,900 (since that's $100 less than he'd pay for a one-bedroom apartment, where he'd also be smoke-free). Tom, for his part, would be $100 a month better off in the two-bedroom apartment if his share of the rent were $1,100. That's $900 less than he'd pay in a one-bedroom apartment, but he'd need $800 of that savings to compensate for the fact that he can no longer smoke at home.

As discussed in chapter 7, these valuations typically depend in part on how much income the parties have. In this example, Sam might have been willing to pay more to avoid smoke than Tom was willing to pay to continue smoking simply because Sam had more income than Tom. Critics on the left often object to the cost-benefit test because it employs valuations that depend on people's ability to pay. Why, they ask, should rich people be advantaged in this way? The answer, as we saw in chapter 7, is that participants themselves get outcomes they like better when costs and benefits are measured by willingness to pay. Using any other valuations could preclude transactions that both parties would want to go forward.

For example, suppose a dictator decreed that differences in willingness to pay based on income differences be ignored in decisions like the one facing Tom and Sam. If the two men had been required to split the rent equally for a shared apartment, Tom would never have agreed to share living space in the first place. Rather than pay $1,500 a month to share a two-bedroom apartment in which he couldn't smoke, he'd have preferred to live alone for $2,000.

Sharing the two-bedroom apartment on the terms described creates a clear gain for each party. There's no coherent sense in which those terms could be said to violate anyone's rights. After all, each man had the right to live alone, so could have easily avoided the arrangement if he'd wanted to. It would thus make no sense for Tom to complain that he no longer has the option of smoking at home. That's true, but he received more than adequate compensation for that fact by saving $900 a month in rent. Nor would it make sense for Sam to complain that he's paying an unfairly high share of the rent. Tom needed to give up something he valued to make the joint living arrangement worthwhile, and he wouldn't have agreed to do that if Sam's share of the rent had been significantly smaller.

In light of the alternatives they faced, an arrangement like the one described—compromises and all—creates the maximum possible degree of autonomy for the two men. Autonomy is about being able to do what you want to do. The shared living arrangement doesn't require Sam to give up anything he values. And by putting an additional $100 a month in his pocket, it makes the list of things he can do longer than before. Tom's agreement not to smoke at home was a significant sacrifice in his eyes, yes. But he received something he valued even more in return—namely an extra $900 a month to spend. So while the list of things he can now do is missing an important element, it has additional elements that he considers more valuable than the one he gave up. So he, too, enjoys greater autonomy.

The point I stress from this example is that it's in *everyone's* interest to arrive at efficient solutions to any problem that stems from activities that cause harm to others. It doesn't matter what the problem is. It can be smoke. It can be noise. Or it can be a positional arms race for access to the best schools. It doesn't matter who the actors are. They can be Republicans or Democrats, Catholics or Protestants, high school dropouts or college graduates. They can be rational libertarians or Tea Party members.

The example just discussed highlights the importance of Coase's observation that externalities are reciprocal. Tom, who wants to smoke at home, is not a perpetrator. Sam, who wants smoke-free living quarters, is not a victim. The two simply confront a problem that it is in their interest to solve as cheaply as they can. Until people implement efficient solutions to the problems confronting them, it will always be possible to rearrange things so that each person has a new list of options that she likes better than the one she had before—in short, so that everyone has more autonomy. Again, efficiency is a prerequisite for maximum autonomy.

A Thought Experiment

With that point in mind, let's consider some specific examples of the kinds of regulations a rational libertarian might willingly embrace. Astute readers may have noticed that the apartment-sharing example resembles the society-formation example discussed in chapter 8. As in the earlier exercise, let's again imagine that you and 999 others have just emerged from an ark after an epic flood that destroyed all existing social arrangements. Your assignment is to form societies and begin civilization anew.

The terms of this exercise are again designed to be maximally advantageous to persons who care strongly about personal autonomy. Most important, membership in each new society is strictly voluntary. No one can make you join a society against your wishes, and the rules of each society will be enacted only in accordance with procedures to which each and every member of that society has agreed.

You, a rational libertarian, and the 999 others represent a random sample from the distribution of human talent and temperament. You and a much smaller number of others like you are from the extreme tail of that distribution in terms of your desire for autonomy. By temperament, you're extreme libertarians, but you're not ideologues. If you join a society that limits your freedom of action, it will be only because you saw it as in your interest to accept those limits.

As before, every society that forms is entitled to a proportional share of the land and other property that survived the flood. A society composed of one hundred persons, for example, would constitute 10 percent of the world's population and would thus claim 10 percent of all existing land and other property. How that property is to be distributed is for the members themselves to resolve. They might give everyone an equal share. Or they might distribute only a small portion of the property in advance, and then allow members to purchase the rest with whatever money they receive under the distribution rules they adopt. Or they could form a society in which all property was held in common in perpetuity. All options are on the table.

Talent and temperament are again assumed to be perfectly observable, so you'd know whom you'd be joining. Once you and others agree to form a society, you're free to earn as much as your efforts and abilities permit under the rules adopted.

As discussed in chapter 8, important outcomes hinge on the identities of those you choose to join. If most of them were highly productive, your society would be able to purchase more and better public goods than would be possible if they were less productive. But there would also be a downside, which is that you'd be at a disadvantage in the bidding for positional goods. Only a fraction of the home sites in any society have views, for example, and if most people find views desirable, you'd be unlikely to get one if you were one of society's least productive members.

In chapter 8, I argued that such considerations would be only one among many factors that might incline people to favor some degree of progressivity in the tax systems they adopt. If a rational libertarian wants to form a society with less productive others, thereby to gain advantage in the bidding for positional goods, those others might respond by demanding compensation through the tax system. It would then be up to the libertarian to decide whether joining on those terms was attractive.

In light of the dismal history of the communist and other collectivist economies, participants in this exercise might well agree to relegate the production of most goods and services to private markets. But as we saw in chapter 9, income prospects in competitive markets are inherently uncertain. Minuscule differences in talent or performance and seemingly unimportant random events often give rise to enormous differences in market rewards. Reflecting on that fact, even a rational libertarian might wish to consider supplementing market incomes with some form of social safety net. Once members have agreed to the institutions and governing rules for their societies, however, they're free to spend their incomes as they wish.

I note in passing that this exercise is in at least one important respect very different from the famous thought experiment proposed by the moral philosopher John Rawls.[1] Rawls asked readers to imagine themselves behind a veil of ignorance that shielded them from knowing what their own talents and temperaments were. He argued that distribution rules chosen from behind such a veil would be presumptively fair, since people wouldn't know which particular rules would work to their advantage. Rawls argued that rules chosen under these circumstances would permit an increase in income inequality only if it served to raise the income of society's poorest member. Although others have argued that most people behind a veil of ignorance would permit more inequality than that, there is broad agreement that the Rawlsian thought experiment provides a strong rationale for taking aggressive steps to limit inequality.

One could argue that the exercise I propose is unfair because people know their talent levels in advance and therefore have the power to exclude those unlucky enough to be born without much talent. It's a cogent objection. But unlike the Rawlsian exercise, the purpose of mine isn't to describe what a fair society would look like. It's to describe what kind of society a rational libertarian would choose to join. I make no claim that society *should* be structured to resemble one that a rational libertarian would want to join. Rather, my claim is that such a society would be strikingly similar to the modern welfare state.

Might the mythical John Galt, protagonist of Ayn Rand's novel *Atlas Shrugged*, voluntarily join a society like that? Rand said she wrote her novel "to show how desperately the world needs prime movers and how viciously it treats them."[2] But the exercise I'm proposing puts libertarian prime movers in the catbird's seat. John Galt would have no reason to fear vicious treatment. But even though the exercise is stacked heavily in his favor, the power it accords him is primarily defensive in nature. He can avoid distasteful terms that others might want to impose on him. But he cannot dictate terms to others.

Practical Reasons for Compromise

At the outset, a rational libertarian will dismiss out of hand the movement libertarian's claim that all taxation is theft. In addition to national defense, a host of other goods that we value can't be produced, or can't be produced well, by the private sector. Private toll roads are economical under some circumstances, for example, but erecting tollbooths at every intersection of a dense urban grid would be impractical. It's much more effective to have government build and maintain those roads with tax revenue. A rational libertarian will also accept the fact that taxation must be mandatory. Voluntary tax contributions would generate nowhere near enough revenue to provide the public goods and services we want.

The most compelling reason for a rational libertarian to consider compromise in this exercise is the advantage inherent in larger populations.
As discussed in chapter 8, for example, a common feature of many public
goods is that they must be provided in the same quantity and quality for
all citizens. The more citizens there are to share their costs, the cheaper
they become for everyone. A rational libertarian might thus choose to join
others in a society even if he knew they favored a somewhat different mix
of public goods and services than he did. The obvious downside would
be that he'd have to make tax payments to support some public goods
he didn't favor. But there would also be a larger population to share the
cost of the public goods he wanted, which might make his taxes lower on
balance.

John Galt and kindred spirits might dream of a society populated only by
prime movers like themselves, for there would then be no need for compromise. On brief reflection, however, they'd surely have second thoughts.
Who'd launder their shirts in a society like that? Who'd respond when their
houses caught fire? Who'd collect their garbage? Having to spend a good
portion of their days performing such tasks for themselves would actually
constitute a serious sacrifice in autonomy.

One of Adam Smith's most profound insights was that production often
grows explosively when we divide tasks and specialize. Consider, for example, his widely quoted account of how specialization led to a several-
hundredfold increase in productivity in an eighteenth-century Scottish pin
factory:

> One man draws out the wire, another straightens it, a third cuts it, a
> fourth points it, a fifth grinds it at the top for receiving the head; to make
> the head requires two or three distinct operations. . . . I have seen a small
> manufactory of this kind where only ten men were employed . . . [who]
> could, when they exerted themselves, make among them about twelve
> pounds of pins in a day. There are in a pound upwards of four thousand
> pins of middling size. Those ten persons, therefore, could make among
> them upwards of forty-eight thousand pins in a day. Each person, there-
> fore, making a tenth part of forty-eight thousand pins, might be consid-

ered as making four thousand eight hundred pins in a day. But if they had all wrought separately and independently, and without any of them having been educated to this peculiar business, they certainly could not each of them have made twenty, perhaps not one pin in a day.[3]

But Smith also realized that the full advantages of such specialization are possible only with sufficient population density. Thus, he wrote,

> As it is the power of exchanging that gives occasion to the division of labour, so the extent of this division must always be limited by the extent of that power, or, in other words, by the extent of the market. . . . In the lone houses and very small villages which are scattered about in so desert a country as the highlands of Scotland, every farmer must be butcher, baker, and brewer, for his own family. In such situations we can scarce expect to find even a smith, a carpenter, or a mason, within less than twenty miles of another of the same trade. The scattered families that live at eight or ten miles distance from the nearest of them, must learn to perform themselves a great number of little pieces of work, for which, in more populous countries, they would call in the assistance of those workmen. . . . A country carpenter . . . is not only a carpenter, but a joiner, a cabinet-maker, and even a carver in wood, as well as a wheel-wright, a plough-wright, a cart and waggon-maker.[4]

I'm assuming, plausibly, that libertarians constitute only a small proportion of the thousand people charged with forming new societies in this exercise. Even if the number of people involved in the exercise were considerably larger, John Galt would relegate himself to a very small society indeed if he were unwilling to join one that included people with views different from his own. Unless we're willing to dismiss the logic of Adam Smith's claim that division and specialization of labor constitute the foundation of economic prosperity, we're forced to conclude that a society consisting only of staunch libertarians would also be a very poor society, at least in comparison to others with significantly larger populations.

Would John Galt Agree to a Mandatory Savings Program?

With that fact in mind, let's confront John Galt with the decision of whether to join a group whose members share his views except for those on one particular issue, the question of whether to adopt a mandatory savings program. The group wants to raise all tax rates 10 percent and deposit the additional revenue in savings accounts for each citizen that would be accessible only after retirement. They favor this program not because they believe themselves to be shortsighted or irrational. Nor is it their aim to make life more difficult for libertarians. Rather, they want the program because they believe it will mitigate the consequences of a positional arms race for houses in neighborhoods served by good schools.

As noted repeatedly, a good school is a relative concept. It's one that is better than other schools in the same environment. Most parents want their children to attend such schools, but only 50 percent of all students can attend schools in the top half of the quality distribution at any moment, no matter how much parents bid for houses in good school districts.

The upshot is that young parents confront a painful dilemma. They can save enough while young to support a comfortable standard of living in retirement, or they can use most of their savings to bid for a house in a better school district. The problem, as discussed earlier, is that when all raid their savings, they succeed only in bidding up the price of access to good schools. The group wants to mitigate this problem by placing part of their current income in savings accounts that are beyond their reach until retirement.

Let's suppose John Galt and his fellow libertarians are initially offended by the very idea of this proposal. Ignoring Coase's insight that externalities are reciprocal, they ask, "What right does the government have to force us to save?" The others, however, are unmoved by the objection and declare their intention to go ahead with the plan, with or without the libertarians. I'll suppose that there's no other large group Galt and his friends could join that would reject this proposal. Their choice, then, is to form a small society on their own in which they retain the right to decide for themselves how much to save each month, or else join a much larger society in which they'd be forced to save at least a certain amount each month.

If they joined the larger society, they'd be able to share the costs of public goods and services with more people. Also, the mandatory savings tax isn't like other taxes, because the money would be invested in accounts with their names on them. At retirement, they'd get every cent back, plus the compound interest that had accumulated. Because of greater division and specialization of labor, they'd also enjoy substantially higher pretax incomes. In all probability, then, their after-tax incomes would be substantially higher in the larger society. If their weekly income net of the savings tax and all other taxes would be higher if they joined the larger society, on what grounds could it be rational for them not to?

To protect their autonomy? That would indeed be a strange conception of autonomy. If they'd have more disposable income in the larger society (even neglecting the fact that they'd be getting the mandatory savings deposits back at retirement), and no additional restrictions, they'd actually have much more autonomy in the larger society.

Safety Regulation

The same logic would apply if the only disagreement were that the larger group wanted to regulate workplace safety. Galt and his friends might point out that such regulations would deprive them of the right to decide for themselves whether to accept additional risk for higher pay. Yes, but the larger group doesn't desire these restrictions because they're know-it-all busybodies. They want them because of the fundamental Darwinian conflict between individual and group incentives with respect to risky choices. As discussed in chapter 3, riskier jobs pay more because safety devices cost money. So if some workers accept riskier jobs, they're able to increase their bidding for houses in better school districts, a trade that makes perfect sense to them as individuals. Yet when all make the same move, the result they'd hoped for doesn't materialize. As when people deplete their savings, the end result is simply to bid up the prices of houses in the better school districts.

Galt and his friends remain skeptical. The fact remains, however, that the proportion of people who want to regulate safety is much higher than the proportion who don't. Because a larger society can achieve greater division and specialization of labor and share the cost of public goods more broadly, it's hardly fanciful to imagine that the after-tax wage in the safer jobs in the larger society would actually be higher than the after-tax wage in the more dangerous jobs in the smaller society that doesn't regulate safety.

Galt and his friends may still refuse to join, claiming that autonomy matters more than anything else to them. But in so doing, they will have revealed themselves to be irrational. No rational persons who value autonomy above all else would choose an option under which they enjoy considerably less autonomy than they could have had. The safer jobs in the larger society would have made them less likely to lose their autonomy to crippling accidents. The higher after-tax incomes in the larger society would have broadened their options in countless other ways. They'd have had more choices about where to vacation, more choices about where to go out for dinner. They'd have had the options of working fewer hours each week, or of retiring earlier. And so on.

There are many competing definitions of rationality in philosophy and economics. But almost all versions of the concept require that a rational person pursue his goals in the most efficient manner available. If Galt and his friends opt for lower autonomy because they're unwilling to yield to the majority's positions on issues like savings or safety, we're forced to conclude either that they're irrational or else that they don't really value autonomy nearly as much as they claim to.

What about Rights?

"People have rights" is the opening sentence in *Anarchy, State, and Utopia*, the philosopher Robert Nozick's landmark defense of the libertarian position.[5] Many libertarians will object that my exercise demonstrates only that majorities often have the power to run roughshod over minorities. Majorities often do have that power, to be sure. To prevent them from abusing it, the constitutions of all successful civilizations enshrine many specific individual rights. No country, for example, grants anyone the right to kill you, or steal your car, or prevent you from voting. Many societies grant wide latitude for public speech, even when people say things that deeply offend the majority. But giving the majority what it wants is not always, or even generally, a violation of anyone's rights.

Again, regulations are data. No country has chosen to make it unconstitutional to regulate savings. Nor has any country declared it unconstitutional to regulate safety. Those observations may tell us something. If libertarians want to assert that people have a right to be exempt from such regulations, they must accept the burden of explaining where that right comes from.

Someone is going to be disadvantaged no matter which way these contested issues are resolved. In the case of savings, for example, refusal to regulate means that many will enter retirement with insufficient savings. But if we regulate savings, some will be forced to save more than they wish to. In the case of safety, refusal to regulate means that some will feel compelled to take excessive risks. But if we regulate, some will have to buy more safety than they want to. If libertarians insist that concern for the second group in each case should trump concern for the first, they must explain why.

Deciding whether to join a society with others who favor some rules you don't like is obviously different from deciding whether to share an apartment with someone who smokes. But for present purposes, the decisions have two important elements in common. Note first the importance of economies of scale in each. Sharing space with others—either in an apartment or in a society—typically entails having to compromise, but the resulting cost savings can easily make those compromises worth accepting.

Second, note that in both examples, monetary valuations provide the common metric for identifying the most efficient ways to limit harm. As discussed in chapter 7, these valuations typically depend in part on how much income the parties have. But given their incomes, it's those valuations that *should* be used for assigning weights. As noted earlier, using any other valuations could preclude transactions that all parties would want to go forward.

Some libertarians may object that the Coase framework's emphasis on cost-benefit analysis isn't necessarily appropriate for all matters pertaining to human rights. Perhaps so. But we're not talking about all matters pertaining to human rights. We're talking about everyday public policy decisions, each one of which typically has only a small impact on anyone's lifetime wealth.

People are long-lived creatures. During a typical lifetime, everyone will be affected by literally tens of thousands of public policy decisions. Taking only those actions whose benefits exceed their costs doesn't guarantee that each person will receive net benefits from every policy adopted. Every change generates both winners and losers. But if the cost-benefit test is the decision rule, virtually everyone will come out a net winner in the long run. It's like taking a favorable gamble thousands of times. Heads you win $4, tails you lose $3. You could lose several times in a row. But if the coin is unbiased and you flip it thousands of times, you're virtually certain to come out ahead.

Would anyone be unfairly disadvantaged by using the cost-benefit test as society's decision rule? Since costs and benefits are measured by willingness to pay, the preferences of people with higher incomes tend to receive greater weight, because high-income people are generally willing to pay more for what they want. That could be a problem if the things they want are systematically different from what others want, which is undoubtedly so in many domains.

As discussed in chapter 7, however, if low-income people have the power to reject the cost-benefit approach—as they could in this exercise by refusing to join any society that proposed to use it—they could always do better by accepting it in return for additional income transfers. And because having a larger, more diverse society makes increased division and specialization of labor possible, it would be in the interest of others to make that concession. But once the bargain was struck, willingness to pay would be the relevant metric for weighing different alternatives.

The bottom line is that if society's rules don't make the total economic pie as large as possible, they squander an opportunity to enhance the personal autonomy of every citizen. Again, when the economic pie is larger, it's always possible for everyone to have a larger slice than before, and that means having the option to do more things.

Libertarians would thus have cogent reasons for agreeing to form broader coalitions than they could if they excluded others with different views. The advantage would be that per-capita incomes would be significantly higher than in the necessarily smaller coalitions consisting only of libertarians. They'd have to abide by rules that eliminate certain options or make them more expensive, as in the examples of mandatory savings and safety regulation just discussed. But they'd also enjoy many new options. If the new ones were of greater value than those sacrificed, as they almost surely would be in the context of the savings and safety examples, it would be irrational for libertarians not to join.

People are not, of course, free to form new societies whenever it suits them. As a practical matter, almost everyone is born into an existing society, and it would be a formidable hurdle indeed to try to organize a new one. Life as we know it is thus like the second variant of Coase's framework, in which transaction costs make it impractical to negotiate efficient private solutions to problems caused by externalities. In such cases, Coase suggested, society should define property rights and adopt institutions that would steer parties toward the solutions they'd have agreed to among themselves if negotiation had been practical.

Here again, his framework emphasizes the importance of efficiency. It suggests, for example, that if one group wants to regulate workplace safety but another doesn't, the question should be resolved by comparing how much the opposing sides are willing to pay to have things their way.

Safety regulations have their greatest impact on workers at the lower end of the income scale. Libertarian prime movers like John Galt typically work under much safer conditions than those required by regulation. Rational libertarians should thus be willing to pay very little to avoid safety regulation. And since the workers who favor safety regulation greatly outnumber the libertarians who oppose it, the cost-benefit test would almost surely rule in favor of safety regulation.

Libertarians might object that it violates their right to decide for themselves how much safety to buy. But defending that right means denying others the right to limit the amount of risk they permit themselves to take. Libertarians need to explain why the first right is more important to defend than the second.

If rational libertarians would indeed have chosen to join the larger group that wanted safety regulation in a world with zero transaction costs, how can they then insist that safety regulation robs them of an essential right? The high transaction costs of the world we live in mean that one group or the other will not be able to get what it wants. What argument can libertarians offer to explain why wishes of the larger group should be discounted? How could a group that claims to celebrate freedom above all else argue for a result that people never would have endorsed in an environment in which everyone had complete freedom of choice? Could there possibly be some other framework for thinking about rights that would be more congenial to a libertarian's ear than Coase's framework? What would it be? A religious text? If so, which one?

A Libertarian Welfare State?

A rational libertarian who reflects carefully about the traditional libertarian position will find it difficult to defend. I have granted every traditional libertarian assumption—that markets are perfectly competitive, that consumers are essentially rational, and that government may not restrict behavior except to prevent undue harm to others. To this list I have added only one substantive element namely the completely uncontroversial observation that many important aspects of life are graded on the curve. It's that observation that causes the traditional libertarian position to collapse.

The link between reward and relative performance underlies the divergence between Adam Smith's view of the competitive process and Charles Darwin's—or, more accurately, the divergence between Smith's modern disciples' view and Darwin's. The former believe that competitive forces channel greedy individuals to behave in ways that produce maximum advantage for society as a whole. Darwin, in contrast, understood that competition molded behavior in ways that benefit the individual. As we saw in chapter 2, such behaviors sometimes benefit society as a whole, but not always. In particular, when individual payoffs depend on relative position, individual and collective interests generally diverge.

If positional competition, not exploitation by powerful employers, is what leads workers to accept excessive risk, libertarians cannot argue that safety regulation robs them of their right to choose individually. Intelligent libertarians know better than to object to a military arms control agreement on the grounds that it limits signatories' freedom to build as many bombs as they want to. That's the explicit rationale for such agreements. Those who sign them realize they'll build too many bombs if they're free to choose individually. Safety regulation is a positional arms control agreement, so of course it limits individual choice. That's exactly what those whose own choices it limits want it to do!

In arenas in which reward depends on relative performance, we invariably see positional arms races. And almost without exception, participants adopt positional arms control agreements that limit what would otherwise be mutually offsetting expenditures. As noted earlier, auto racing associations limit engine displacement; sports leagues impose roster limits; school districts impose mandatory kindergarten start dates; and so on. To object to such constraints on the grounds that they limit individual freedom is to miss the point entirely.

Some libertarians insist that relative position isn't very important to most people. But that's a losing argument. Even a minimally competent and informed debater could demolish it without effort. Libertarians must eventually concede that relative position matters, but many may still want to insist that it shouldn't. They'll object that allowing public policy to be shaped by positional concerns would be to legitimize and encourage negative emotions like jealousy and envy. We discount the preferences of sadists and masochists in the design of public policy, they'll say, and we should also discount any preferences that stem from jealousy and envy.

But that's a losing argument, too, because positional concerns exist quite apart from such emotions. It's an incontestable property of the human nervous system that evaluation is shaped by context. Unless a car is faster than most other cars in the same local environment, it won't seem fast. If a house is significantly smaller than most other houses in a local environment, it will seem small, irrespective of its absolute size. As we saw in chapter 5, when context shapes evaluation more in some domains than others, spending patterns are distorted. People spend too much on context-sensitive categories like houses, jewelry, and cars, and too little on less context-sensitive categories like safety, savings, and leisure. Those same distortions would be present in a world completely devoid of jealousy or envy.

Libertarians might continue to insist that progressive taxation violates their rights. But as we saw in chapter 8, any other form of taxation would deprive the most prosperous members of society of the mix of public and private goods and services they'd most prefer. Libertarians might insist that higher taxes on the most prosperous members of society will make the economic pie smaller. But as we saw in chapter 10, there is little evidence for that position. On the contrary, as we saw in chapter 11, a well-designed tax system actually makes the economic pie larger, by discouraging behaviors that cause more harm than good. If we all spent a little less on weddings and coming-of-age parties, the people we celebrate would still feel just as special. If we all discharged fewer tons of CO_2 into the atmosphere, we could reduce the odds of catastrophic global climate change.

As John Stuart Mill maintained, the government may legitimately restrict individual behavior to prevent undue harm to others. But heavy-handed regulation is almost never the most effective means to that end. As our experience with pollution taxes has demonstrated, it's generally better to discourage harmful behavior by making it more expensive than by prohibiting it outright. Society's interest lies in reducing the total amount of harmful behavior, not in reducing harmful behavior by specific individuals. The tax approach keeps total costs to a minimum while restricting options as little as possible, because it concentrates harm reduction in the hands of those who accomplish it most cheaply.

Antitax, antigovernment rhetoric has prevented us from taking greater advantage of that simple insight. As we saw in chapter 4, some countries have reasonably honest governments that reliably deliver valued public goods and services. Every rational person would want to live under such a government. But good government doesn't just happen. It must be nurtured carefully. Starve-the-beast rhetoric surely hasn't helped us forge the kind of society most of us want to live in.

We need good government because individual and societal goals are often squarely in conflict. When they are, it's naïve to expect an invisible hand to produce good outcomes. The good news is that intelligent tax policy can often guide us to better outcomes unintrusively. Simply by taxing behaviors that cause harm to others, we could easily afford to maintain our roads and bridges without having to make any painful sacrifices in private consumption.

Although the traditional libertarian position does not withstand careful scrutiny, I was never under any illusion that theories or evidence would compel committed ideologues to change their minds. But in writing this book, my hope was that it might persuade at least some antigovernment activists to rethink their uncritical opposition to collective action. There remains a pivotal role in public debate for those who care most passionately about personal autonomy. Almost no one wants a government that tries to regulate every behavior that somebody, somewhere, might find annoying. A truly effective government would focus only on behaviors that cause real harm that others cannot easily avoid on their own. It would try to discourage those behaviors with the lightest touch possible.

To have a government like that would be to have a successful libertarian welfare state. To get there, we'll need a new generation of libertarians who are willing to accept legitimate restraints on their own behavior, while continuing to battle ferociously to prevent government from intruding any more than necessary.

Every generation has had its doomsayers. But unlike those of previous generations, who were mostly religious fanatics, ours are the planet's most distinguished scientists. They tell us there's a good chance we'll burn up if we don't act forcefully and quickly to reverse global warming. The policy instrument that would accomplish that goal is simple and well understood—essentially some variant of a stiff carbon tax. The costs we'd have to bear would be modest. Yet it appears we'll take no action.

What stands in our way are antitax, antigovernment zealots driven by a philosophy that, on close examination, collapses under its own weight. They're in control of the conversation at the moment, but they're not invincible. Win or lose, we should fight them. Looking back on it all, would you feel comfortable if you hadn't?

Cynical friends caution that I'm naïve to believe we can do better. I'm just tilting at windmills, they say. Perhaps. But as Cervantes reminds us in the words of Don Quixote, "Too much sanity may be madness—and the maddest of all—to see life as it is, and not as it ought to be."[6]

NOTES

Chapter One: Paralysis

1. John Maynard Keynes, *The General Theory of Employment, Interest, and Money,* Basingstoke, Hampshire, U.K.: Palgrave Macmillan, 2007 (originally published in 1936).

2. Nevada Department of Transportation, FAQs, http://www.nevadadot.com/about/faqs/.

3. *State of the Union with Candy Crowley,* interview with Mitch McConnell, CNN, July 18, 2010, http://transcripts.cnn.com/TRANSCRIPTS/1007/18/sotu.01.html.

4. A. P. Sokolov, P. H. Stone, C. E. Forest, R. Prinn, M. C. Sarofim, M. Webster, S. Paltsev, C. A. Schlosser, D. Kicklighter, S. Dutkiewicz, J. Reilly, C. Wang, B. Felzer, J. Mclillo, and H. D. Jacoby, "Probabilistic Forecast for 21st Century Climate Based on Uncertainties in Emissions (without Policy) and Climate Parameters," MIT Joint Program on the Science and Policy of Global Change, Report 169, January 2009.

5. Jane Mayer, "Covert Operations: The Billionaire Brothers Who Are Waging a War against Obama," *New Yorker,* August 30, 2010, pp. 44–55.

6. Adam Smith, *An Inquiry into the Nature and Causes of the Wealth of Nations,* State College, PA: Penn State University, 2005, p. 364 (originally published in 1776).

7. Ibid., p. 111.

8. For a comprehensive account of how laissez-faire enthusiasts have often misrepresented Adam Smith's positions, see Amartya Sen's introduction to the 250th-anniversary edition of Smith's *The Theory of Moral Sentiments,* New York: Penguin, 2009.

9. Charles Darwin, *The Origin of Species, 6th London Edition,* The Literature Project, 2000–2010. Modern biologists have pressed the claim that selection sometimes occurs at the group level. See, for example, David Sloan Wilson, *The Natural Selection of Populations and Communities.* Reading, MA: Benjamin Cummings, 1980; David Sloan Wilson, "The New Fable of the Bees," in *Advances in Austrian Economics,*

Vol. 9, Greenwich, CN: JAI Press, 2004, pp. 201–220; David Sloan Wilson and Edward O. Wilson, "Rethinking the Theoretical Foundation of Sociobiology," *Quarterly Review of Biology* 82, 2007: 327–348; and A. J. Field, "Why Multilevel Selection Matters," *Journal of Bioeconomics* 10, 2008: 203–238. For present purposes, the important point is that traits favored because they confer advantage at the individual level are often disadvantageous to larger groups.

10. Burney J. Le Boeuf, "Male-Male Competition and Reproductive Success in Elephant Seals," *American Zoologist* 14(1), 1974: 163–176.

11. Thomas C. Schelling, *Micromotives and Macrobehavior,* New York: W. W. Norton, 1978.

12. See, for example, Richard Thaler and Cass Sunstein, *Nudge,* New Haven, CT: Yale University Press, 2007.

13. John Stuart Mill, *On Liberty,* State College, PA: Penn State University, 1998 (originally published in 1859).

14. Others have offered cogent objections to the principle. See, for example, Joel Feinberg, *Harm to Others,* New York: Oxford University Press, 1987.

15. See, for example, the statement of Congressman Dan Burton (R, IN): http://burton.house.gov/issues/tax-reform.

Chapter Two: Darwin's Wedge

1. Adam Smith, *An Inquiry into the Nature and Causes of the Wealth of Nations,* State College, PA: Penn State University, 2005, p. 213 (originally published in 1776).

2. Galbraith developed these ideas in two widely discussed books, *The Affluent Society,* Boston: Houghton Mifflin, 1956, and *The New Industrial State,* Boston: Houghton Mifflin, 1967.

3. For a detailed history of the Edsel, see Thomas Bonsall, *Disaster in Dearborn: The Story of the Edsel,* Stanford, CA: General Books, 2002.

4. This claim merits qualification to the extent that it is *relative* speed among gazelles that determines which ones are caught and eaten. An old joke describes a camper who awoke to see his friend frantically putting on his running shoes as an angry bear approached their campsite. "Why bother?" he asked. "Don't you know there's no way you'll be able to outrun that bear?" "I don't have to outrun him," the friend responded, "I just need to outrun *you.*"

5. Richard H. Thaler and Cass R. Sunstein, *Nudge,* New Haven, CT: Yale University Press, 2007.

6. See, for example, Peter Richerson and Robert Boyd, *Not by Genes Alone: How Culture Transformed Human Evolution,* Chicago: University of Chicago Press, 2004.

7. See, for example, Richard Rorty, "The Brain as Hardware, Culture as Software," *Inquiry* 47(3), 2004: 219–235.

8. The question of how such motives might have evolved in relentlessly competitive environments was the subject of my 1988 book, *Passions within Reason: The Strategic Role of the Emotions,* New York: W. W. Norton.

9. For a detailed survey of this evidence, see chapter 2 of my 1985 book, *Choosing the Right Pond: Human Behavior and the Quest for Status,* New York: Oxford University Press.

10. For a review of studies of the relationships among local rank, serotonin, and testosterone, see Robert H. Frank, *Luxury Fever,* New York: Free Press, 1999, chapter 9.

11. Richard Easterlin, "Will Raising the Incomes of All Increase the Happiness of All?" *Journal of Economic Behavior and Organization* 27, 1995: 35–47. More recently, Betsy Stevenson and Justin Wolfers have shown that average happiness is also positively related to average income over time within countries, and across countries at any moment: "Economic Growth and Subjective Well-Being: Reassessing the Easterlin Paradox," *Brookings Papers on Economic Activity,* Spring 2008: 1–87.

12. Erzo Luttmer, "Neighbors as Negatives: Relative Earnings and Well-Being," *Quarterly Journal of Economics* 120(3), August 2005: 963–1002.

13. See chapter 8 of my 1985 book, *Choosing the Right Pond.*

14. See, for example, Ori Heffetz, "Conspicuous Consumption and the Visibility of Consumption Expenditures," Princeton University Department of Economics mimeo, 2004; Luis Rayo and Gary Becker, "Evolutionary Efficiency and Happiness," University of Chicago Department of Economics mimeo, 2004; and Laurie Simon Bagwell and Douglas Bernheim, "Veblen Effects in a Theory of Conspicuous Consumption," *American Economic Review* 86, June 1996: 349–373.

Chapter Three: No Cash on the Table

1. See, for example, Greg Hundley, "Why and When Are the Self-Employed More Satisfied with Their Work?" *Industrial Relations* 40(2), April 2001: 293–316; and Matthias Benz and Bruno S. Frey, "Being Independent Raises Happiness at Work," *Swedish Economic Policy Review* 11, 2004: 95–134.

2. See, for example, Andrew J. Oswald, Eugenio Proto, and Daniel Sgroi, "Happiness and Productivity," Department of Economics Working Paper, University of Warwick, March 2009, which extends earlier findings by Wright and Staw and that workers with happier dispositions tend to be more productive: T. A. Wright and B. A. Staw, "Affect and Favorable Work Outcomes: Two Longitudinal Tests of the Happy Productive Worker Thesis," *Journal of Organizational Behavior* 20, 1998: 1–23.

3. Sam Bowles, David Gordon, and David Weisskopf, *Beyond the Wasteland,* Garden City, NY: Anchor Doubleday, 1983, pp. 167, 168.

4. Herbert Gintis, "The Nature of the Labor Exchange and the Theory of Capitalist Production," *Review of Radical Political Economics* 8, 1976: 36–54.

5. Adam Smith, *An Inquiry into the Nature and Causes of the Wealth of Nations,* State College, PA: Penn State University, 2005, p. 19 (originally published in 1776).

6. For a discussion, see Benjamin Klein, Robert G. Crawford, and Armen A. Alchian, "Vertical Integration, Appropriable Rents, and the Competitive Contracting Process," *Journal of Law and Economics* 21, October 1978: 297–326.

7. For detailed discussions of Walmart's labor practices, see Steven Greenhouse, *The Big Squeeze,* New York: Knopf, 2008; and in Nelson Lichtenstein, *The Retail Revolution,* New York: Metropolitan, 2009.

8. On this point see Bethany Moreton, *To Serve God and Wal-Mart,* Cambridge, MA: Harvard University Press, 2009.

9. For a more detailed account of this explanation, see chapter 8 of my 1985 book, *Choosing the Right Pond: Human Behavior and the Quest for Status,* New York: Oxford University Press.

10. Richard Thaler and Cass Sunstein, *Nudge,* New Haven, CT: Yale University Press, 2007, p. 251.

11. Thomas C. Schelling, *Micromotives and Macrobehavior,* New York: W. W. Norton, 1978.

12. Karl Marx, *Capital,* New York: Modern Library, 1936, pp. 708–709.

13. See, for example, the title essay in my 2004 book, *What Price the Moral High Ground?* Princeton, NJ: Princeton University Press.

14. Paul Samuelson, "A Note on the Pure Theory of Consumers' Behaviour," *Economica* 5, 1938: 61–71.

Chapter Four: Starve the Beast—But Which One?

1. Ronald Utt, "The Bridge to Nowhere: A National Embarrassment," Heritage Foundation, October 20, 2005.

2. Project on Government Oversight, http://www.pogo.org/pogo-files/reports/national-security/defense-waste-fraud/ns-wds-19990901.html.

3. "Conservative Advocate," *Morning Edition,* National Public Radio, May 25, 2001, http://www.npr.org/templates/story/story.php?storyId=1123439.

4. Peter Schrag, *Paradise Lost: California's Experience, America's Future,* New York: New Press, 1998.

5. Ibid., p. 8.

6. For more extended discussion of these points, see B. C. Sheldon and S. Verhulst, "Ecological Immunology: Costly Parasite Defences and Tradeoffs in Evolutionary Ecology," *Trends in Ecology and Evolution* 11, 1996: 317–321.

7. For a persuasive argument that this problem has grown substantially worse in recent decades, see Robert Reich, *Supercapitalism,* New York: Vintage, 2007.

8. Adam Liptak, "Justices, 5-4, Reject Corporate Spending Limit," *New York Times,* January 21, 2010, http://www.nytimes.com/2010/01/22/us/politics/22scotus.html.

9. Lauren Etter, "Economic Crisis Forces Local Governments to Let Asphalt Roads Return to Gravel," WSJ.com, July 17, 2010, http://online.wsj.com/article/SB10001424052 748704913304575370950363737746.html.

10. "Oakland Road Commissioners Divert Money for 'Pothole Emergency,'" PR Newswire, April 19, 1997.

11. Bruce Van Voorst, "Why America Has So Many Potholes," *Time,* May 4, 1992, pp. 64–65.

12. John Maynard Keynes, *The General Theory of Employment, Interest, and Money,* Basingstoke, Hampshire, U.K.: Palgrave Macmillan, 2007 (originally published in 1936).

13. Lee Ohanian, "How Stimulating Is Stimulus?" Forbes.com, June 17, 2009, http://www.forbes.com/2009/06/16/stimulus-arra-government-spending-krugman-prescott-opinions-contributors-ohanian.html.

14. Peter A. Diamond, "A Framework for Social Security Analysis," *Journal of Public Economics* 8(3), December 1977: 275–298.

15. Etter, op. cit.

16. http://www.transparency.org/publications/publications.

17. http://www.transparency.org/policy_research/surveys_indices/cpi/2007.

18. Selim Algar and Andy Geller, "Daddy's $10M 'Bad' Mitzvah," *New York Post,* October 26, 2007, http://www.nypost.com/p/news/national/item_YOwmAGCrVERbnta G5BN2XO.

19. MaryEllen Fillo, "MTV's 'Sweet 16' show drives fad for lavish birthday parties," *Hartford Courant,* July 31, 2007, http://www2.ljworld.com/news/2007/jul/31/mtvs_sweet_16_show_drives_fad_lavish_birthday_part/.

20. Bethany Kandel, "With This Dress, I Thee Wed and Wed and Wed," *New York Times,* January 31, 2009, http://www.nytimes.com/2009/02/01/fashion/weddings/01field notes.html.

21. Sarah Wilkins, "For Richer, For Poorer," *Mother Jones,* January–February 2005, http://motherjones.com/politics/2005/01/richer-or-poorer.

22. For a more detailed survey of these distributional shifts, see my 2007 book, *Falling Behind: How Rising Inequality Harms the Middle Class,* Berkeley, CA: University of California Press.

23. Robert H. Frank, Adam Seth Levine, and Oege Dijk, "Expenditure Cascades," Social Science Research Network Working Paper, October 2010, http://papers.ssrn.com/sol3/papers.cfm?abstract_id=1690612.

24. Kelly Evans, "Size of New Homes Starts Shrinking as Builders Battle Housing Slump," *Wall Street Journal*, September 12, 2007, p. A1.

Chapter Five: Putting the Positional Consumption Beast on a Diet

1. Fred Hirsch, *Social Limits to Growth*, Cambridge, MA: Harvard University Press, 1976.

2. See, for example, chapter 7 in my *Falling Behind: How Rising Inequality Harms the Middle Class*, Berkeley, CA: University of California Press, 2007.

3. Other authors, however, have identified conditions under which positional concerns could lead to higher savings rates. See, for example, H. L. Cole, G. J. Mailath, and A. Postlewaite, "Social Norms, Savings Behavior, and Growth," *Journal of Political Economy* 100(6), 1992: 1092–1125; and Giacomo Corneo and Olivier Jeanne, "Social Organization, Status, and Savings Behavior," *Journal of Public Economics* 70(1), 1998: 37–51.

4. Again, see *Falling Behind*, op. cit., chapter 7.

5. See, for example, chapter 8 in my *Choosing the Right Pond: Human Behavior and the Quest for Status*, New York: Oxford University Press, 1985.

6. See, for example, Sara J. Solnick and David Hemenway, "Is More Always Better? A Survey on Positional Concerns," *Journal of Economic Behavior and Organization* 37, 1998: 373–383; Sara J. Solnick and David Hemenway, "Are Positional Concerns Stronger in Some Domains Than in Others?" *American Economic Review, Papers and Proceedings* 95, 2005: 147–151; F. Alpizar, F. Carlsson, and O. Johansson-Stenman, "How Much Do We Care about Absolute versus Relative Income and Consumption?" *Journal of Economic Behavior and Organization* 56, 2005: 405–421; and Charles Kerwin, Erik Hurst, and Nick Roussanov, "Conspicuous Consumption and Race," University of Chicago, mimeo, 2007, http://faculty.chicagogsb.edu/erik.hurst/research/race_consumption_april2007_applications.pdf.

7. Robert H. Frank, *Luxury Fever*, New York: Free Press, 1999; and Robert H. Frank, *Falling Behind*. Other authors have also discussed tax remedies for positional externalities. See, for example, Michael Boskin and Eytan Sheshinski, "Optimal Redistributive Taxation When Individual Welfare Depends on Relative Income," *Quarterly Journal of Economics* 92(4), 1978: 589–601; Yew Kwang Ng, "Diamonds Are a Government's Best Friend: Burden-Free Taxes on Goods Valued for Their Values," *American*

Economic Review 77(1), 1987: 186–191; Norman Ireland, "On Limiting the Market for Status Signals," *Journal of Public Economics* 53, 1994: 91–110; and Richard Layard, *Happiness: Lessons from a New Science,* London: Penguin, 2005.

8. For a detailed discussion, see Laurence Seidman, *The USA Tax: A Progressive Consumption Tax,* Cambridge, MA: MIT Press, 1997.

9. Loan repayments would be added to the savings total, thereby reducing potential tax liability. New borrowing would be subtracted from savings, increasing the potential tax. For homeowners annual housing consumption would be counted as the implicit rental value of their houses.

10. Robert H. Frank, "The Frame of Reference as a Public Good," *Economic Journal* 107, November 1997: 1832–1847.

11. Milton Friedman, "The Spendings Tax as a Wartime Fiscal Measure," *American Economic Review* 33(1), Part 1, March 1943: 50–62.

12. Laurence S. Seidman, *Pouring Liberal Wine into Conservative Bottles: Strategy and Policies,* Lanham, MD: University Press of America, 2006.

13. For example, annual consumption for a family that earned $2 million and saved $300,000 would be $1.7 million, and the surtax would be levied on $1.2 million, the amount by which the family's consumption exceeded $500,000.

Chapter Six: Perpetrators and Victims

1. See, for example, H. Kaplan and K. Hill, "Food Sharing among Ache Foragers: Tests of Explanatory Hypotheses," *Current Anthropology* 26, 1985: 223–246.

2. Even the outspoken Richard Epstein, an avowed libertarian on most issues, acknowledged the legitimacy of utilitarian constraints on some libertarian principles. See Richard A. Epstein, "Nuisance Law: Corrective Justice and Its Utilitarian Constraints," *Journal of Legal Studies* 8(1), 1979: 49–102.

3. A notable champion of the earlier view was A. C. Pigou, in *The Economics of Welfare,* 4th ed., London: Macmillan, 1932, http://www.econlib.org/library/NPDBooks/Pigou/pgEW.html.

4. Ronald H. Coase, "The Federal Communications Commission," *Journal of Law and Economics* 2, October 1959: 1–40.

5. Ibid., p. 26.

6. Ibid., p. 27.

7. http://econc10.bu.edu/economic_systems/Theory/Contemp/Coase.htm#Stigler.

8. Ronald H. Coase, "The Problem of Social Cost," *Journal of Law and Economics* 3, October 1960: 1–44.

9. See, for example, A. M. Diamond, "Most Cited Economic Papers and Current Research Fronts," *Journal of Citation Studies* 50, Part 2, 1989: 10–15.

10. Ronald H. Coase, "The Nature of the Firm," *Economica*, New Series, 4(16), November 1937: 386–405.

11. See, for example, Armen Alchian and Harold Demsetz, "Production, Information Costs, and Economic Organization," *American Economic Review* 62, December 1972: 777–795; Richard M. Cyert and James G. March, *A Behavioral Theory of the Firm*, Englewood Cliffs, NJ: Prentice-Hall, 1963; Michael Jensen and William Meckling, "Theory of the Firm: Managerial Behavior, Agency Costs and Ownership Structure," *Journal of Financial Economics* 3(4), 1976: 305–360; Sanford Grossman and Oliver Hart, "Takeover Bids, the Free-Rider Problem, and the Theory of the Corporation," *Bell Journal of Economics* 11, Spring 1980: 42–64; and Oliver Williamson, *Markets and Hierarchies: Analysis and Antitrust Implications*, New York: Free Press, 1975.

12. Libertarians who are critical of Coase's framework tend to focus on a presumed right of early arrivers to continue pursuing their activities without restriction. See, for example, Hans-Hermann Hoppe, "The Ethics and Economics of Private Property," chapter 2 in Enrico Colombatto, ed., *The Elgar Companion to the Economics of Property Rights*, Cheltenham, U.K.: Edward Elgar, 2004. But if granting such rights is efficient, defending them is of course consistent with Coase's framework.

13. See, for example, Steven Holmes and Cass R. Sunstein, *The Cost of Rights: Why Liberty Depends on Taxes*, New York: W. W. Norton, 1999.

14. My erudite Cornell colleague Robert Hockett reminds me that before coming to the United States, Coase had been a colleague of the British economist and über-consequentialist Nicholas Kaldor, a celebrated champion of cost-benefit analysis.

15. The example comes from Bernard Williams. See J.J.C. Smart and Bernard Williams, *Utilitarianism: For and Against*, Cambridge: Cambridge University Press, 1973.

16. *Loving v. Virginia*, 388 U.S. 1 (1967).

17. I summarize the evidence on this point in chapter 6 of *Luxury Fever*, New York: Free Press, 1999.

Chapter Seven: Efficiency Rules

1. Clinton Executive Order 12866, 3 CFR 638 (1993).

2. For convenience only, I assume here that the amount one is willing to pay to acquire an object is the same as the price at which one would be willing to sell it. In some settings, willingness to pay is significantly less than willingness to accept. But in such cases, the examples could be modified to make the same points by assuming that both values for one party exceed both values for the other. In cases in which valuations overlap, the "best" destination for a good may depend on where it starts out.

3. S. J. Pokharel, G. A. Bishop, and D. H. Stedman, "On-Road Remote Sensing of Automobile Emissions in the Los Angeles Area: Year 2 Final Report Prepared for CRC," March 2001, http://www.feat.biochem.du.edu/assets/databases/Cal/LA_year_2_CRC00.pdf; "CARB Throws a Hail-Mary Regulation," Patrick Bedard, *Car and Driver,* November 2001, p. 134.

4. "Exploring the Role of Pricing as a Congestion Management Tool," Searching for Solutions: A Policy Discussion Series, No. 1, Federal Highway Administration and Federal Transit Administration, Washington, D.C., July 23, 1991.

5. See, for example, Michael O'Hare, Lawrence Bacow, and Debra Sanderson, *Facility Siting and Public Opposition,* New York: Van Nostrand Reinhold, 1983; and Howard Kunreuther and Paul Kleindorfer, "A Sealed-Bid Auction Mechanism for Siting Noxious Facilities," *American Economic Review* 76(2), May 1986: 295-299.

Chapter Eight: "It's Your Money . . ."

1. Liam Murphy and Thomas Nagel, *The Myth of Ownership,* New York: Oxford University Press, 2001.

2. Liam Murphy and Thomas Nagel, "Tax Travesties," *Boston Globe,* January 26, 2003, http://brothersjuddblog.com/archives/2003/01/we_hold_these_suggestions_to_b_1.html.

3. For a brilliant summary of the relevant literature that goes on to break exciting new ground, see Robert Hockett, "Taking Distribution Seriously," Cornell University Law School working paper, 2011.

4. Robert H. Frank, "Are Workers Paid Their Marginal Products?" *American Economic Review* 74(4), September 1984: 549-571.

5. Mohammad Qamar uz Zaman, "Review of the Academic Evidence on the Relationship between Teaching and Research in Higher Education," U.K. Department for Education and Skills Research Report RR506, 2004.

6. See, for example, Robert H. Frank, "Are Workers Paid Their Marginal Products?"; Jeffrey Pfeffer and A. Davis Blake, "Determinants of Salary Dispersion in Organizations," *Industrial Relations* 29, Winter 1990: 38-57; and Jeffrey Pfeffer and A. Konrad, "Do You Get What You Deserve? Factors Affecting the Relationship between Productivity and Pay," *Administrative Science Quarterly* 35, June 1990: 258-285.

7. Robert H. Frank and Robert M. Hutchens, "Wages, Seniority, and the Demand for Rising Consumption Profiles," *Journal of Economic Behavior and Organization* 21, 1993: 251-276; and Robert H. Frank, *What Price the Moral High Ground?* Princeton, NJ: Princeton University Press, 2004, chapter 6.

8. David Neumark and Andrew Postlewaite, "Relative Income Concerns and the Rise in Married Women's Employment," *Journal of Public Economics* 70, 1998: 157-183.

9. Erzo Luttmer, "Neighbors as Negatives," *Quarterly Journal of Economics: Relative Earnings and Well-Being* 120, 2005: 963–1002.

10. I defend this claim at greater length in chapter 6 of my 1985 book, *Choosing the Right Pond: Human Behavior and the Quest for Status*, New York: Oxford University Press.

Chapter Nine: Success and Luck

1. For an excellent, accessible summary, see Joseph LeDoux, *The Emotional Brain*, New York: Simon and Schuster, 1998.

2. Ibid., p. 165.

3. National Taxpayers Union, "Who Pays Income Taxes and How Much?" ntu.org/tax-basics/who-pays-income-taxes.html.

4. Ken Rudin, "Dreading a Tie in the Electoral College," National Public Radio, http://www.npr.org/template/story/story.php?storyId=4093121.

5. Instapundit.com, Comment of the Day, June 27, 2010, pajamasmedia.com/instapundit/101928/.

6. Leonard Mlodinow, *The Drunkard's Walk: How Randomness Rules our Lives*, New York: Vintage, 1990, chapter 10.

7. Quoted by Malcolm Gladwell, *Outliers*, New York: Pantheon, 2008, pp. 54, 55.

8. Ibid., Chapter 1.

9. K. Anders Ericsson, Michael J. Prietula, and Edward T. Cokely, "The Making of an Expert," *Harvard Business Review*, July–August, 2007, http://www.coachingmanagement.nl/The%20Making%20of%20an%20Expert.pdf.

10. Ibid., p. 3.

11. Robert H. Frank and Philip J. Cook, *The Winner-Take-All Society*, New York: Free Press, 1995, chapter 4.

12. *Business Week* Annual CEO Compensation Survey, April 9, 2001, www.businessweek.com/careers/content/apr2001/ca2001049_100.htm.

13. Frank and Cook, op. cit.

14. Sherwin Rosen, "The Economics of Superstars," *American Economic Review* 71, December 1981: 845–858, quote on p. 845.

15. Xavier Gabaix and Augustin Landier, "Why Has CEO Pay Increased So Much?" *Quarterly Journal of Economics* 123(1), 2008: 49–100.

16. See, for example, James Quirk and Rodney D. Fort, *Pay Dirt: The Business of Professional Team Sports*, Princeton, NJ: Princeton University Press, 1992.

17. For an engaging history of the IBM turnaround, see Doug Garr, *IBM Redux: Lou Gerstner and the Business Turnaround of the Decade*, New York: Harper Paperbacks, 2000.

18. Frank and Cook, op. cit.

19. According to a 1988 study, nearly half of American CEOs had at least twenty

years' tenure with the organizations they led. See Louis Boone and David Kurtz, "CEOs: A Group Profile," *Business Horizons,* July–August 1988, pp. 38–42.

20. See, for example, Paul Pierson and Jacob Hacker, *Winner-Take-All Politics,* New York: Simon and Schuster, 2010.

21. Amy F. Woolf, "Nonproliferation and Threat Reduction Assistance: U.S. Programs in the Former Soviet Union," Congressional Research Service, February 4, 2010.

Chapter Ten: The Great Trade-Off?

1. http://socialismdoesntwork.com/killing-the-goose-tha-lays-the-golden-eggs/.

2. "Business Bulletin," *Wall Street Journal,* March 26, 1997, p. A1.

3. Alberto Alesina and Dani Rodrik, "Distributive Politics and Economic Growth," *Quarterly Journal of Economics,* 109(2), May 1994: 465–490.

4. http://www.princeton.edu/odoc/faculty/grading/faq/#comp000047219e980000000b7278c0.

5. See, for example, Michael Lewis, *Liar's Poker,* New York: W. W. Norton, 1979.

6. For references to studies that document these and other forms of overconfidence, see Thomas Gilovich, *How We Know What Isn't So,* New York: Free Press, 1991, pp. 77–78.

7. Garrett Hardin, "The Tragedy of the Commons," *Science* 162, 1968: 1243–1247.

8. For a more detailed discussion of the incentive problems that lead to superfluous entry into winner-take-all markets, see Robert H. Frank and Philip J. Cook, *The Winner-Take-All Society,* New York: Free Press, 1995, chapter 6.

9. Jenny Anderson and Andrew Ross Sorkin, "Bill Is Offered to Increase Tax on Private Equity," *New York Times,* June 23, 2007, http://www.nytimes.com/2007/06/23/business/23tax.html.

10. Robert D. Yaro, "An Investment We Have to Make," *New York Times,* October 14, 2010, http://www.nytimes.com/roomfordebate/2010/10/13/will-we-ever-have-high-speed-trains/an-investment-we-have-to-make.

11. U.S. Department of Energy, "The Smart Grid: An Introduction," 2008, http://www.oe.energy.gov/1165.htm.

Chapter Eleven: Taxing Harmful Activities

1. A. C. Pigou, in *The Economics of Welfare,* 4th ed., London: Macmillan, 1932, http://www.econlib.org/library/NPDBooks/Pigou/pgEW.html.

2. For an excellent case study, see Gary W. Dorris, "Redesigning Regulatory Policy: A Case Study in Urban Smog," PhD dissertation, Department of Applied Economics and Management, Cornell University, 1996.

3. Joseph Kruger and Melanie Dean, "Looking Back on SO_2 Trading: What's Good

for the Environment Is Good for the Market," *Public Utilities Fortnightly,* August 1, 1997, http://www.pur.com/pubs/2616.cfm.

4. A. P. Sokolov, P. H. Stone, C. E. Forest, R. Prinn, M. C. Sarofim, M. Webster, S. Paltsev, C. A. Schlosser, D. Kicklighter, S. Dutkiewicz, J. Reilly, C. Wang, B. Felzer, J. Melillo, and H. D. Jacoby, "Probabilistic Forecast for 21st Century Climate Based on Uncertainties in Emissions (without Policy) and Climate Parameters," MIT Joint Program on the Science and Policy of Global Change, Report 169, January 2009.

5. "Climate Change Policy and CO_2 Emissions from Passenger Vehicles," Congressional Budget Office, October 6, 2008, http://www.cbo.gov/ftpdocs/98xx/doc9830/10-06-ClimateChange_Brief.pdf.

6. http://inhofe.senate.gov/.

7. Jonathan Leape, "The London Congestion Charge," *Journal of Economic Perspectives* 20(4), Fall 2006: 157–176.

8. Henry Goldman, "New York City Council Approves Manhattan Traffic Fees," Bloomberg.com, April 1, 2008, http://www.bloomberg.com/apps/news?sid=at9mizGXi7y4&pid=newsarchive.

9. Keith Bradsher, *High and Mighty,* New York: Public Affairs, 2002.

10. Jonathan Gruber and Sendhil Mullainathan, "Do Cigarette Taxes Make Smokers Happier?" *Advances in Economic Analysis and Policy* 5(1), 2005: 1–43.

11. T. K. Greenfield and J. D. Rogers, "Who Drinks Most of the Alcohol in the U.S.? The Policy Implications," *Journal of Studies on Alcohol and Drugs* 60(1), January 1999: 78–89.

12. Philip J. Cook, *Paying the Tab: The Costs and Benefits of Alcohol Control,* Princeton, NJ: Princeton University Press, 2007.

13. N. Gregory Mankiw, "Can a Soda Tax Save Us from Ourselves?" *New York Times,* June 5, 2010, http://www.nytimes.com/2010/06/06/business/06view.html.

Chapter Twelve: The Libertarian's Objections Reconsidered

1. John Rawls, *A Theory of Justice,* Cambridge, MA: Belknap Press of Harvard University Press, 1971.

2. Harriet Rubin, "Ayn Rand's Literature of Capitalism," *New York Times,* September 15, 2007, http://www.nytimes.com/2007/09/15/business/15atlas.html.

3. Adam Smith, *An Inquiry into the Nature and Causes of the Wealth of Nations,* State College, PA: Penn State University, 2005, book 1, chapter 1 (originally published in 1776), http://www.online-literature.com/adam_smith/wealth_nations/3/.

4. Ibid., book 1, chapter 3.

5. Robert Nozick, *Anarchy, State, and Utopia,* New York: Basic Books, 1974.

6. www.sirclisto.com/cavalier/spain.htm.

absolute consumption, 24–25, 40
absolute income, 23, 44
ACAP. *See* Aviation Consumer Action Project
acid rain, 176, 177, 178
advertising, consumer tastes affected by, 19
Aesop, 157
Afghanistan, corruption in, 56
agriculture, income transfers in, 113, 115–16
Agriculture, U.S. Department of, 115–16
airplanes, overbooked, 106–10, 179
Alaska, Bridge to Nowhere in, 46–47, 51
alcohol taxes, 185–87
Alesina, Alberto, 160
Allen, Paul, 144
Alpha magazine, 162
American Economic Review, 82
Americans for Tax Reform, 47
Anarchy, State, and Utopia (Nozick), 207
animals, competition among. *See* natural
    selection
antigovernment slogans, 168–71, 194–95
antlers, 21, 72–73
apartment-sharing example, 195–99
Archer, Bill, 119
arms races: in sports, 67–68; in workplace
    safety, 212. *See also* military arms races
athletes. *See* sports
Atlanta (Georgia), interracial couples in, 95–97
Atlas Shrugged (Rand), 202–7
autonomy, personal, 194–211; in apartment-
    sharing example, 195–99; link between

efficiency and, 196, 199; reasons to compro-
    mise, 202–11; and retirement savings, 205–6,
    208, 210; and safety regulations, 206–7, 208,
    210–11; in society-formation example,
    199–207; taxes as reduction of, 194; value of,
    to libertarians, 194–95. *See also* freedom
Aviation Consumer Action Project (ACAP),
    108–10, 179

bank loans: cost-benefit test for, 161; to
    labor-managed firms, 32–34
bankruptcies, role of luck in, 142
baseball, 67–68, 153, 154
Baumann, Bob, 55
Beatles (band), 147
bicycle helmets, 187–92
Bill and Melinda Gates Foundation, 145
Bloomberg, Michael, 182–83
brain, human: emotional reactions in, 140–41;
    evolution of, 24; relative position in, 25–26
Bridge to Nowhere, 46–47, 51
broadcast rights, 86–87
Bush, George H. W., 142
Bush, George W.: income tax cuts by, 3, 119, 155,
    170; spending cuts by, 155, 170; on trickle-
    down theory, 160

CAB. *See* Civil Aeronautics Board
California: pollution from cars in, 113;
    Proposition 13 in, 48–49; starve-the-beast
    strategy in, 47–50

campaign finance: government waste reduction through reform of, 51; perception of corruption in, 57

Canada, lack of corruption in, 56

cap-and-trade system, 181

capital gains tax rate, 163

capitalism: assumption of greed in, 33; labor-managed firms in, 32–34; task specialization in, 43

car(s): congestion fees for, 113–14, 182–83; context in evaluation of speed, 26; gasoline prices' effect on design of, 181; need for corporations in industry, 90; pollution regulations for, 113; taxing by weight, 183–84

carbon dioxide tax, 179–82; cap-and-trade system as, 181; and climate change, 4, 179–82, 215; pace of implementation of, 4, 180–81

carried interest, 163

Carter, Jimmy, 112

cash-on-the-table metaphor, 31, 32, 35–36, 43

CEOs: before-tax versus after-tax incomes of, 154–55; competition in hiring of, 153–54; decision leverage of, 151–52; income growth of, 1, 61, 149–55; relationship between pay and ability of, 149–55; spending by, 60, 78

Cervantes, Miguel de, 215

Chicago Board of Trade, 177

children: helmet rules for, 187–89. See also schools

Citizens United v. Federal Election Commission, 51

Civil Aeronautics Board (CAB), 108

civil servants, in good government, 57

classical musicians, 150

class warfare, 29

Clean Air Act of 1990, 176–77

climate change: barriers to action on, 3–4, 181–82, 214–15; and carbon dioxide tax, 4, 179–82, 215; scientific estimates of pace of, 3–4, 180

Clinton, Bill, 103

Coase, Ronald, 85–99; career of, 85–86; as consequentialist, 94–97; cost-benefit analysis in framework of, 91–99, 209; and income differences, 100–102; on negotiation of efficient contracts, 86–91, 124, 178, 196, 210; noise damage example of, 86–89, 91–94, 100; and pollution tax, 177–78; and progressive income tax, 126, 137; summary of arguments of, 195–96; on transaction costs, 91, 137

cognition, interdependence of emotion and, 140–41

collective action problems: in animal species, 21; in markets, 9–10; in sports, 9

collective economies, failure of, 122, 201

common good, in invisible-hand theory, 7, 9–10

competition: flaws in process of, 7, 19–20, 22, 30; individual versus group benefits from, 7–8, 17, 19–23; insufficient, as cause of market failures, 11, 18, 30; invisible-hand view of, 6–10, 17–18, 211–12; in labor markets, 37–38; libertarian assumptions about, 11, 22; in military arms races, 66; misunderstandings about, 6; negative outcomes of, 7–10, 18; relative performance in, 8–9, 21; Smith's versus Darwin's view of, 7, 17–18, 211–12. See also invisible hand; natural selection

compromise, reasons for libertarians to, 202–11

computer operating systems, 144–45

congestion fees, 113–14, 182–83

Congress, U.S.: agricultural policies of, 115; on carried interest, 163; on climate change, 3–4; on income transfers, 113; perception of corruption in, 57; on pollution permits, 176–77. See also House of Representatives; Senate

consequentialists, 94–97

Conservation Reserve Program (CRP), 116

conservatives: on government as problem, 5; on progressive consumption tax, 82. See also libertarian(s)

constitutions, limitations on individual rights in, 208

consumer(s): advertising's effect on tastes of, 19; as beneficiaries of invisible hand, 6–7, 18; libertarian assumptions about, 11, 22–23; rationality of, 11, 23

consumer saving. See savings

consumer spending: by CEOs, 60, 78; context of, 68–74, 75; effects of progressive consumption tax on, 77–79, 80–81; expenditure cascade in, 61–62, 77–78; harm caused by, 78; on positional goods, 70–72; waste in, 59–61, 62, 63

consumption: context of, 26, 61–62, 65; in economic downturn of 2008, 53; relative versus absolute, 24–25, 40

consumption beast, positional, 63

consumption surtax, progressive, 82–83

consumption tax, flat or value-added, 82
consumption tax, progressive, 76–83; approach
    to implementation of, 77, 82–83; direct and
    indirect effects of, 77; effects on consumer
    spending and saving, 77–79, 80–81; effects
    on social welfare, 80–81; versus income tax,
    efficiency of, 81, 167–68; luxuries under,
    76–77; obstacles to establishing, 81–83;
    pollution tax compared to, 79–80; supporters
    of, 81–83; tax revenue from, 78–79, 80–81
consumption tax, regressive, 82
context: of consumption, 26, 61–62, 65; in
    emotional responses, 140–41; of government
    regulations, 75–76; of housing, 68–72; lack
    of, in economic models, 27–29, 69–72;
    of military arms races, 65, 70; relative
    importance of, in different settings, 68–74,
    75–76; role in evaluation, 26–27, 28, 213; of
    workplace safety, 69–72
contracts, negotiation of efficient, 86–91, 124–25,
    178, 196, 210
Cook, Philip, 149–50, 153, 186
Cornell University, 134, 150–51
corporate executives. See CEOs
corporations: campaign contributions by, 51;
    reasons for existence of, 90–91
corruption, government, 56–57
Corruption Perceptions Index (CPI), 56–57
cost-benefit analysis: of hiring decisions, 161;
    individual rights under, 209
cost-benefit analysis, of harmful activities
    versus freedom, 91–118; alternatives to, 103,
    118; consequentialists versus deontologists
    on, 94–97; income differences in, 100–106;
    liberal hostility to, 110–11; morality of, 91–97;
    in pollution reduction, 174–75; in public
    policy, 102–4, 116–18, 209; rights in, 93–99,
    209; willingness to pay in, 101–11, 118, 197–98;
    in workplace safety, 36–39, 210
CPI. See Corruption Perceptions Index
CP/M operating system, 144
critical thinking, impaired by ideology, 35
CRP. See Conservation Reserve Program
culture, in human behavior, 24
curve, grading on, 11, 23–24, 41–42, 211

Darwin, Charles: economists' influence on, 16;
    as intellectual father of economics, 16–17;
    and market failures based on individual

versus group interests, 22–23, 30, 40–45, 85,
    138; on population density, 85; on positional
    versus nonpositional goods, 72–74; on
    relative performance, 8–9, 21, 23–24; versus
    Smith, on competition, 7, 17–18, 211–12. See
    also natural selection
data, regulations as, 75–76, 208
decision leverage, of CEOs, 151–52
deficit(s): aversion to, as argument against
    economic stimulus, 3; misconceptions about,
    13; reduction of, through taxes on harmful
    activities, 14–15
deliberate practice, in development of expertise,
    148
Denmark, lack of corruption in, 56
deontologists, 94–97
Digital Research, 144
Director, Aaron, 89
directory assistance, 114–15
Domenici, Pete, 81–82
Dubose, Ronald, 58–59

Earned Income Tax Credit (EITC), 113
economic downturn of 2008, 52–55;
    consumption in, 53; government role in
    recovery from, 2–3, 53–55; savings rates in,
    78; unemployment in, 2, 53–55
economic efficiency. See efficiency
economic growth: all taxes as inhibitor of, 13,
    157–58; and income inequality, correlation
    between, 159–60; lower taxes as inhibitor of,
    162–64, 167–68, 213; from taxes on harmful
    activities, 158; trickle-down theory of, 157–62;
    after World War II, 1
economic models: context-free, 27–29, 69–72;
    of human motivation, 24–25; of retirement
    saving, 54
economic recoveries, government role in, 2–3,
    53–55
economics, Darwin as intellectual father of,
    16–17
economic stimulus: critics of, 2–3, 54–55; recent
    need for, 2–3, 54–55; from temporary tax
    cuts, 83
economic surpluses, in efficient provision of
    public goods, 124, 125–26
economies, collective, failure of, 122, 201
Edsel, 19
education. See schools

efficiency: in definition of rationality, 207; of income tax versus progressive consumption tax, 81, 167–68; link between autonomy and, 196, 199; in negotiation of contracts, 86–91, 124–25, 178, 196, 210

efficient public policies: barriers to, 111–18; income transfers in, 104, 111–18, 123–26; in provision of public goods, 123–26; willingness to pay in, 109, 118, 123

effluent taxes. *See* pollution taxes

EITC. *See* Earned Income Tax Credit

elephant seals, 8

elk, 21, 30, 72–73

emissions taxes. *See* pollution taxes

emotional reactions: context in, 140–41; to income taxes, 141–42; interdependence of cognition and, 140–41

energy crisis of 1979, 112

Energy, U.S. Department of, 155

energy policy, U.S.: cap-and-trade system in, 181; climate change in, 3–4

England, congestion fees in, 182

entitlement programs, future of, 170–71

environmental factors, in success, 146–47

environmental groups, on pollution taxes, 177

environmental pollution. *See* pollution

envy, 29, 212–13

Ericsson, K. Anders, 147–48

Etter, Lauren, 55

Europe: congestion fees in, 182; gasoline prices in, 181; government corruption in, 56; government regulations in, 84. *See also* *specific countries*

evaluation, role of context in. *See* context

evolution theory, influence of economics on, 16. *See also* natural selection

expenditure cascades: and income inequality, 61–62; and progressive consumption tax, 77–78, 80; and regressive consumption tax, 82

expertise, development of, 147–48

exploitation, of workers, 36

E-ZPass system, 113–14

failures, role of luck in, 142–43

fairness, in social hierarchies, 131

famines, 25, 73

farmers, income transfers to, 113, 115–16

Federal Communications Commission, 86–87

"Federal Communications Commission, The" (Coase), 86–89

Fidler, Lewis A., 183

Fillo, MaryEllen, 60

financial crisis of 2008, 52–55; consumption in, 53; government role in recovery from, 2–3, 53–55; savings rates in, 78; unemployment in, 2, 53–55

financial markets: cost-benefit test for loans in, 161; and labor-managed firms, 32–34

financial services industry: competition in hiring in, 154; income in, 162–63; over-crowding in, 162, 163–66; tax rates on, 163, 167; as winner-take-all labor market, 163–66

Finland, lack of corruption in, 56

first-come, first-served rule, 107–8, 110

fishery example, 164–66

fitness, reproductive, 7–8, 20–21, 24, 25

flat consumption tax, 82

food scarcity, 25

Ford, 19

Ford, Henry, 19

Fox News Channel, 5

France, bicycle helmets in, 189–90

free agency, in sports, 153

freedom, constraints on: in arms control agreements, 66, 67; libertarians on acceptable reasons for, 10–11, 195; shallow thinking about, 10–11; to solve collective action problems, 9; workplace safety regulations as, 41, 71, 72. *See also* harmful activities, constraints on freedom to prevent

free markets: government-as-problem argument for, 5; libertarians' expectations regarding outcomes in, 22–23

free-rider problem, 124–25

Friedman, Milton, 82, 89

Gabaix, Xavier, 152

Galbraith, John Kenneth, 18–19

Galt, John (character), 202–7

Gann, Paul, 48

gasoline tax: critics of, 13; effect on prices, 180–81; in energy crisis of 1979, 112; pace of implementation of, 180–81

Gates, Bill, Jr., 144–45, 147

Gates, Bill, Sr., 145
gazelles, 20
General Theory of Employment, Interest, and Money, The (Keynes), 53
genetic factors, in success, 146–47
genetic mutations, individual versus group benefits from, 7–8, 20–21. *See also* natural selection
Georgia, interracial couples in, 95–97
Germany, CEO income in, 152
Gerstner, Louis V., Jr., 153
Gladwell, Malcolm, 146
globalization, and CEO income growth, 152, 154
global warming. *See* climate change
golden eggs fable, 157, 163, 170
government: corruption in, 56–57; good, obstacles to, 55–59, 214; as source of problems, rise of concept, 4–5
government policy. *See* public policy
government regulations: as all bad, 75; on broadcast rights, 86–87; Coase on harm prevention through, 85–91; as data, 75–76, 208; European, 84; examples of common, 75; versus individual rights, 208–11; on oversold flights, 108–10; on pollution, 14, 175; population density and, 84; reasons for having, 75–76, 84; as social engineering, 13–14, 122–23; versus taxation, to prevent harm, 13–14, 79–80, 123, 172–74, 213
government role: in addressing flaws in consumer rationality, 23; in economic recoveries, 2–3, 53–55; in maintenance of property rights, 120; necessity of, 5–6
government spending, 46–63; in economic recoveries, 2–3, 53–55; nondiscretionary increases in, 170–71. *See also* government waste; infrastructure spending
government spending cuts: by Bush (George W.), 155, 170; decision framework for making, 155–56; harm caused by, 2–3, 14, 51–55
government waste, 46–63; all spending as, 2; examples of existing, 14, 46–47; parasite-host analogy for, 50–51; presidential promises on, 170; versus private sector waste, 59–61, 62, 63; problems with examples of, 58–59; reasons for, 46–47, 50–51; starve-the-beast strategy against, 47–50
grandfather clock example, 104–6

grants, research, 133–35
Great Depression, 53
greed, assumption of, in capitalism, 33
Greenspan, Alan, 157
group interests. *See* common good; individual versus group interests

Haiti, corruption in, 56
happiness: in labor-managed firms, 31; and relative position, 27
hard work, in success, 143–48
harm: from consumer spending, 78; direct versus indirect forms of, 11–12; from government spending cuts, 2–3, 14, 51–55; measurement of, 12. *See also* indirect harm
harmful activities: examples of, 14; laws and regulations on, 13–14, 85–90; perpetrators and victims in, 87, 90, 92, 93; reciprocal nature of, 87, 97, 195–96
harmful activities, constraints on freedom to prevent, 84–99; bicycle and motorcycle helmet rules as, 187–92; Coase on, 85–99; hockey helmet rules as, 8–9, 30, 42, 44–45; income differences in, 100–102; Mill's principle for, 9, 10, 12, 85, 98; negotiation of efficient contracts on, 86–91; by regulation versus taxation, 13–14, 79–80, 123, 172–74, 213; rights in, 93–99, 207–11; weighing costs in, 85. *See also* cost-benefit analysis; tax(es), on harmful activities
harmful activities tax. *See* tax(es), on harmful activities
head tax, 125
hedge fund managers: excessive number of, 164, 166–67; income of, 162–64
helmets: bicycle, 187–90; hockey, 8–9, 30, 42, 44–45; motorcycle, 190–92
high-fructose corn syrup, 192, 193
Hightower, Jim, 142
hiring decisions: competition in, 153–54; cost-benefit analysis of, 161
Hirsch, Fred, 70
hockey: helmets in, 8–9, 30, 42, 44–45; luck in success in, 146, 156
Hoover, Herbert, 53
Hossa, Marian, 156
House of Representatives, U.S.: on cap-and-trade system, 181; on climate change, 4; on IRS budget, 3

housing: context in evaluation of, 68–72; in economic downturn of 2008, 53; expenditure cascades in, 61–62, 77–78, 80; under progressive consumption tax, 77, 78–79

human motivation: culture in, 24; economic models of, 24–25; evolution of brain and, 24; relative position in, 25–26

Hurricane Katrina, 57

IBM, 144–45, 153

Iceland, lack of corruption in, 56

ideology, critical thinking impaired by, 35

ignoramitocracy, 3, 4

incentive to work, and income tax rates, 158–60

income: absolute versus relative, 23, 44; and happiness, 27; misconceptions in invisible-hand theory about, 23, 44; myth of ownership of, 120–21; per capita, and government corruption, 56–57; as positional good, 73–74; in winner-take-all labor markets, 148–55, 166

income growth: of CEOs, 1, 61, 149–55; fundamental shift in pattern of, 61–62; after World War II, 1, 61

income inequality: in cost-benefit analysis, 100–106; and economic growth, correlation between, 159–60; in efficient provision of public goods, 123–26; and expenditure cascades, 61–62; in public policy decisions, 102–4, 111–12; rise of, in U.S., 61; and willingness to pay, 101–11, 198

income tax, 119–39; consumption tax as alternative to, 76–77, 80; consumption tax as supplement to, 82; in efficient provision of public goods, 123–26; emotional reactions to, 141–42; and incentive to work, 158–60; libertarian objections to, 6, 119–21, 123, 157; marginal rates for, 77; morality of, 119–21; in myth of ownership, 120–21; perception of overtaxation, 141–42; versus progressive consumption tax, efficiency of, 81, 167–68

income tax, progressive: efficient provision of public goods through, 124–26; justifications for, 124–31; libertarian rationale for, 126–31, 137–38; mindless slogans opposing, 169; and rank, 126–31

income tax cuts: under Bush (George W.), 3, 119, 155, 170; as inhibitor of economic growth,

162–64; temporary, effectiveness of, 83; trickle-down theory of, 157–62

income transfers: in efficient public policies, 104, 111–18, 123–26; libertarian objections to, 104, 111, 117, 123–26

indirect harm, 11–12; in Coase framework, 98; libertarians on, 11–12, 44; measurement of, 12; taxes on activities causing, 187

individual rights. *See* rights

individual self-interest, in economic models of motivation, 24–25

individual versus group interests, 19–23; market failures caused by incompatibility of, 22–23, 30, 40–45, 85, 138; in modern interpretations of invisible-hand theory, 7, 9–10, 17, 211–12; in natural selection, 7–8, 17, 19–21; population density and, 85; Smith's skepticism about compatibility of, 7; in tragedy of the commons, 34, 164–68; in workplace safety, 9–10, 42–45

Industrial Revolution, 43

information revolution: and CEO income growth, 150, 151, 154; and government waste, 51

infrastructure spending: cost of postponing, 2–3, 51–52; dependence of wealthy on, 120–21; need for, 1–2, 171; through progressive consumption tax, 81; after World War II, 1

Inhofe, James, 181

innovation, in invisible-hand theory, 6, 17–18

Instapundit, 142–43

Institutional Investor, 162

insurance, workman's compensation, 41

Integrated Global Systems Model, 4, 180

interest, carried, 163

Intergovernmental Panel on Climate Change, 180

Internal Revenue Service (IRS), cuts to budget of, 3

interracial couples, 95–97

investments: as positional goods, 73–74; public, dependence of property rights on, 120

invisible hand of the market: assumptions underlying, 22–23; context not considered in, 27, 29, 69–72; key insights of, 6–7, 17–18; modern misinterpretations of, 7, 17, 211–12; negative outcomes of, 7–10, 18; problems

with theory, 6–10, 22–23; understanding of competition in, 6–10, 17–18, 211–12; and workplace safety, 9–10, 36–39, 43–44, 70–71
IRS. *See* Internal Revenue Service
"It's your money" rhetoric, 119–21, 139, 155–56

Japan, CEOs in, 152, 159
Jarvis, Howard, 48
Jarvis-Gann Amendment (California), 48–49
job creation: payroll tax cuts in, 13, 14; by small businesses, 160–62
John M. Olin Foundation, 5
Journal of Law and Economics, 89
justice: of progressive taxation, 169; in social hierarchies, 131

Kahn, Alfred, 115
Katrina, Hurricane, 57
Kennedy, John F., 1
Ketchikan (Alaska), Bridge to Nowhere in, 46–47, 51
Keynes, John Maynard, 2, 53
Kildall, Gary, 144, 145
Kin smartphone, 19
Koch, Charles, 4–5
Koch, David, 5
Koch Industries, 5

labor laws, impact of violations of, 39–40
labor-managed firms, 31–35; economic benefits of, 31–32; history of, 32; productivity in, 31–32; reasons for lack of proliferation of, 32–35; social justice in, 31
labor markets: lack of mobility in, 38; rank in, 131–36; skepticism about competition in, 37–38. *See also* winner-take-all labor markets
labor specialization: development of, 43, 100; and productivity, 43, 203–4
Landier, Augustin, 152
laws, as social engineering, 13–14, 122–23. *See also specific types*
leisure time, versus income, 73
Leopold's record store, 32, 34, 35
liability, for harmful activities, 91, 92
liberals: on cause of market failures, 11, 18–19, 30, 84, 138; hostility toward cost-benefit analysis among, 110–11; on progressive income tax, 126

libertarian(s): on acceptable reasons to constrain freedom, 10–11, 195; antitax slogans of, 168–71, 194–95; basic assumptions of, 11, 22–23, 211; on before- versus after-tax incomes, 154–55; Coase embraced by, 86, 94, 98–99, 178; as consequentialists versus deontologists, 94; Darwin's view of competition and, 17, 22, 211–12; expectations regarding outcomes in free market, 22–23; flaws in framework of, 11, 23; on government as source of problems, 4–5; on indirect harm, 11–12, 44; influence on public discourse, 4–5; on Mill's harm principle, 10, 98; on progressive income tax, 125–31, 137–38; rational, definition of, 195, 207; reasons for compromise by, 202–11; in society-formation example, 127–31, 199–207; on taxes as social engineering, 13–14, 122–23; on taxes as theft, 6, 119, 154, 202; type of government preferred by, 22, 23, 195; value of autonomy to, 194–95
libertarian objections: to helmet rules, 9, 189–92; to income taxes, 6, 119–21, 123, 157; to income transfers, 104, 111, 117, 123–26; to pollution tax, 177–79; to progressive consumption tax, 83; to regulation of harmful activities, 86; to relative position, role of, 29, 212–13; to workplace safety regulations, 41, 43, 206–7
Libertarian Party, 4
liberty. *See* freedom
loans: cost-benefit test for, 161; to labor-managed firms, 32–34
Locke, John, *The Second Treatise of Civil Government,* 119
Lockheed, 58–59
London, congestion fees in, 182
luck, 140–56; in antitax slogans, 169–70; denial of role of, 142–44, 146–48; in environmental and genetic factors, 146–47; of Gates (Bill), 144–45; in sports, 145–46, 156; strengthening of relationship between success and, 154
luxuries: identification of goods as, 76–77; as positional goods, 76; progressive consumption tax on, 76–77

majority rights, versus minority rights, 207–11
Malthus, Thomas, 16
Mankiw, Greg, 193

mansions, in expenditure cascades, 61–62, 77–78. *See also* housing
marginal tax rates: income, 77; progressive consumption, 77
market economy: collective action problems in, 9–10; versus collective economy, 122. *See also* free markets; invisible hand
market failures, 30–45; context as key to understanding, 27; Darwin on individual versus group interests as cause of, 22–23, 30, 40–45, 85, 138; flaws in conventional accounts of, 31, 84, 138; ideological versus critical thinking about, 35; and labor-managed firms, 31–35; liberals on cause of, 11, 18–19, 30, 84, 138; Smith on cause of, 18; and workplace safety, 36–39
Marx, Karl, 43
Massachusetts Institute of Technology (MIT), 4, 180
mating, in natural selection, 7–8, 20–21, 24, 25
Mayer, Jane, 4–5
McCain, John, 160
McConnell, Mitch, 3
Medicare program, 170
merit, in success, 142–44
methane, 180
Microsoft, 19, 144–45
middle class, after World War II, 1
military arms races, 64–68; competition in, 66; conditions leading to, 65–66; context of, 65, 70; control agreements on, 64, 66; logic of, 64–66; versus other arms races, 67–68
Mill, John Stuart, harm principle of, 85, 98; and helmet rules, 9; indirect harm in, 12; misunderstandings of, 10, 85, 98; and taxes on harmful activities, 187, 188, 189, 190, 213
Minneapolis, bridge collapse in, 81
minority rights, versus majority rights, 207–11
MIT. *See* Massachusetts Institute of Technology
Mlodinow, Leonard, 144–45
money, impact of development of, 100
morality: consequentialists versus deontologists on, 94–97; of cost-benefit analysis, 91–99; of income taxes, 119–21
motivation. *See* human motivation
motorcycle helmets, 190–92
MS-DOS, 145
Murdoch, Rupert, 5

Murphy, Liam, 121
musicians, classical, 150
Myanmar, corruption in, 56

Nader, Ralph, 108, 179
Nagel, Thomas, 121
national defense, government role in, 5, 6
natural selection: central premise of, 19–20; individual versus group interests in, 7–8, 17, 19–23; positional versus nonpositional goods in, 72–73; relative performance in, 8–9, 21, 23–24; reproductive fitness in, 7–8, 20–21, 24
"Nature of the Firm, The" (Coase), 90–91
negotiation, of efficient contracts, 86–91, 124–25, 178, 196, 210
Nepal, poverty in, 120–21
Netherlands, lack of corruption in, 56
neurophysiological responses, to relative position, 26–27
Nevada State Department of Transportation, 2
New York City, congestion fees in, 182–83
New Yorker, 4–5
New York State: helmet rules in, 188–89; soda tax in, 192
New York State Public Service Commission, 114–15
New York Yankees, 67–68
New Zealand, lack of corruption in, 56
Nobel Prize, 85
noise damage examples: doctor versus factory, 86–89, 91–94, 100; violin music, 100–102
nonpositional goods: context in evaluation of, 70–72; Darwinian perspective on, 72–74; definition of, 70; taxes on, 76
Norquist, Grover, 47
Norway, lack of corruption in, 56
Nozick, Robert, *Anarchy, State, and Utopia*, 207
nuclear materials, loose, 155
Nudge (Thaler and Sunstein), 23
Nunn, Sam, 81–82

Occupational Safety and Health Administration, 41
Ohanian, Lee, 54
On Liberty (Mill), 9, 10
Organisation for Economic Co-operation and Development, 160
overfishing, 164–66

oversold flights, 106–10, 179
ownership, myth of, 120–21

Paradise Lost (Schrag), 49
parasite-host analogy, 50–51
party planning, 59–61, 77–78, 80
paternalism, and soda taxes, 192
Paterson, David, 192
Paterson, Tim, 144, 145
Paulson, John, 163
payroll tax: benefits of cutting, 14, 112; as tax on
    useful activities, 13
Peace Corps, 120
performance, and pay, in winner-take-all labor
    markets, 148–55. *See also* relative performance
perpetrators, of harmful activities, 87, 90, 92,
    93
Pigou, A. C., 172
Pigouvian taxes, 172–74. *See also* tax(es), on
    harmful activities
political barriers: to action on climate change,
    3–4, 181–82, 214–15; to efficient public policy,
    111–18; to progressive consumption tax,
    81–83
political careers, luck in success of, 142
political donations, in support of government-
    as-problem message, 4–5
political system, U.S., paralysis in, 2, 3, 195
pollution: from cars, 113; differences in cost of
    reducing, 14, 79–80, 174–77; inefficiency of
    traditional regulation of, 175; optimal level
    of, 174–75
pollution taxes, 172–83; on carbon dioxide, 4,
    179–82; cleanup costs with, 175–77; and
    climate change, 4, 179–82; congestion fees as,
    113–14, 182–83; critics of, 177–80; differences
    in cost of avoiding, 14, 79–80, 175–77;
    efficiency of, 175–77; pace of implementation
    of, 4, 180–81; permits as form of, 176–77, 178;
    and price of goods, 178, 180; versus
    regulation of pollution, 14, 175; on sulfur
    dioxide, 172–79
poor, the: effect of congestion fees on, 183;
    income transfers to, 104, 111–16; role of luck
    in lives of, 142–43; willingness to pay among,
    102–4, 108–10
population density: and degree of government
    regulation, 84; and task specialization, 204

positional arms races: in military, 65; in sports,
    67; in workplace safety, 212
positional consumption beast, 63
positional externalities: definition of, 68; in
    rank, 127; taxation to limit, 79
positional goods: context in evaluation of,
    70–72; Darwinian perspective on, 72–74;
    definition of, 70; taxes on, 76
practice time, in development of expertise,
    147–48
Princeton University, 162
private sector: negotiation of efficient contracts
    in, 86–91, 124–25, 178, 196, 210; willingness
    to pay in, 102, 104–6, 197–98
private-sector waste: expenditure cascades in,
    61–62; versus government waste, 59–61, 62,
    63; ways of cutting, 63
"Problem of Social Cost, The" (Coase), 89–90
productivity: in labor-managed firms, 31–32;
    and rank, 127–33; in society-formation
    example, 127–31, 200–201; and task
    specialization, 43, 203–4; and wages, 132–35
professors, productivity of, 133–35
profit motive, in invisible-hand theory, 6, 17–18
progressive consumption surtax, 82–83
progressive consumption tax. *See* consumption
    tax, progressive
progressive income tax. *See* income tax,
    progressive
progressives, flaws in understanding of
    markets, 11
Project on Military Procurement, 47
property rights, government role in
    maintenance of, 120
property taxes, in California, 48–49
Proposition 13 (California), 48–49
Prozac, 26–27
public discourse, libertarian influence on, 4–5
public goods: dependence of property rights
    on, 120; differences in valuation of, 123–26;
    efficient provision of, 123–26; as non-
    positional goods, 74; under progressive
    consumption tax, 80–81; under progressive
    income tax, 124–26; willingness to pay for,
    123
public policy: cost-benefit analysis in, 102–4,
    116–18, 209; income differences in decisions
    in, 102–4, 111–12; income transfers in, 104,

public policy (*continued*)
111–18, 123–26; willingness to pay in, 102–4,
106–11, 118. *See also* efficient public policies
public radio example, 102–4, 111–12
public transportation, 171

QDOS, 144–45

Rand, Ayn, *Atlas Shrugged,* 202–7
rank, 126–38; dependence of reward on, 11;
evolution of concern about, 25, 26–27; in
labor market, 131–36; outside labor market,
136–37; and progressive income tax, 126–31;
reciprocal nature of, 126–27; and relative
productivity, 127–33; valuation of high, 129,
130, 133–38. *See also* relative position
rationality: consumer, 11, 23; efficiency in
definition of, 207; libertarian, 195, 207
Rawls, John, 201–2
Reagan, Ronald: antigovernment views of, 57;
and income transfers, 112, 113; on military
arms races, 64, 66; on taxes, 119
Reardon, Susan, 60
regressive consumption tax, 82
regulations. *See* government regulations
relative consumption, importance of, 24–25
relative income, 23, 44
relative performance: CEO pay by, in
winner-take-all markets, 150; dependence
of reward on, 9, 211–12; in natural selection,
8–9, 21, 23–24
relative position: in human brain, 25–26;
importance of, 23–26, 29, 212–13; libertarian
rejection of role of, 29, 212–13; in natural
selection, 8–9, 21, 23–24; neurophysiological
responses to, 26–27. *See also* rank
rent controls, 113, 116
reproductive fitness, 7–8, 20–21, 24, 25
Republican Party, on cap-and-trade system, 181
research grants, 133–35
retirement savings: in economic models versus
real life, 54; mandatory, 205–6; reasons for
libertarian compromise on, 208, 210
revealed preference doctrine, 44
reward: dependence on rank, 11; dependence
on relative performance, 9, 211–12
Reynolds, Glenn, 142–43
Ricardo, David, 16

rights, 207–11; constitutional limitations on,
208; cost-benefit analysis of, 93–99, 209;
versus government regulations, 208–11;
majority versus minority, 207–11
right-wing think tanks, on government as
problem, 5
roads. *See* infrastructure spending
Rodrik, Dani, 160
Roosevelt, Franklin, 53
Rosen, Sherwin, 150

safety. *See* workplace safety
sales tax, national, 82
Sams, Jack, 144–45
savings: mandatory, 205–6; as nonpositional
good, 74; in progressive consumption tax,
77–79; reasons for libertarian compromise
on, 208, 210
Scaife, Richard Mellon, 5
Schelling, Thomas, 8–9, 30, 42
schools: ability to send children to best, 10,
25–26, 40–41, 128, 205; government
regulation of, 75; as positional goods, 74;
quality of, as relative concept, 10, 40, 128, 205
Schrag, Peter, *Paradise Lost,* 49
Scotland, task specialization in, 203–4
second-hand smoke, 184–85
Second Treatise of Civil Government, The
(Locke), 119
Seidman, Laurence, 82–83
self-interest. *See* individual self-interest
Senate, U.S.: on cap-and-trade system, 181; on
climate change, 4; on progressive consumption tax, 81–82; on soda tax, 192
serotonin, 26–27
Sierra Club, 177
Singapore, lack of corruption in, 56
Skorton, David J., 150–51
slippery slope argument, 193
slogans, antitax, 168–71, 194–95
small businesses: job creation by, 160–62; as
labor-managed firms, 32; in trickle-down
theory, 160–62
Smith, Adam: versus Darwin, as intellectual
father of economics, 16–17; skepticism about
good market outcomes, 7, 18; on task
specialization, 43, 203–4; *The Wealth of
Nations,* 16, 18, 33. *See also* invisible hand

smoking, taxes on, 184–85
social engineering: flaws in arguments about taxes as, 13–14, 122–23; pollution tax as, 181
socialismdoesntwork.com, 157
social justice, in labor-managed firms, 31
Social Security, 170
social welfare, effects of progressive consumption tax on, 80–81
society-formation example, 127–31, 199–207
soda taxes, 192–93
Somalia, corruption in, 56
Soviet Union: failure of collective economy of, 122; nuclear materials in, 155
special occasions, 59–61, 77–78, 80
species, competition in. See natural selection
spending. See consumer spending; government spending
sports: arms races in, 67–68; competition in hiring in, 153, 154; luck in, 145–46, 156; relationship between pay and ability in, 153; steroids in, 12, 67
sports utility vehicles (SUVs), 183–84
starve-the-beast strategy, 47–50
Steinbrenner, George M., 67–68
steroids, 12, 67
Stigler, George, 89
success, 140–56; in antitax slogans, 169–70; denial of role of luck in, 142–44, 146–48; development of expertise in, 147–48; environmental and genetic factors in, 146–47; of Gates (Bill), 144–45, 147; merit in, 142–44; in sports, 145–46, 156; strengthening of relationship between luck and, 154; talent and hard work in, 143–48; in winner-take-all markets, 148–55
sulfur dioxide pollution, 172–79
Sunstein, Cass, 23, 41
Supreme Court, U.S.: on campaign finance, 51; on interracial marriage, 95
Sutton, Willie, 171
SUVs. See sports utility vehicles
Sweden, lack of corruption in, 56
Switzerland, lack of corruption in, 56

talent, in success, 143–48
task specialization, 43, 203–4
tax(es): as inhibitor of economic growth, 13, 157–58; libertarian objections to, 6, 119–21;

need for mandatory, 6, 168–69, 202; slogans opposing, 168–71, 194–95; as social engineering, 13–14, 122–23; as theft, 6, 119, 154, 168–69, 202; trickle-down theory of, 157–62. See also specific types
tax(es), on harmful activities, 13–15, 172–93; alcohol taxes as, 185–87; causing indirect harm, 187; economic growth caused by, 158; and helmet rules, 187–92; and Mill's harm principle, 187, 188, 189, 190, 213; versus regulations, 13–14, 79–80, 123, 172–74, 213; slippery slope argument against, 193; soda taxes as, 192–93; tax on vehicle weight as, 183–84; tobacco taxes as, 184–85; versus useful activities, 13–15, 122. See also consumption tax, progressive; pollution taxes
tax cuts: payroll tax, 13, 14, 112; trickle-down theory of, 157–62. See also income tax cuts
tax rates: capital gains, 163; for hedge fund managers, 163, 167; marginal, 77; on top earners, impact on economic growth, 158, 162–64, 167, 213
tax reform: antitax slogans in conversation about, 168–71; essential questions to consider in, 168; need for fundamental, 81
tax revenue: from harmful versus useful activities, 13–15, 122; IRS budget cuts and, 3; from progressive consumption tax, 78–79, 80–81
Tea Party, 5, 181
technology. See information revolution
testosterone, 27
Thaler, Richard, 23, 41
tobacco taxes, 184–85
Tonga, corruption in, 56
tragedy of the commons: individual versus group interests in, 34; and labor-managed firms, 33–34; in winner-take-all markets, 164–68
transaction costs: Coase on, 91, 137, 178; definition of, 91
Transparency International, 56
transportation, public, 171. See also infrastructure spending
trickle-down theory, 157–62

unemployment: in economic downturn of 2008, 2, 53–55; payroll tax cuts and, 13, 14

United States government. *See* government
University of Chicago, 85–86, 89
university presidents, 150–51
Uzbekistan, corruption in, 56

vacation time, versus income, 73
value-added tax, 82
vehicles: congestion fees for, 113–14, 182–83;
    gasoline prices' effect on design of, 181;
    taxing by weight, 183–84. *See also* car(s)
victims, of harmful activities, 87, 90, 92, 93

wages: and productivity, 132–35; and rank,
    132–33. *See also* income
Wall Street Journal, 51–52
Walmart, 39–40
Washington, D.C., soda tax in, 192
water-filter example, 124–26
Wealth of Nations, The (Smith), 16, 18, 33
wealthy, the: Bush tax cuts for, 3, 119, 155, 170;
    dependence on infrastructure, 120–21; under
    progressive income tax, 124–26; tax rates on,
    impact on economic growth, 158, 162–64,
    167–68, 213; willingness to pay among,
    101–11, 123
weddings, 61
welfare state, 202, 214
well-being, 26–27

willingness to pay, 101–11; and income inequality,
    101–11, 198; and individual rights, 209; in
    private sector, 102, 104–6, 197–98; for public
    goods, 123; in public policy, 102–4, 106–11, 118
winner-take-all labor markets, 148–55; financial
    services industry as, 163–66; income in,
    149–55, 166; tragedy of the commons in,
    164–68
work, incentive to, 158–60
worker(s): exploitation of, and workplace safety,
    36; task specialization by, 43, 100, 203–4;
    value of workplace safety to, 36–39, 41, 71
worker-managed firms. *See* labor-managed
    firms
workman's compensation insurance, 41
workplace safety: context in evaluation of,
    69–72; cost-benefit analysis in, 36–39, 210;
    individual versus group interests in, 9–10,
    42–45; value of, to workers, 36–39, 41, 71
workplace safety regulations: arguments
    supporting, 41–45; critics of, 41, 43, 71, 72,
    208; versus individual rights, 208, 210–11;
    libertarian objections to, 41, 43, 206–7; as
    positional arms control agreement, 212;
    reasons for libertarian compromise on,
    206–7, 210–11; U.S. regime of, 41
World Bank, 160
World War II, income growth after, 1, 61